# Early Childhood Teacher Research

What is early childhood teacher research and why is it important? How does a teacher researcher formulate a research question and a plan for doing research? How do teachers apply research results to effect change? *Early Childhood Teacher Research* is an exciting new resource that will address the sorts of questions and concerns that pre- and in-service teachers of young children frequently have when engaging in teacher research.

Accessible and interactive, this book touches upon the important issues every early childhood teacher should know—the uniqueness of early childhood teacher research, reasons for doing it, and how to do it. In this comprehensive guide, Kathryn Castle explores each stage of teacher research, from conceptualization, generating research questions, identifying data sources, gathering and analyzing data, interpreting results, sharing results, to taking action based on results.

Special features included in each chapter:

- **Teacher Researcher Notebook** prompts for the reader to record ideas for research questions and to develop a plan for doing research.
- **From the Field** provides rich examples of real life early childhood teacher researchers and their perspectives on doing teacher research.
- **Reflections** ask readers to pause and think deeply about relating content to their own situations.
- **Exploration** of additional content, websites, resources, and activities are located in each chapter to help the reader go further in constructing their knowledge of teacher research.

**Kathryn Castle** is Professor and Chuck & Kim Watson Endowed Chair in Education in the School of Teaching and Curriculum Leadership at Oklahoma State University.

# Early Childhood Teacher Research

## From Questions to Results

KATHRYN CASTLE

Routledge
Taylor & Francis Group

NEW YORK AND LONDON

2011000738

First published 2012
by Routledge
711 Third Avenue, New York, NY 10017

Simultaneously published in the UK
by Routledge
2 Park Square, Milton Park, Abingdon, Oxon OX14 4RN

*Routledge is an imprint of the Taylor & Francis Group, an informa business*

© 2012 Taylor & Francis

*Library of Congress Cataloging in Publication Data*
Castle, Kathryn.
Early childhood teacher research: from questions to results / Kathryn Castle.
     p. cm.
1. Child development—Research. 2. Early childhood education—Research. I. Title.
LB1139.23.C389 2011
372.21072—dc22                                                    2011010779

ISBN: 978–0–415–87758–9 (hbk)
ISBN: 978–0–415–87759–6 (pbk)
ISBN: 978–0–203–83568–5 (ebk)

Typeset in Sabon and Neue Helvetica
by Book Now Ltd, London

Printed and bound in the United States of America on acid-free paper by
Walsworth Publishing Company, Marceline, MO.

SUSTAINABLE
FORESTRY
INITIATIVE

Certified Sourcing
www.sfiprogram.org
SFI 00000
*The SFI label applies to the text stock.*

# Dedication

This book is dedicated to Kristi Dickey, Annie Ortiz, Andrea Rains, Jackie Needham, Sandra Bequette, and all early childhood teacher researchers who have the courage and autonomy to dare to live their questions and meet the challenges of the work.

# Contents

# Preface

## Early Childhood Teacher Research: From Questions to Results

The cover design of this book is a colorful jigsaw pattern symbolic of what it means to do teacher research. In puzzling over questions that they raise for themselves about the complex world of teaching young children, early childhood teacher researchers fit the jigsaw pieces of data together in ways that connect to create a whole picture of what they are studying. Reflecting on the whole puzzle picture they have constructed of the results of their study gives teachers new perspectives, new knowledge, and insights into their own teaching and children's learning leading to greater understanding and action to do things better. The different colors and textures of each puzzle piece symbolize diversity and connectedness that exist in early childhood settings. The process of solving the puzzle can be challenging when pieces that look like they would fit, do not, necessitating a rethinking of what goes with what. Sometimes the puzzle pieces fit smoothly into a meaningful pattern. At the end of the process, a new image or understanding is constructed. At other times there may be missing pieces or extra pieces that call for new questions and further study. The process is both exhilarating and satisfying but also frustrating and challenging as any meaningful learning process tends to be.

This book explores the puzzling that early childhood teachers do as they study questions important to their professional work with children. It serves as a text for early childhood students and professionals interested in learning about early childhood teacher research and how to do it. The book is designed to actively engage the reader in participation with others including the teacher researchers described in the book in exploring the possibilities of teacher research within the numerous contexts and age groups of early childhood programs (birth through age 8). Early childhood teacher educators will find in the book examples for their students of teachers using an evidence-based approach, basing their practice on results from their own teacher research studies.

The following questions provide a structure for the content in the book:

- What is early childhood teacher research and why is it important?
- How does a teacher researcher formulate a teacher research question and a plan for doing research?
- How does a teacher use existing data to answer research questions?

- How are data collected and analyzed in teacher research?
- What are ways to share results with others?
- How do teachers apply research results to making changes?
- What roles do collaborative group participation and group protocol discussions play in teacher research?

The book can be used as a main textbook in a course on teacher research, in a research course with content on teacher research, as a textbook in an early childhood methods course, or read by those who want to learn more about early childhood teacher research to improve their practice.

## Audience

The book is written for those preparing to be early childhood teachers in community colleges, two-year, four-year, alternative, and graduate level programs. It is also written for in-service teachers who want to know about early childhood teacher research. The book contains examples of parallels between the National Board process and teacher research and would serve as a resource for those early childhood teachers preparing for National Board Certification.

*Early Childhood Teacher Research* is aimed at early childhood professionals in child care, preschool, and primary education programs, but may also appeal to elementary teachers who teach or are preparing to teach at the primary level. The topic of teacher research is increasingly being taught in educational programs such as pre-service and in-service teacher education in courses and practicum experiences. It is a topic that has become incorporated into national standards such as those of the National Board for Professional Teaching Standards and National Board certification, standards of the National Association for the Education of Young Children, and of the National Council for the Accreditation of Teacher Education. The book may serve early childhood teacher educators seeking a text on teacher research and help them meet accreditation requirements in their courses related to evidence-based teaching. This book may be used in early childhood or primary education courses that focus on inquiry and teacher inquiry such as courses on Methods of Early Childhood Education or culminating courses such as senior level capstone courses. It may also serve as a text for graduate level students who may not be familiar with teacher research.

## Author Stance

My background is in early childhood/elementary curriculum studies. I have been an early childhood teacher, teacher educator, and teacher researcher and I know the challenges of teacher research. It isn't easy doing teacher research, but it is the most meaningful work a teacher can do to gain a deepening understanding of how to do things better for young children. My teaching role at Oklahoma State University involves teaching basic and advanced courses in teaching and in teacher research. I work with teachers in the field as a mentor and facilitator of their teacher research studies. I do teacher research on my own teaching and collaborate with colleagues in teacher research.

I believe that teacher research reflects a constructivist approach to education because it is a means for constructing professional knowledge through the process of questioning one's work and systematically studying teaching and learning in order to do what is in children's best interests regardless of the reward system in place and the barriers in the way. It is a form of constructivist teacher autonomy. Through studying and teaching about teacher research and doing teacher research, I have come to believe that teacher research has the potential to transform schooling from the inside like no other educational reform has been able to do.

## Features of the Book

This book is written for early childhood professionals from the perspective of an early childhood educator. While there are other books on the topic of teacher research, few address the field of early childhood education across the age span of birth through age 8 in the same way this book does. This book contemplates the type of teacher research that early childhood professionals conduct so that early childhood education readers can relate to the examples and see how they might apply the content to their own situations. The term teacher research used in this book is specifically focused on the work that early childhood teachers do.

The book contains special features designed to engage the reader in reflection, journaling, and further explorations of content and resources. The book uses interactive devices including **Reflections**, the **Teacher Researcher Notebook, From the Field**, and **Explorations** in each chapter. **Reflections** ask readers to pause and think deeply about relating content to their own situations. Each chapter asks the reader to make an entry in their **Teacher Researcher Notebook** so that by the end of the book, the reader will have many ideas recorded in the notebook for teacher research questions and development of a plan for doing teacher research. The feature called **From the Field** provides rich examples of real life early childhood teacher researchers and their perspectives on doing teacher research. **Explorations** of additional content, websites, resources, and activities are located in each chapter to help the reader go further in constructing their knowledge of teacher research. In addition, the **Glossary** at the end of the book gives definitions of terms found in bold type throughout the book that may be unfamiliar to the reader. Readers can consult the Glossary as a helpful resource in understanding the content in the book.

## Content

The book begins with an overview of early childhood teacher research, the relationship of teaching and research, the uniqueness of early childhood teacher research, reasons for doing it, and examples from the field of early childhood teacher research. Research is presented from the professional literature supporting teacher research. The book also shows how to do teacher research from formulating research questions to data collection and analysis to sharing results and making changes based on results. The reader is offered a variety of resources including website information and practice data sets.

Most of the book is focused on how to do early childhood teacher research from conceptualizing it, generating research questions, identifying data sources, gathering and analyzing data, interpreting results, sharing results with others, taking action based on results, and joining early childhood teacher research collaborative groups. Each chapter gives examples of early childhood teacher research studies done by real teachers in the field.

The book consists of eight chapters followed by Appendices with practice data sets and a Glossary of terms used throughout the book. The title of each chapter is in the form of a question. The question format is used to focus and engage the reader in actively searching for answers.

**Chapter One: What is Early Childhood Teacher Research?** This chapter is about what is unique to the field of early childhood education and what is unique about early childhood teacher research. This chapter sets the stage for the rest of the book by defining what is meant by early childhood teacher research and giving reasons for doing it including support from professional literature on the topic. Examples of real early childhood teachers and their teacher research studies help bring the topics to life and help acclimatise readers to the book.

**Chapter Two: What is the Purpose of Early Childhood Teacher Research?** This chapter invites the reader to consider the role of early childhood teacher research in the professional development of early childhood teachers in pre-service, in-service, and graduate level programs. It juxtaposes what good teaching is with what teacher research is all about. It begins by exploring what readers may currently be doing that is teacher research and that can develop into a teacher research agenda. It identifies purposes of doing teacher research including documentation of children's learning, assessment including portfolio assessment, and movement toward quality teaching. This chapter addresses how teacher research may help meet professional standards including working toward National Board of Professional Teaching Standards certification.

**Chapter Three: Where Will Puzzlement and Wondering Lead?** Chapter Three is a pivotal chapter because the content is critical to beginning the teacher research process. This chapter is about the primary role of questioning in the teacher research process and guides readers through many exercises to help them generate their own teacher research questions. This chapter will give readers a multitude of ways to think about possible questions and where they might originate in the professional work of teachers. For early childhood students, examples will be given of questions coming from coursework and practicum experiences. For early childhood professionals, examples will be given of questions that arise from teaching and classroom life.

**Chapter Four: Why Plan?** This chapter is about planning a teacher research study once a question has been formulated and refined. Various teacher research designs are explained including qualitative, quantitative, and mixed methods designs. A template for developing a teacher research study complete with a timeline is given with each aspect of the plan explained. Examples show the role of planning in the success of teacher research studies. Ethical issues such as confidentiality, child and parental consent, and working with human subject review boards are addressed.

**Chapter Five: Data, Data, Who Has the Data?** This chapter explores what data are and the purpose they serve. It gives examples of appropriate data sources for early childhood teacher research including existing data, teacher journals, child artifacts and work samples, surveys, interviews, and other documents. Data artifacts from teacher research studies are used to provide examples of data sources. The relationship of each research question and its connection to a data source is emphasized. The main point of this chapter is to show that data come from the everyday life and activities of the classroom.

**Chapter Six: What Do Data Reveal?** The primary purpose of this chapter is how to analyze and interpret data. Data analysis methods are presented including qualitative, quantitative, and mixed methods analysis techniques including descriptive and inferential statistics. Data sets in the book's appendix serve as examples that readers can use to practice various data analysis methods. Validity, reliability, and how to establish trustworthiness are addressed.

**Chapter Seven: Who Might Be Interested?** The focus of this chapter is on various ways to share research findings. Examples are given for presenting results in informal and formal ways including sharing with colleagues, presenting at professional meetings, posting results online and writing results for publication in professional magazines, journals, and other documents. Examples are provided for how to write a conference proposal, how to write a manuscript for publication, and the review system for manuscripts. Information on existing teacher researcher collaborative groups and on forming collaborative groups is given. This chapter contains lists of resources such as online teacher research groups.

**Chapter Eight: What Comes After Research is Completed?** This is the final chapter that brings the book full circle. This chapter presents information on using teacher research results to take action, make changes, and make improvements in teaching and in children's learning. The chapter addresses action plans and advocacy efforts at the individual, program, and community levels. It provides examples of types of collaborative groups formed by teacher researchers to facilitate research studies. It also shows how to use results to decide on what to research next and thus begin a new teacher research cycle. The use of protocols in teacher research is discussed with many examples that are used for various teacher research purposes including formulating research questions, studying children's work, and deciding on next steps at the completion of a teacher research study. The book ends with examples of how teaching becomes transformed through teacher research.

# Acknowledgments

I would like to acknowledge and thank all those who contributed to this book in so many ways. First I would like to say thanks to young children, including my grandsons Sawyer and Beau, who inspire teachers to do their best everyday and to engage in teacher research to make things better for children. Next I want to acknowledge my students, who are my teachers, for their enthusiastic energy in undertaking the challenge of learning about teacher research and planning the most meaningful teacher research studies. Thanks to those who generously shared their teacher research with me: Kristi Dickey, Annie Ortiz, Andrea Rains, Jackie Needham, Sarah Sturzenbecker, Caren Feuerhelm, Peggy Lisenbee, Joy Modenbach, Holly Schuler, Karen Rogers, Sarah Chimblo, Lori Beasley, and Rhonda Hover.

I am grateful to my colleague, Pam Brown, for her friendship and collaboration and for introducing me to the Writing Project and its Teacher Inquiry Communities. I would like to acknowledge Max van Manen for his inspiring work in hermeneutic phenomenology, for his book *Researching Lived Experiences*, and for helping teachers understand that research is doable and they are the insiders in the best position to do the research.

Thanks to my friends and family, to Adam, Clint, and Melanie, and especially to my husband Douglas B. Aichele who supported me throughout the process, and to my dog, Lilly for her companionship.

I offer special thanks to my editor, Heather Jarrow, who attended my conference presentation and encouraged and supported me to do this book. In addition, I give thanks to the reviewers for all their comments and suggestions for this book: Patricia A. Crawford, Amy Halliburton Tate, and Sally Peña.

I hope that readers of this book will be inspired to do teacher research just as I have been inspired by the special people mentioned here to write about the importance of doing it.

# one
# What is Early Childhood Teacher Research?

*Please think of the children first. If you ever have anything to do with their entertainment, their food, their toys, their custody, their day or night care, their health care, their education—listen to the children, learn about them, learn from them.* Think of the children first.

Fred Rogers (2003, p. 168)

## How My (the author of this book) Teacher Research Journey Began

Young children are fascinating. Young children are vulnerable. My research journey began as a young woman caring for a two year old boy, Michael, while his mother, my sister, worked. There was a cat in their home that Michael liked to hold very much. His mother would tell him and remind him not to put his mouth on the cat. She lectured him very sternly about germs and dirt. I don't think he understood her lectures, but he did understand that she would get upset when he did this. He was not deterred by her reprimands. He continued to put his mouth on the cat. I was puzzled and curious that he would persist even when his mother would punish him. Research typically begins with puzzlement about something that doesn't quite make sense.

My study of Michael began with puzzlement and a question: Why would Michael continue to put his mouth on the cat, even when he was being punished for it? My study ended with wonder. In between the question and the wonder, I became a "child watcher" of Michael, trying to understand his motivation while I was caring for him. I watched him very closely, wondering what he was thinking. I observed him and the cat at close range. I noticed that he wasn't really putting his mouth on the cat. He was putting his cheek very close to the cat's body and just close enough that when he would do this, the cat's fur would stand on end, barely reaching his face. He was very gently and softly rubbing his cheek just close enough to the fur to feel its softness, similar to the tickle of a feather gently brushing against your cheek.

I was so surprised to see his eyes light up and an enormous smile appear on Michael's face when he gently brushed against the cat. He seemed to get great pleasure from this experience. The sequence of my research began with a puzzling situation, then a question, then systematic observation, then data gathering, and finally interpretation of the data. My interpretation was that Michael was getting such positive sensory feedback

1

from the cat that disobeying his mother was worth the price of the thrill! Reflecting on this situation hit me like a bolt of lightning: young children thrive on sensory experiences. Michael knew what he was doing and that his mother didn't approve. But he did it anyway.

My study did not end at this point. I felt I had to share my findings with my sister. She was afraid Michael would catch a disease from putting his mouth on the cat. She also thought he was doing this just to spite her. She said his behavior was a result of being in the "Terrible Twos" phase of development. I shared my observations with her including my interpretation of what was happening. She got it! Then we talked about substituting other fur-like, clean, and acceptable objects for his sensory exploration. As a result, the power struggle between Michael and his mother over the cat was resolved.

This experience fueled my desire to work with young children and their families. I wanted also to do more research like this. Although I wasn't a teacher at the time, I do think I regarded Michael with developing "teacher eyes" focused on his learning, well-being, and interests. I have been an early childhood teacher, professor, and researcher for many years now. I have witnessed the value of teacher research in improving teaching and learning experiences for children. I think teacher research is quietly reforming schooling because teachers are more likely to apply results from their own research to their teaching than results from distant researchers outside classrooms.

This chapter is about the unique qualities of early childhood teacher research. Have you already started your own teacher research journey? Have you experienced situations that didn't quite make sense to you and you wondered what was going on? Have you ever wondered why babies usually crawl before they walk or why some children learn to read at age 4 while others have great difficulty, or how you might help generate a love of books in young children? If you have a curiosity about young children and why they do what they do, then you just might be an early childhood teacher researcher! This book should help you in your journey.

---

### TEACHER RESEARCHER NOTEBOOK

 Begin to keep your own Teacher Researcher Notebook and choose a format that best fits your learning style. You might choose a spiral notebook, loose-leaf notebook, or go digital. Plan to record entries in your notebook from prompts in this book. Occasionally you will be asked to revisit entries and reinterpret their meaning, so choose a format that is easily accessible to you.

---

### TEACHER RESEARCHER NOTEBOOK ENTRY #1

Your first entry asks you to:

Try to recall a research study that you remember, possibly from a class you took or from the news media, and write down what you thought was significant about the study. Then think about reasons you remember this particular study and write about the significance this study has for you. For example, recent research says that infants need to be placed on their backs for sleeping to help prevent sudden infant death syndrome. If you have an infant or care for infants, it would be important for you to know about this research. Can you think of a similar research study?

Next reflect on a time you either had a question about your own teaching or the teaching of someone else such as a teacher you might have had. For example as an early childhood teacher, I might ask, "I wonder if all my children have equal access to my teaching, or if only a few are getting most of my attention?" Write a question about teaching and reflect on why this question is important to you.

Now consider the two entries you just wrote. Do they have anything in common? What do these examples show about the importance of research? How important do you think it is to do teacher research in early childhood?

## Teaching and Research

Teaching has been defined as to assist others to learn. Research has been defined as to systematically search and search again looking for answers to your questions. When you combine the act of teaching with the act of researching, you get teacher research: a systematic approach to studying teaching for the improvement of teaching and learning (Lankshear & Knobel, 2004). Teacher research in early childhood is very special because it puts children first in better understanding how teaching affects children's learning. In this book about teacher research in early childhood, you will learn what it is, why it is important, how to do it, and how to use results to improve the early childhood experience for the children in your care.

The reason many enter the field of early childhood education is to care and educate young children. The field is focused on the young child from birth through age eight, preschool through third grade. Some say they enter the field because they love children and have experiences taking care of them. Others say they want to give children better experiences than they had as children. These reasons may motivate individuals to enter, but will not sustain them in the field over the long term. Early childhood professionals who stay have found ways to continue learning about how children learn and develop and what they need from the adults in their lives. Just as children grow, early childhood professionals also need growth experiences in their knowledge of what it takes to be an early childhood practitioner and they continuously seek ways to improve what they do in putting children first.

Why did you consider early childhood care and education as a career? What have you learned about children and their learning that you bring into daily activities with them? How did you learn it? Early childhood practitioners who question what they do and how it affects the children in their care, use what they learn to improve what they do. A systematic approach to this learning cycle is teacher research. Early childhood teachers who do teacher research use results to improve practice, improve the learning situation for children, and put children first. They can articulate to others what they are doing and why because they study their own teaching. They have data and documentation to support what they do. For example, when a teacher engages 4 year olds in storytelling activities and records which children can retell a story and which ones have difficulty, the teacher is actually collecting data that will help improve teaching and document to parents and others what children are learning.

This chapter is about what is unique to the field of early childhood education and what is unique about early childhood teacher research. Here you will find examples of such research and reasons for doing it. Before you continue reading this chapter, record any questions you may have about early childhood teacher research in your teacher researcher notebook. As you read, seek answers to your questions and record any new questions that come to mind.

## Spiral of Teacher Research

Doing teacher research can be considered as a spiral process that begins with a question and ends with taking action or improvement of the teaching/learning situation that then leads back to new questions (Ellis and Castle, 2010). It is not circular because research results bring new understandings and knowledge that result in professional development in an ongoing cycle as in the spiral depicted in Figure 1.1. The upward cycle indicates that knowledge does not stay stagnant or the same, but grows with a teacher's learning experiences and understanding that comes from doing teacher research.

**FIGURE 1.1  Teacher Research Process**
Source: Adapted from Ellis and Castle (2010)

## What is Unique About Early Childhood Teaching?

Early childhood teaching is unique in several ways including its focus on the child, the age group involved, a special pedagogical orientation to children, the role of the family and community, and the multiple contexts in which early childhood programs reside.

## Focus on the Child

Early childhood teaching is a special area in the field of education that is focused on the child. A whole child approach to early childhood teaching facilitates children's development in all areas: physical, socio-emotional, cognitive, and aesthetic. Early childhood teachers recognize that children develop at their own pace and with their own unique developmental profile including special needs (Hooper & Umansky, 2004). The professional knowledge base in early childhood includes not only content areas such as mathematics and methods for teaching it, but also knowledge of how children develop and how they come to construct knowledge including mathematical knowledge (Geist, 2009). Working with children requires comprehension and knowledge of not just academic subjects, but knowledge of children, developmental patterns, and how to facilitate learning and development including accommodating various learning styles and special needs.

Teachers in middle and secondary schools aren't as concerned with developmental knowledge because at those levels the primary focus is not so much on the learner as it is on the subject matter content to be taught. That is not to say that teachers of older students ignore developmental patterns and milestones, but rather that adolescent learners do not experience the rapid shifts and dramatic developmental changes that younger children do. The first three years of life are particularly packed with rapid growth spurts and developmental milestones (Copple & Bredekamp, 2009; Frost, Wortham, & Reifel, 2008). In the early childhood years (0–8), young children grow from babies highly dependent on adults into functioning 8 year olds who have learned how to communicate, get around, read and write, make and keep friends, appreciate art, beauty, and nature, and inquire about the world and how it works. These are amazing feats in such a short eight years!

## Early Childhood is a Special and Vulnerable Age

Not only is the focus on the child in early childhood teaching, but also on the special age of the child in early childhood programs. Early childhood practitioners work with the youngest age group in the human life span: birth through age eight. Children are more vulnerable than older students, but young children are the most vulnerable of all. Young children are the most vulnerable because what happens to young children can leave long lasting effects including detrimental ones (Stanford & Yamamoto, 2001). The younger the child, the more damaging the detrimental effects can be. For example, infants who do not bond with a primary caregiver, may have long lasting relationship difficulties throughout their personal development. Young children who are abused or traumatized may experience long lasting effects such as learning difficulties that interfere with success in school and that are most difficult to overcome (Hooper & Umansky, 2004). Young children are also most vulnerable because they rely on adults to make decisions for them and take care of their needs. They are not yet capable of making abstract decisions that affect their welfare and rely on adults for daily needs, guidance, and nurturance. Teachers of young children have a special responsibility not only to their learning but also to their well-being.

## Pedagogical Orientation

Pedagogy is the study of the teaching–learning relationship. The early childhood teacher plays a critical role in the care and education of children. A unique and special pedagogical orientation distinguishes early childhood teaching from other professions. This pedagogical orientation is about teaching that is focused on doing what is in the best interests of the young child (van Manen, 1991). It involves consistently being mindful that young children are at the center of the early childhood program. Of course, no one can always know what is in the best interests of each child, but it is the responsibility of the early childhood teacher to always strive to do what is in each child's best interests and to reflect on consequences of decisions for making improvements for next time. Intentional teaching for what is good for children reflects a pedagogical orientation that keeps early childhood practitioners asking, What is the best thing to do? What is the best thing to do for this child in this situation? What is the best thing to do for all the children in my care? What is the best thing to do that will help children learn? (Epstein, 2007) Such questions can become the foundation for doing teacher research.

## Family and Community Involvement

The level of family and community involvement is nowhere higher than it is in early childhood programs. Families of the youngest children tend to be much more involved in their children's experiences than at any other level of education. Parents may interact with early childhood professionals on a regular basis as they drop off and pick up their children. Even programs that provide alternate means of transportation offer opportunities for families to engage with the program. And many programs are located in community facilities such as childcare centers, churches, or community buildings used for educational purposes. Family and community involvement are recognized goals for the early childhood professional and play an important role in children's success in school (Copple & Bredekamp, 2009).

## Multiple Contexts

Another unique characteristic that differentiates early childhood teaching from other teaching is that it occurs in multiple contexts. While elementary teaching is generally done in schools, early childhood teaching may occur in schools, childcare centers, and in infant and toddler programs. Early childhood programs are varied and located in a variety of settings including homes, centers, churches, schools, shopping centers, museums, and nursing homes. Early childhood programs also vary a great deal and include infant and toddler programs, preschool, kindergarten, and primary (first through third grades). Early childhood programs may vary in sponsorship and goals as reflected in Head Start, Montessori, and other curriculum models. Early childhood programs blend caring for young children with educating them (Copple & Bredekamp, 2009).

## What is Unique About Early Childhood Teacher Research?

The following are examples of Early Childhood Teacher Research Questions:

■ What do 2 year olds think about?

- Is naptime really important?
- What activities will 3 year olds choose if given a choice?
- In what ways can I communicate with children and their families who are learning English?
- Does Time Out help children learn responsibility?
- How can I get boys more involved in literacy activities?
- Do girls' preferences for dramatic play over block play interfere with their mathematical knowledge construction?

The same things that make early childhood teaching unique also apply to early childhood teacher research. Focus on the child will be at the center of early childhood teacher research. Regardless of the research questions asked, children will take priority in the research. Teachers may systematically study children's learning choices, book preferences, play activities, mathematical understanding, and social group dynamics. They may select certain planned projects to study what children learn in project work. But children's needs must come first in any inquiries that they do, even to the extent of abandoning the study if they perceive that it interferes with children's daily activities in the program.

## Teaching and Teacher Research

Early childhood teacher researchers integrate their research with their program goals and activities. The difference between the early childhood teacher and teacher researcher is that the teacher researcher systematically studies her teaching and children's learning. Teacher researchers systematically scrutinize what they do and use results to make changes in the program (Pine, 2009).

For example, a kindergarten teacher who does morning meeting time everyday may want to study the time of the morning that will maximize children's participation. She may vary the time of morning it is done. For one week she may do morning meeting at the very beginning of the day when children first arrive. The next week she may have center time first and morning meeting following center time. Her research question may be: In what ways does the scheduled time of morning meeting affect children's participation in morning meeting?

For data collection, she may keep a journal for two weeks recording her observations and thoughts about children's participation in the two approaches. During each morning meeting time, she may use a check sheet to record the number of times individual children participate in each session including checking who participates and the type of participation: asking questions, volunteering information, making constructive comments, or disrupting the group. If available, she may even have an assistant who records participation during the meeting sessions for her.

She may also ask children to tell her when they prefer to have the morning meeting time. This would give her three data sources: her journal entries, check sheet participation frequencies and types, and children's preferences. She would then analyze the data, draw some conclusions, and use the results to schedule future morning meetings. She may find out that the two times she has studied make no difference in children's participation. At that point, she may study other times morning meeting may be offered or decide that the time it is offered is not much of an issue with children's participation. If she is concerned about lack of participation, she may decide to study different teaching techniques to promote more participation.

You may be thinking that this example reflects what good teaching is all about. You may ask, What is the difference between just good teaching and teacher research? Some educators think they are the same (Hubbard & Power, 1999). Others say that systematic study and acting on results distinguish teacher research from teaching (Hopkins, 2002). What do you think?

## Children's Age and Teacher Research

Early childhood teacher research is done with the youngest age groups. Early childhood teachers are responsible most of all for the safety and well-being of the children in their care. Issues related to young children and other types of research include the possibilities of coercion to participate in the research, lack of informed child assent, research that detracts from children's needs, and lack of confidentiality (Mertler, 2009). All of these issues will be dealt with in detail in the chapters to follow. These issues are more typical of other types of outsider research and less typical of teacher research. But coercion of children to participate can be an issue when the research involves activities that are not part of the routine activities of the regular program. Because young children tend to respond to teachers as authority figures, they tend to think they must do what teachers tell them to do. It is important to keep this in mind when doing teacher research and make sure that children are not doing things merely for purposes of the research. Unlike other types of research, most teacher research focuses on what teachers and children do in the regular program and does not impose external treatments or interventions from the outside. Teacher research is insider research (Cochran-Smith and Lytle, 2009).

Teacher research usually reflects existing program goals and objectives. The idea is to study what is already being done in the program. Teacher research attempts to study how to make the program better. Early childhood teacher researchers typically do research because they are motivated to improve education for young children including improving their own teaching and growing in their professional knowledge.

## Reasons to Do Early Childhood Teacher Research

There are many reasons to do early childhood teacher research. Some do teacher research for their own purposes, not intending to share results with others. Others may want to share their significant findings with others, particularly other teachers who may benefit. In general, the primary reason is to improve teaching and learning.

### To Deepen Understanding of Teaching

One reason to do early childhood teacher research is to deepen one's understanding of teaching and what it means to work with young children. Teacher research becomes a tool to contemplate the meaning of teaching and add to one's knowledge of teaching strategies in order to become a wiser teacher. Teacher research can help an early childhood teacher find answers to the question, Am I doing what I intend to do in my teaching? For example, a teacher may have the perception that he is sensitive to children's cultural backgrounds and teaching for inclusiveness and diversity. Keeping a teacher research journal may help him better understand the ways in which he does this in his verbal communications with children. The journal becomes a reflective tool to help him record his thoughts and observations. He can analyze his journal entries looking for patterns of inclusiveness in communications. Analysis may confirm or disconfirm his perceptions and give him direction for future communications.

## To Help Solve Problems

The earlier example of the kindergarten teacher who wanted to find the best time for morning meeting to maximize children's participation, is an example of teacher research that helps solve problems. Teachers who have a problem, such as lack of student motivation, can use teacher research as a tool to find better ways to engage children's interests. Results of one study may not solve the problem, but may help teachers clarify the problem and refine their research questions so that they will eventually solve the problem.

## To Improve Teaching and Learning

Teachers use results from their teacher research to make changes in their teaching that improve the learning situation for children. For example, a third grade teacher was concerned that children were having difficulty staying on task in doing their seatwork. In analyzing what he was doing before and after he assigned the work, he found that the set of instructions he was giving children prior to doing their work was too long resulting in their inattention to what he was asking them to do. He decided to make changes in the way he gave instructions. The changes he made resulted in more on task behavior and learning from the assignments.

## For Professional Development

Teacher research can be a form of professional development. Teacher research engages the teacher in thinking about teaching and new teaching approaches and strategies. Teachers who do teacher research learn not just about how to do it, but also about new approaches to teaching they can incorporate into their knowledge base. Teacher research helps teachers to develop their professional knowledge base, teaching skills, and also mentoring skills in helping other teachers, particularly beginning teachers.

## To Contribute to the Early Childhood Knowledge Base

When teacher researchers share results form their studies, they add to the knowledge base in the field. Their results shared at meetings, conferences, on websites, and in written publications, such as teacher research journals, help others looking for information on particular topics or problems. The collective body of knowledge from teacher research is quite impressive. Access to the studies of other teachers gives teachers ideas to try in their own teaching and encouragement to do teacher research. The idea is if other teachers can do this, maybe I can too. Teacher research is currently changing the face of schooling (Hendricks, 2009). Chapter Two will provide even more reasons for doing teacher research and give many examples of teacher research studies.

## From the Field

Abena is a college student majoring in early childhood education. One of her practicum experiences is in a local Head Start program for 4 year olds. Her college supervisor has asked students to come up with a question about their work they can ask and get answered during their 6-week practicum experience. Abena wasn't sure what the focus of her study would be. She tried out several ideas before she settled on her question: What role does having a friend play for an immigrant child in adjusting to the program? Abena has decided to focus on one immigrant male child, Uday, who has been excluded from play activities by the other children in the program. Abena has decided to encourage a friendship relationship between this child and another boy, Max, who is friendly and demonstrates social skills in interactions with other children.

Abena works closely with the Head Start teacher who has encouraged Abena to do the research. Abena creates opportunities for Uday and Max to work together in centers and to sit together during group times. She plans activities that pair the boys up such as working jointly on making a collage, writing a story, and building a village. She keeps a teacher research journal in which she records her observations of the boys' interactions, the level of participation that Uday shows in the group, and her own reflections on the extent to which this friendship has helped Uday become more accepted and included in the group. At the end of the 6-week practicum, Abena writes a report of her findings that she shares with her supervisor and the Head Start teacher. Her report summarizes the systematic approach she took in collecting, analyzing, and interpreting data and provides specific recommendations for encouraging friendship relationships in the future.

## REFLECTIONS

What do you think about Abena's study?

What have you done or are currently doing in your teaching that could be considered teacher research?

In what ways can you picture yourself as an early childhood teacher researcher?

What strengths do you bring to early childhood teaching? To teacher research?

What burning questions do you have about teaching young children?

## Explorations

Visit the website of the National Association for the Education of Young Children (www.NAEYC.org) and take the link to Voices of Practitioners then to Teacher Research Articles. Find an example of early childhood teacher research that is interesting to you. What is the main research question? Who is asking the question? What is the purpose of the study? What are the methods of data collection and analysis? How might results be used to improve educational experiences of young children? Why does this study have meaning for you? Share your findings with others.

Choose one of the websites below to explore for ideas about teacher research and teacher research studies:

Reprint of "How Do I Learn How to Do Action Research?" by Jack Whitehead at http://www.ncsu.edu/meridian/2000wint/action/index.html
http://www.lupinworks.com/jn/
http://gse.gmu.edu/research/tr/
http://oldweb.madison.k12.wi.us/sod/car/carhomepage.html

## References

Cochran-Smith, M., & Lytle, S. L. (2009). *Inquiry as stance: Practitioner research for the next generation*. New York: Teachers College Press.

Copple, C., & Bredekamp, S. (Eds.) (2009). *Developmentally appropriate practice in early childhood programs serving children from birth through age 8* (3rd edition). Washington, DC: National Association for the Education of Young Children.

Ellis, C., & Castle, K. (2010). Teacher research as continuous process improvement. *Quality Assurance in Education*, 18(4), 271–285.

Epstein, A. S. (2007). *The intentional teacher, choosing the best strategies for young children's learning*. Washington, DC: National Association for the Education of Young Children.

Frost, J. L., Wortham, S. C., & Reifel, S. (2008). *Play and child development* (3rd edition). Columbus, OH: Pearson Merrill Prentice Hall.

Geist, E. (2009). *Children are born mathematicians*. Columbus, OH: Merrill Pearson.

Hendricks, C. (2009). *Improving schools through action research*. Columbus, OH: Pearson.

Hooper, S. R., & Umansky, W. (2004). *Young children with special needs* (4th edition). Columbus, OH: Pearson Merrill Prentice Hall.

Hopkins, D. (2002). *A teacher's guide to classroom research*. Philadelphia: Open University Press.

Hubbard, R. S., & Power, B. M. (1999). *Living the questions, a guide for teacher-researchers*. York, ME: Stenhouse Publishers.

Lankshear, C., & Knobel, M. (2004). *A handbook for teacher research*. New York: Open University Press.

Mertler, C. A. (2009). *Action research* (2nd edition). Thousand Oaks, CA: Sage.

Pine, G. J. (2009). *Teacher action research*. Thousand Oaks, CA: Sage.

Rogers, F. (2003). *The world according to Mister Rogers*. New York: Hyperion.

Stanford, B. H., & Yamamoto, K. (Eds.) (2001). *Children and stress*. Onley, MD: Association for Childhood Education International.

van Manen, M. (1991). *The tact of teaching*. Albany, NY: State University of New York Press.

# two
# What is the Purpose of Early Childhood Teacher Research?

*I love the voice of teacher research. It encompasses the personal and professional points of view that are who we are as teachers.*

Third Grade Teacher Researcher

This chapter shows the role of early childhood teacher research in the professional development of early childhood teachers. It juxtaposes what good teaching is with what teacher research is all about. It explores what readers may currently be doing that is already teacher research and that can develop into a teacher research agenda. Multiple purposes of teacher research are presented including documentation of children's learning, assessment including portfolio assessment, and movement toward quality teaching. This chapter addresses how teacher research may help meet professional standards including working toward National Board of Professional Teaching Standards certification.

## What Teachers Already Do That Can Become Teacher Research

The idea of doing teacher research may be a bit intimidating to those who haven't considered it and to those who view research as a capital R endeavor, something that others removed from the classroom do. In order to get beyond these perceptions, it helps to consider what you are currently doing in your teaching that could be enlisted as data for a systematic study about your teaching and possible changes to your work. For example, if you currently gather any of the items listed below, consider these things as possible data sources that are already at hand and that you could use to answer your own questions about your teaching, children's learning, and your educational program:

- Children's drawings
- Examples of children's written work such as journal entries, worksheets, narratives, and assignments
- Photos/videos of children's block constructions, sand play, dramatic play enactments, and performances

- Anecdotal notes you have taken about children's activities
- Rubric assessments of children's performance
- Quizzes/tests
- Records of children's progress
- Children's portfolio items, such as written stories and illustrations, used to show long-term progress.

Chapter Five expands upon these data sources with examples from teacher research studies.

Taking inventory of what you already have that could become data sources to answer your teacher research questions is a good thing to do before beginning a study. You may find that in order to answer your teacher research questions, you don't need more data, but just need to do a systematic study of the data you currently have. Teachers who considered their current data sources in light of the questions they wanted to answer explain how getting research started can be quick and easy:

> I had photos of my preschoolers' block constructions that I could use as data to answer my research question about what children learn through block play.

> I wanted to find out if reading comprehension, specifically sequencing, was learned better by my third graders in small group or large group work. I found I could use my existing rubric assessments to analyze by small/large groups.

> Our program requires that we complete forms making anecdotal notes on our four-year-old children's activities during center time. I wanted to study what choices individual children were making and how their choices were reflected in their learning. I used my existing anecdotal records to study that question.

---

### Explorations

If you currently teach, take inventory of possible existing data sources you have access to. Make a list of all the ways children's learning is documented in your program. Review the list reflecting on some teacher research questions you might ask and could get answered with your existing data sources.

If you are not currently teaching, then conduct a brief interview of an early childhood teacher, asking about existing ways children's learning is documented in her program. Make a list of existing data sources and review the list thinking about possible teacher research questions that the data sources from her program may help to answer. Keep your list and set of questions in your Teacher Researcher Journal for possible future teacher research projects.

## Role of Teacher Research in Professional Development

As Chapter One indicated, teacher research can be done for many purposes including for professional development, to become a better teacher, and to make a professional contribution to the field. For many experienced teachers who do teacher research as a part of their everyday teaching lives, teacher research is just good teaching. It is what good teachers do naturally in order to answer questions they have about teaching and learning (Hubbard & Power, 1999). As one teacher said, "I now realize that as a kindergarten teacher, I can be a researcher too." Teachers who are thinking about the impact they are making on children will question what they are doing and whether it is making a difference. Answering this question is a form of teacher research that helps a teacher better understand her children's learning and make necessary changes. This spiraling process results in professional development and understanding. Teachers who don't question their work don't usually grow as professionals.

The professional life of a teacher has a certain developmental progression to it (Steffy, Wolfe, Pasch, & Enz, 2000). It may even begin in childhood with an interest in imitating a teacher or playing "school". The passion to enter teaching is often driven by a desire to help people, especially to help them learn. This passion to become an educator may lead one to get an education to prepare oneself for teaching. Such an education may be to enter a 2, 4, 5 year, or graduate teacher education program at a college or university. It may also lead one into a teacher training program or alternative teacher certification pathway. Whatever pathway you have chosen will eventually put you in a classroom to work with young children. As you begin a teaching career, you may have many questions about what to do. As you get these questions answered and gain valuable teaching experience, your questions may become more systematic in terms of gaining answers you can use to document the difference you are making in children's lives.

At this point you may be drawn to teacher research either as an individual teacher or with a group of trusted colleagues. Your own teacher research will help you better understand how you are meeting educational goals and how to better articulate your work to others including to parents and administrators. In the sections that follow you will find examples of teacher research that is done at various stages of teachers' professional development.

### Pre-Service Teacher Research

Various forms of teacher inquiry may be part of teacher education programs at both the undergraduate and graduate levels. Many teacher education programs that meet accreditation standards of the National Council for Accreditation of Teacher Education (NCATE) prepare students to engage in **evidence based teaching**—teaching focused on documenting that learning has occurred with evidence of that learning, such as assessments of child performance and achievement. Teacher education students may be asked to prepare lessons with clear performance objectives, implement lessons with children, and then assess the extent to which the objectives were accomplished as evidenced by an analysis of children's performance as a result of the lesson. Increasingly teacher education programs must demonstrate evidence based teaching of students in the programs (Cochran-Smith, 2006).

For example, an undergraduate pre-service teacher education program offers a course entitled Literacy in Early Childhood Education. One requirement in the course is for students to work in a preschool classroom and teach literacy lessons based on mandated literacy objectives for the preschool level. Students are evaluated not only on the lesson they prepare but also on the assessment and documentation of children's learning from the lesson. Benjamin, a pre-service teacher in the program taking the Literacy in Early Childhood course, prepared a lesson for his practicum setting in a 4-year-old classroom. His literacy objective from the state mandated list for 4-year-old programs was for children to understand and comprehend literature such as a children's book. He chose the book *Friends* by Helme Heine (1986) to share with his group of children. He then prepared a lesson plan complete with the literacy objective and a description of the planned group time read aloud and discussion of the book.

In addition to the mandated objective, Benjamin asked himself another question. He really wanted to know what children might learn about the meaning of friendship by listening to and discussing this particular book. He thought it was important for young children to learn how to be a friend through children's literature, class discussions about friendship and what it looks like, sounds like, and feels like, role playing various friendship scenarios using puppets, and through his own modeling and pointing out to children instances of what friends do for each other.

Benjamin's assessment of the literacy objective was to determine children's understanding of the story by their responses to questions about the story. He hoped to learn to what extent they understood the friendship behaviors of the book characters and the extent to which they were able to retell the story. In his documentation of children's learning, he wrote that all eight children were able to describe the friendship behaviors of the characters, four children were able to give specific examples of other types of friendship behaviors they had experienced, and three children could retell the story with no errors. In his teacher journal, he wrote about what he thought children had learned about friendship and described several anecdotes he observed of children helping each other and making comments about how their behavior was similar to the characters in the book.

What makes this an example of teacher research? Benjamin extended his thinking about children's learning by asking what they were learning and systematically documenting their learning in his assessment and in the journal he kept. Benjamin's own interest in children's learning about friendship motivated his behavior and resulted in his ability to answer his own "research" question. Teacher research is about systematically studying teaching and learning and applying results to new situations. Such activity leads to a deeper understanding of teaching. Such activity also helps pre-service teachers to learn that the process of teacher research leads to becoming a good teacher.

## In Service Teacher Research

In service teachers who do teacher research may be motivated in similar ways as Benjamin to learn more about children's understanding in order to improve teaching. In service teachers who do teacher research tend to be either more experienced teachers wanting to improve their teaching or teachers who are around other teachers doing teacher research who are intrigued by the results and wish to be part of the process. In service teachers may also become interested in doing teacher research in an attempt to demonstrate evidence and documentation of children's learning to others as well as to themselves.

An example of an in service teacher research study comes from a third grade teacher, Jan, who wanted to document children's mathematics learning to show evidence of their learning to her administrator and to parents. One state mandated learning objective for third grade math was to develop problem-solving strategies. Jan wanted to find out whether children learned problem solving better from the required math curriculum or from playing math games requiring strategy. She set about to do a systematic study by dividing her class in half and engaging one half in the mandated curriculum and one half in game playing. After four weeks she assessed their problem solving and switched the groups so that the game group then participated in the math curriculum and the mandated curriculum group engaged in game playing. At the end of four more weeks (eight weeks altogether) she gave a similar problem solving assessment to all children. The final assessment asked children to solve the problem of transporting rehabilitated sea turtles back to the beach to be turned loose, where only 3 sea turtles maximum fit per truck, with a maximum of 4 available trucks for transporting, and 31 turtles needing to be transported. Children were asked to show as many strategies for solving the problem as they could. Then she compared their performance in terms of the number of strategies each child demonstrated to correctly solve the problem in both the first and second assessments. In comparing the performance of the two groups, Jan found no significant differences in their ability to solve the problem with at least one strategy, but the group that played games first and then participated in the math curriculum demonstrated a greater number of problem solving strategies than the other group had in both assessments. She therefore decided to change her teaching by incorporating game playing first before introducing the mandated curriculum.

What makes this an example of teacher research? Again this teacher conducted a systematic study of two different ways to teach problem solving. She collected and analyzed assessment data and used results to make changes in her teaching. Conducting the study gave her a more informed understanding of children's problem solving strategies plus the evidence to apply what she learned to her teaching in making modifications in her program.

## Graduate Level Teacher Research

Many graduate programs now require either a course in teacher research or a unit on teacher research in other courses. Many experienced teachers who have been teaching for a few years may first hear about teacher research in a graduate class. They may be asked to plan and conduct a teacher research study in their own classroom. For example, Tamara, a first grade teacher working on a master's degree in early childhood education, was required to take two research courses. She chose a course on Teacher Research because she thought she might be able to apply it to her teaching. Course requirements included planning and conducting a teacher research study on a question chosen by each student in the class. Tamara had never thought about doing her own research and had difficulty posing a teacher research question.

Engaging in a structured class discussion called a **protocol** (see Chapters Three and Eight for additional information on protocols) used in the teacher research course on refining research questions gave her insight into what she wanted to do in her own teacher research project. Tamara worked in a school on the state school improvement list that had been told to improve their test score results or they would face being taken over by the state department of education. There was much pressure on the teachers at Tamara's school to show test score increases. In fact, recess had been eliminated two years earlier in order for teachers to devote maximum time to improving test scores.

Tamara was worried most about her students' math scores, and brainstormed what she could do to improve them. She had heard about a school in which fifth graders were allowed to sit and bounce on large inflated fitness balls while doing their school work. The classroom she read about had only fitness balls, no chairs, for children to sit on. The fifth grade teacher and children seemed to like the situation and reported being more interested in doing school work as a result of being able to move on the balls.

Tamara decided that her first grade students might benefit from having more opportunities for movement, especially since their recess time had been taken away. Tamara planned a study of using fitness balls with her students to increase math test scores and increase her students' interest in math. She collected baseline math test scores from her students then implemented math time with fitness balls. After a period of four weeks, she collected math test scores and compared them to the baseline scores. In addition, she interviewed seven children at random about their interest in math before and after using fitness balls. Not only did her math scores improve but also children enjoyed their opportunities for physical movement that had previously been denied to them. Based on their interview responses, all seven children indicated more interest in math after using the fitness balls than before the balls were available. Tamara had begun her graduate Teacher Research class with few ideas about teacher research and ended it with a successful teacher research project that increased her enthusiasm for doing teacher research and benefited her first grade students.

These are a few of the examples of teachers coming to teacher research. The next section gives additional examples of how teachers can take what they currently do and transform it into systematic study called teacher research.

---

### REFLECTIONS

Where are you in your career development? Are you preparing to become an early childhood teacher or are you a teacher already? Reflect on your own professional development and identify places in your own professional development that would lend themselves to doing teacher research. If you are in a teacher preparation program, where in the program, such as in a course or practicum, could you see yourself doing teacher research? If you are a teacher, what activities do you engage in that could evolve into teacher research?

---

## From Current Teaching Practices to Teacher Research

Chapter One asked you to reflect on what you are currently doing that might be considered teacher research. Some teachers who answered this question indicated they already observe children's behaviors looking for their interests and needs and what they might be learning. They interact with children and make mental or written notes about what children say or how they interact with others. Teachers ask themselves questions about certain children such as why a child doesn't seem to be interested in learning. They plan and work with children in daily activities and project work collecting children's work, evaluating their work, and recording the extent to which a child's work represents accomplishment of program objectives, whether a child may benefit from special services, and what needs to be changed in the program. Teachers reflect on their own teaching and its impact on learners and try new ways of doing things to help children learn. How many of these things have you done? When done systematically, these activities can be part of a teacher research study. The following section gives a few examples of what teachers do that can become teacher research.

## Anecdotal Observation Notes

As part of routine practice, many early childhood teachers make notes of significant happenings and children's behaviors during small and large group activities and free choice time. **Anecdotal notes** can be made on the fly as events happen or after the fact at later times when a teacher has an opportunity to write about the event. Anecdotal notes usually include the date, time interval, context of what is happening, children's names/ initials, and a brief description of the event. Anecdotal notes are commonly used by teachers to help in making written profiles of individual children for reflection on what they might need next to advance their learning and to share with parents in progress reports. Teachers may record notes when events happen or they may record on a systematic timeline such as once a week for each child.

Guoping, a teacher in a 3-year-old program, made anecdotal records both on a timeline of every two weeks as well as when significant things happened that she wanted to capture. She found that she recorded more frequent anecdotal records and events happening in the block building and dramatic play areas than any other area. She wondered if the reason for this was that more significant child behaviors happened in blocks and dramatic play or if she was more aware of events happening in those areas due to the higher noise levels in those areas getting her attention. She decided to study in which areas of the room more significant events were happening. She planned to observe the same amount of time in each area over the course of two weeks and then to tally the events recorded in her anecdotal notes by frequency and type of events. She discovered that significant events were mostly equally divided across areas but that some more quiet areas did not draw her attention the way that noisy areas did. She concluded based on analyzing her data that she needed to focus her attention more equally across areas. In this example, the teacher used existing anecdotal data she was already collecting, but made the collection of the data more systematic in order to more conclusively answer her question.

## Children's Project Work

Project work or the Project Approach (Katz & Chard, 2000) is implemented by many early childhood teachers to encourage children's interests in pursuing their own questions about things such as nature, machines, events, cultural traditions, and a variety of other topics that have relevance for children. Children express their learning about project topics in their activities, drawings, writing, and play. Teachers document children's learning by analyzing the products of their project work. In order to find out what children might be learning from a project on the nature of a wheat field, Anne, a kindergarten teacher, planned for children's activities related to the project by bringing into the classroom many books, videos, and materials. She brought in wheat, setup a field trip to a local wheat field, scheduled a local farmer to speak to the class, and created many activities related to the wheat field for children to experience including expressive art, math, literacy, science (which included a baking activity), and social studies.

What might move this project into becoming a teacher research study? Anne had taken a workshop on documenting children's learning. She wanted to use what she learned to show that project work integrated all areas of the kindergarten curriculum. Her teacher research question became: To what extent do children learn math, science, social studies, literacy, and expressive arts in project work on a wheat field? She collected samples of children's project work such as their drawings and writings about the stages in growing wheat, their artwork using various parts of a wheat plant for paint brushes, photos of their constructions of a wheat field outside the classroom, and their group dictated stories about why wheat is important. She studied these child artifacts looking for concepts indicating children's learning. With the children's help, she created a **documentation panel** showing the stages of the project and displaying children's work with captions about their learning. The documentation panel was displayed in the hallway outside the classroom for other students, teachers, and parents to study. Anne connected what children learned to the mandated kindergarten objectives. She presented her project to other teachers and to her principal as evidence that children learn through project work. Other teachers then decided to conduct their own teacher research projects because they too wanted to document what their children were learning.

## Assessment

Young children should be assessed in appropriate ways that do not add undue stress to their lives. Early childhood teachers conduct assessments in a variety of ways including asking children to engage in self-assessment, which helps teachers and the children themselves to judge the quality of children's own work across time. The National Association for the Education of Young Children (NAEYC) with the National Association of Early Childhood Specialists in State Departments of Education (NAECS/SDE) adopted guidelines for early childhood assessment that say assessment should be:

Developmentally appropriate

Culturally and linguistically responsive

Tied to children's daily activities; inclusive of families

Done with clear, beneficial purposes in order to inform teaching and learning, to identify concerns that may require intervention, and to improve educational interventions.

(NAEYC & NAECS/SDE, 2003)

Early childhood teachers have a responsibility to assess children in appropriate ways to benefit their learning and to identify possible needs for interventions. A single test or single assessment is usually not appropriate for making decisions about children's educational programs. Young children continuously change and are greatly influenced by the context in which assessment is done. Multiple forms of assessment provide a more holistic picture of a child's development: "Assessment is the process of gathering information about children from several forms of evidence, then organizing and interpreting that information." (McAfee, Leong, and Bodrova, 2004, p. 3) Types of assessments include tests, anecdotal records, recorded observations of performance, checklists, rating scales, and authentic assessment based on children's performance (not tests) during the regular educational program (Branscombe, Castle, Dorsey, Surbeck, and Taylor, 2003).

Portfolio assessment refers to collecting artifacts of children's work, such as writing samples, in a portfolio or file so that children's progress can be analyzed and interpreted and shared with others, such as with parents. Items chosen for inclusion in a portfolio provide evidence of children's learning. The **portfolio** represents a long-term record of progress reflecting a teacher's evaluation of the materials as well as the possible self-evaluations that children do when asked to compare an item they produced at the beginning of the year to one at a later point in time and when asked to select and give reasons for their best work.

First grade teacher, Bryon, systematically collected children's work samples that he kept in a portfolio for each child. He evaluated the work samples using a combination of checklists and rubrics that assessed the extent to which children made progress in their learning. Part of each child's portfolio included numerous samples of their writing from the first week of the program. After the first of the calendar year when parent progress reports were due, Bryon wondered what children might learn from assessing their own work. He decided to try to answer this teacher research question using existing portfolio data and systematically focusing only on the area of writing. He held individual conferences with each child and recorded their self-evaluations of their writing from the first week of the program in August to the middle of January. He asked each child to pick a piece of their writing from the first week and to tell him about it while he took notes. He then asked them to pick a current sample of writing and to tell him about it. He then asked each child to compare the two writing samples and to tell him what they viewed as good about their own work. After completion of all individual conferences, Bryon analyzed his notes looking for the reasons children gave for what was good about their work. He classified their responses into the following categories:

> **Non-reflective:** doesn't give any reasons for why the work is good
>
> **Somewhat reflective:** cites a reason or two based on what the child says he likes about the work
>
> **Reflective:** cites several reasons for why the work is both good and needs improvement
>
> **Analytical:** analyzes their own work using standard conventions of writing such as spelling, punctuation, neatness, sequencing of events, characterization, setting, and purpose for the writing.

Bryon concluded that most first graders were somewhat reflective about their own work and that a small number (3) were analytical indicating they had learned some of the standard conventions of writing. He concluded that through self-assessment children became more focused on analysis of what was good or needed improvement in their own writing and began to learn about standard conventions of writing, one of the learner outcomes for his grade level, as a result of their self-evaluations. Based on his analysis of results, Bryon decided to implement writing journals and to provide more time in the program for free writing as well as for teacher prompted writing. In addition, he decided to incorporate self-evaluation of children's own writing and conferencing with them about their self-evaluations into his curriculum.

The previous examples show that teachers in general already have an abundance of data at hand that could be used to do teacher research. The key to moving from what is already being done to teacher research is focusing on a more systematic approach to data gathering and analysis. The chapters that follow will provide information on the systematic approach to teacher research.

## Quality Teaching and Teacher Research

The main thing that quality teaching and teacher research have in common is the aim to make education better for children. Palmer, (2007) finds, "Good teachers possess a capacity for connectedness. They are able to weave a complex web of connections among themselves, their subjects, and their students so that students can learn to weave a world for themselves." (p. 11) Teachers who take an inquiry stance in their teaching (Cochran-Smith & Lytle, 2009) continuously try to weave meaningful connections, question what they do, whether it was the right thing to do, and how to make it better next time. This inquiry stance demonstrates a level of professionalism and care for teaching and learning. Teachers who take such a stance find their voices, know why they do what they do, and can articulate their professional rationale to others. They can also add their voices to the voices of others to make significant changes to benefit students (Pine, 2009). This then becomes a form of professional courage. Taulbert (2006) says, "Courage often allows educators not only to think outside the box but also to take positive steps that may fly in the face of tradition." (p. 105) Teachers demonstrate courage through doing teacher research. Such courage has also been described as **teacher (pedagogical) autonomy**, the ability to make professional judgments and actions based on the right thing to do, taking into consideration all relevant perspectives, and in spite of the reward system in place (Castle, 2006; Kamii, 1985). Autonomous teacher researchers demonstrate an ethic care for children and for the educative process (Noddings, 1992). They study their own teaching in order to make it better and help improve the learning situation for children. In order to become an autonomous teacher researcher, it is important to cultivate existing strengths and to develop new ones.

---

### From the Field

Andrea Rains, elementary teacher researcher, commented on her experiences:

> My teacher research question was, "What can I do to help students understand measurement?" My teacher research enhanced my own professional development. If I had read an article about students measuring it may have given me an idea to toy with or an activity to try out in my room. However, my teacher research was better for my students because it directly involved

*Continued overleaf*

them and I was able to interact with each of my students on a personal level. No staff development or Harvard research article could have done that for my students. I strongly support staff development and professional research articles. But I think that when teacher research is added to a body of research then one's professional development can take place at a much deeper level. The research has a personal meaning and once again, it's from that personal narrative that a teacher gains strength and empowerment.

## Teacher Researcher Strengths

Early childhood teachers uniquely demonstrate many teacher researcher strengths including observation skills, organizational skills, questioning skills, a disposition to be reflective, ability to analyze children's work, and collaborative skills that enable them to work well with others. All of these skills can be developed and become employed when doing teacher research. All are important to systematically answer questions about teaching and learning. To become a teacher researcher it helps to reflect on the researcher strengths you already have and use in your teaching and then consider developing additional researcher strengths.

There is a delightful children's book that can be used to consider your own teacher researcher strengths and compare them to the ones demonstrated by the main character in the book. The book can also be shared with children. The book is *Dear Mr. Blueberry* by Simon James (1991). If possible, read the book looking for the researcher strengths of Emily, the main character. Try to identify as many of Emily's strengths as possible. Then consider your own strengths as compared to those Emily demonstrates in her quest to understand her whale.

The story involves a series of letters between Emily and her teacher, Mr. Blueberry, during the summer months when she is not in school. Emily asks her teacher for information about whales because she saw one in the pond in her backyard. Her teacher discourages her from possibly thinking that a whale could live in her pond, but shares some information with her about whales. Throughout Emily's communications with her teacher and her quest to learn more about whales so that she will know what to feed her whale and how best to care for him, she demonstrates many researcher strengths. She asks questions, seeks information from outside experts and written sources, observes her whale, hypothesizes about her whale's behavior, conducts an experiment with her whale, analyzes her whale's behavior, demonstrates persistence and determination in resisting the obstacles put in her way by her teacher, and her parents, and shows passion through her commitment to her whale, the object of her study. These are the strengths that teacher researchers need to study their own teaching. Each strength can be practiced and developed through the everyday activities of teaching. Emily's experience shows the importance of persistence and determination in following one's questions and discovering where they might lead.

---

**TEACHER RESEARCHER NOTEBOOK ENTRY #2:**

 Create a poem about your own teacher researcher strengths using the format below modified from Ayers (2001) for an autobiographical poem:

Line 1: Your first name
Line 2: Three words that describe your strengths as a researcher
Line 3: A research question you might have asked in the past
Line 4: A research question you would like to pursue
Line 5: Something that would help you live your question
Line 6: One thing you like about research
Line 7: Your last name.

Consider sharing your poem with others. Here is an example:

Kathryn
Observant, passionate, persistent
How do interactions help children learn to take others' perspectives?
What do early childhood teachers need to conduct teacher research?
Collaborations with teachers
Getting results from questions and wonderings
Castle

---

## Quality Teaching Defined by the Profession

Multiple professional associations and boards have attempted to address what is meant by quality teaching. The definitions across groups have similar characteristics primarily centered on the importance of understanding young children and how they develop and learn.

### NAEYC Appropriate Practices for Early Childhood Teachers

The largest early childhood association, the National Association for the Education of Young Children (**NAEYC**), has developed guidelines for appropriate practices set forth in *Developmentally Appropriate Practice in Early Childhood Programs* (3rd edition, Copple and Bredekamp, 2009). These guidelines call for teaching that addresses children's developmental levels, individual differences and cultural backgrounds. The major guidelines of NAEYC's appropriate practices are about:

Creating a caring community of learners

Teaching to enhance development and learning

Planning curriculum to achieve important goals

Assessing children's development and learning

Establishing reciprocal relationships with families. (Copple & Bredekamp, 2009, pp. 16–23).

Copple and Bredekamp (2009) describe what teachers can do to implement the guidelines that lead to excellence in teaching. They say that to be an excellent teacher means implementing the guidelines based on a teacher's knowledge of child development and learning in an intentional way to enhance the educational experience for the individual children in the program. They say that excellent teachers do these things:

Use a wide range of teaching strategies

Scaffold children's learning

Make purposeful use of various learning formats. (Copple & Bredekamp, 2009, pp. 36–41).

Copple and Bredekamp's description of excellence in teaching parallels what teacher researchers do in collecting and analyzing data about children and using results to improve the program for children. For example, on assessment they say:

Assessment information is vital to guide teachers' planning, The excellent teacher uses her observations and other information gathered to inform her planning and teaching, giving careful consideration to the learning experiences needed by the group as a whole and by each individual child. By observing what children explore, what draws their interest, and what they say they do, the teacher determines how to adapt the environment, materials, or daily routines. The teacher can make an activity simpler or more complex according to what individual children are ready for. Then, her follow-up plans can include giving children repeated experiences with an idea or skill to get a solid grasp of it. Effective planning also means considering where the child or group of children might go next.

(2009, pp. 44–45)

## Core Competencies

Similar to the NAEYC guidelines for appropriate practice, many states and local agencies have established sets of competencies that early childhood teachers should strive to achieve. Such competencies are usually complementary to the work of teacher research in advocating teacher activities such as reflection, observation of children, gathering of data about children, analysis of data, and reflection on results to make needed changes in the educational program. One such set of competencies was developed by early childhood professionals in the state of Oklahoma in their 2008 *Oklahoma Core Competencies for Early Childhood Practitioners*. This set of competencies calls for teacher reflection and research in order to demonstrate professionalism. For example, the Child Observation and Assessment Competency calls for teacher observation and authentic assessment to obtain information for curriculum planning and systematic, ongoing evaluation (p. 27). Teachers working toward achieving the competencies or other goals such as teacher certification or national board certification are usually asked to demonstrate skills that can be utilized in teacher research.

## National Board for Professional Teaching Standards (NBPTS)

The National Board for Professional Teaching Standards (**NBPTS**) created in 1987 has now certified over 82,000 teachers and recertified over 2,000 teachers. NBPTS was created to provide a national certification program to certify quality teachers who participate in and pass the certification process. The process may take two years to complete and involves study of one's own teaching, documentation through preparation of a teacher portfolio, and participation in an assessment center that all show one has met the standards for what teachers should know and be able to do. The knowledge, skills, and dispositions that teachers should possess are represented in the NBPTS Five Core Propositions (www.nbpts.org, 2010):

1. Teachers are committed to students and their learning
2. Teachers know the subjects they teach and how to teach those subjects to students
3. Teachers are responsible for managing and monitoring student learning
4. Teachers think systematically about their practice and learn from experience
5. Teachers are members of learning communities.

While all five propositions are important, propositions numbered 4 and 5 directly relate to the activities of teacher research. The board certification process requires teachers to reflect on their teaching and their students' learning and to study their teaching through producing portfolio entries that require systematic collection and analysis of student work.

The NBPTS Early Childhood Generalist Standards for teachers of students ages 3–8 are currently under revision. The existing standards emphasize understanding young children through reflective practice. Teachers undertake national board certification for many reasons. One teacher said, "I had grown past district workshops. I wanted to move to another depth in my professionalism." Teacher research and working toward national board certification have several processes in common including reflection, documentation of learning, systematic study of teaching and learning, and collaboration with others in professional development. The national board process asks teachers to use reflection to systematically analyze goals, individual children's learning over time, videotaped teaching sequences, and their own professional development.

For example, a teacher determines goals for a certain teaching sequence, such as a second grade small group experience with rocks and discussion of the properties of rocks. The teacher videotapes the small group sequence then analyzes it for what the teacher did during the sequence, what children learned, whether goals were achieved, and what the teacher might do to improve the activity. The planning, implementation of the learning activity, collection of data in the form of the video of the group activity and discussion, analysis of the video sequence in terms of teaching and learning, reflection on the analysis including conclusions, and drawing implications about the impact on learning and improvements for the future are the same processes involved in doing teacher research. The national board process is good preparation for teacher research and vice versa. The two processes are so similar because they both reflect a similar view of good teaching:

> Accomplished early childhood teachers recognize the strengths and weaknesses of multiple assessment methodologies and know how to use them effectively. Employing a variety of methods, they systematically observe, monitor, and document children's activities and behavior, analyzing, communicating, and using the information they glean to improve their work with children, parents, and others.
>
> (NBPTS, 2001, p. 15)

This chapter has presented multiple purposes for conducting teacher research. It has shown that teacher research is a form of teacher professional development. Conducting teacher research may help teachers not only improve their programs but also lead to professional development in terms of meeting nationally established standards for excellence in teaching. The chapters that follow are a guide to doing teacher research with accompanying examples from the experiences of early childhood teacher researchers.

---

### Explorations

Review the NAEYC Developmentally Appropriate Practice Guidelines for the age group you are most interested in working with. Make a list of the teacher activities advocated in the guidelines. Then next to each activity, list a complementary teacher research activity. For example, if the teaching activity is to be attentive to infants and toddlers during routines, then a teacher research activity might be to study how attentive you are in daily routines by keeping a teacher researcher journal in which you record anecdotal notes of your activities during daily routines, such as talking to children during diaper changes. Another approach would be to videotape a daily routine, such as exploration time, then analyze the videotape for instances in which you were attentive.

---

## References

Ayers, Wm. (2001). *To teach, the journey of a teacher*. New York: Teachers College Press.

Branscombe, A., Castle, K., Dorsey, A., Surbeck, E., & Taylor, J. (2003). *Early childhood curriculum: A constructivist perspective*. Boston: Houghton Mifflin.

Castle, K. (2006). Autonomy through pedagogical research. *Teaching and Teacher Education*, 22, 1094–1103.

Cochran-Smith, M. (2006). Ten promising trends (and three big worries). *Educational Leadership*, 20–25.

Cochran-Smith, M., & Lytle, S. L. (2009). *Inquiry as stance: Practitioner research for the next generation*. New York: Teachers College Press.

Copple, C., & Bredekamp, S. (Eds.) (2009). *Developmentally appropriate practice in early childhood programs* (3rd edition). Washington, DC: National Association for the Education of Young Children.

Heine, H. (1986). *Friends*. New York: Aladdin Books Macmillan.

Helm, J. H., & Katz, L. (2001). *Young investigators: The Project Approach in the early years.* New York: Teachers College Press and Washington, DC: National Association for the Education of Young Children.

Hubbard, R. S., & Power, B. M. (1999). *Living the questions: A guide for teacher researchers.* York, Maine: Stenhouse.

James, S. (1991). *Dear Mr. Blueberry.* New York: Aladdin.

Kamii, C. (1985). *Young children reinvent arithmetic.* New York: Teachers College Press.

Katz, L. G., & Chard, S. C. (2000). *Engaging children's minds: The Project Approach* (2nd edition). Stamford, CT: Ablex.

McAfee, O., Leong, D. J., & Bodorova, E. (2004). *Basics of assessment: A primer for early childhood educators.* Washington, DC: National Association for the Education of Young Children.

National Association for the Education of Young Children (NAEYC) and the National Association of Early Childhood Specialists in State Departments of Education (NAECS/SDE). (2003). Where we stand on curriculum, assessment, and program evaluation. Retrieved January 24, 2011, from www.naeyc.org/about/positions/cape.asp.

National Board for Professional Teaching Standards (2001). *Early Childhood Generalist Standards* (2nd edition). Arlington, VA: National Board for Professional Teaching Standards.

Noddings, N. (1992). *The challenge to care in schools.* New York: Teachers College Press.

Oklahoma Commission for Human Services. (2008). *Oklahoma Core Competencies for Early Childhood Practitioners.* Oklahoma City, OK: Oklahoma Commission for Human Services.

Palmer, P. J. (2007). *The courage to teach: Exploring the inner landscape of a teacher's life.* San Francisco, CA: John Wiley & Sons.

Pine, G. J. (2009). *Teacher action research.* Los Angeles, CA: Sage.

Steffy, B. E., Wolfe, M. P., Pasch, S. H., & Enz, B. J. (2000). *Life cycle of the career teacher.* Thousand Oaks, CA: Kappa Delta Pi and Corwin/Sage.

Taulbert, C. L. (2006). *Eight habits of the heart for educators.* Thousand Oaks, CA: Corwin.

# three
# Where Will Puzzlement and Wondering Lead?

*I'm a thinker and a whyer.*

5 year old child

Poet Rainer Maria Rilke's quote often cited in the teacher research literature—"Be patient towards all that is unsolved in your heart, and learn to love the questions themselves." (Rogers, 2003, p. 117)—is good advice to all teacher researchers to learn to love the questions that lead to doing the research. This chapter will focus not only on loving the questions but living them or becoming them as well (Hubbard & Power, 1999; van Manen, 1991). Questions and wonderings help lead us to solving problems, deeper understanding, and improving what we do. This chapter will provide guidelines for formulating and refining teacher research questions. Early childhood teachers have long known that young children are full of all kinds of questions that motivate their activities. A resource for answering some common questions that children have is the book, *The Nobel Book of Answers* (Stiekel, 2003), in which the author shares answers from famous Nobel Prize winners, such as Ghandi, to common wonderings that children have about the world and how it works. Teachers sometimes yearn for a similar book that would give them the experts' answers to their most pressing questions. Although not in book form, teacher research is a tool that helps teachers get answers to the important questions in their lives.

When my son was 4 years old, he was a "whyer" who asked so many questions I began to wonder if questioning was becoming his only mode of communication. My son's questions are commonly heard among young children:

Why do giraffes have long necks?

Why can't we see dinosaurs walking around?

Why does the snow go away and where does it go?

When children question, early childhood teachers can help create opportunities for children to live their questions. That is a common early childhood practice. And yet when we have questions and wonderings as teachers, do we do the same for ourselves? Do we create opportunities for us to live our own questions?

In one first grade classroom, children became fascinated with tornadoes and asked many questions such as:

How can we protect ourselves in a tornado?

How fast do they go?

Why do they twist?

How do they destroy things like buildings?

How do animals get lost in tornadoes?

When do they get smaller and bigger?

The teacher stocked the classroom library with books on tornadoes, helped children find websites with scientific information on tornadoes, invited local storm chasers and tornado survivors to class to talk about tornadoes, and set up a tornado construction center where children could create their own tornadoes in plastic bottles. After several weeks of studying tornadoes, the teacher invited another class to hear and see what her class had learned.

This teacher could go beyond helping children question, and do her own teacher research in parallel with the children's inquiry. She could generate a teacher research question such as: What forms of documentation of children's learning best demonstrate their understanding of tornadoes? She could collect artifacts of children's conversations, drawings, stories, and constructions. She could develop a rubric to assess the extent to which children learn through this project. She could analyze the data she collects by comparing assessed knowledge across all artifacts and draw conclusions about children's learning and what to improve in her own teaching. Then she could share her results with other teachers or in a public forum such as at a meeting or on a website.

Just as children learn from questioning, teachers who question also learn. Here are some examples of questions that teachers have asked:

How does weather affect children?

What makes some children more prone to bullying others?

Why should I include games in my math curriculum?

How do children who are socially isolated or rejected gain acceptance from peers?

## Guidelines for Formulating and Refining Teacher Research Questions

**Reflect** on what brought you to early childhood education and on things you wonder about such as how to engage young children in meaningful learning experiences, or why some children do well in school while others do not, or how to reach a child who needs but resists a teacher's help.

**Identify** the things you are passionate about in early childhood education such as a child's right to play, or the effects on young children of too much testing, or how best to teach English language learners and communicate with their families and think of ways to transfer your passion into your professional work.

**Select** a wondering you have or a passion such as how to help young children deal with a parent on a military assignment far from home and read about the topic in the professional literature to find out what others have done to address it.

**Compose** a main question that is clear, focused, calls for more than a yes/no or single word answer and a question not already answered to use in a teacher research study based on your selection of a topic and then compose a few (3 to 5) subquestions each of which might contribute to answer the main question.

**Revise** your main question and subquestions eliminating education jargon such as ADHD (attention deficit hyperactivity disorder) and value laden words such as "best approach". Revise your questions to give them a clear focus and eliminate jargon that an average person would not understand. Rewrite your questions such as yes/no questions to make them lead to more than a one word answer and open them up, such as changing the question "Will children learn phonics from direct instruction?" to "To what extent will children learn phonics from direct instruction?"

**Consult** others such as fellow teachers to review your questions and give feedback.

**Consider** whether each research question will lead to specific data sources to answer the question and change the ones that do not point to data sources.

**Ask yourself** if the study based on your research questions is realistic in terms of your interests and the time and resources needed to complete it then make adjustments where necessary.

## Where Questions Originate

Questioning is very important to learning and is critical to beginning the teacher research process. Questioning plays a primary role in the teacher research process. Teacher research goes nowhere without clearly defined questions. This chapter will illustrate this point by providing a multitude of ways to think about possible questions and where they might originate in the professional work of teachers.

Questions may originate in:

- Wonderings
- Problems
- Interactions with other teachers
- Professional literature
- Daily experiences and passions.

### Wonderings

In our daily lives we wonder about all sorts of things, such as:

Why do they call a blue moon blue when it doesn't look blue?

What makes advertisers think we will buy their products just because they increase the volume on their TV commercials?

I wonder if I could live a day without my cell phone?

Why do I forget where I parked my car when I go to the grocery store?

Will wars ever stop?

How can I find more leisure time?

We wonder especially about things we are passionate about, interested in, or have an investment in. It is the passion, interest, and investment that drive us to find answers and solutions. That is why loving the questions is important and propels us forward, especially in doing teacher research. Wondering is an important first step on the road to investigation. A kindergarten teacher wondered why mostly boys played with the blocks in her classroom. She wondered if boys were intentionally keeping the girls out of their play. Based on her wonderings, she came up with a question to research. Her question was, What happens when I encourage girls to play more with blocks? She spent time studying this question and systematically collecting data that she analyzed. Results disconfirmed her original idea and showed that girls spent less time in the block area even with teacher encouragement, block time for girls only, and dramatic play props added to the block area. The teacher found no evidence that boys were hindering girls from play with blocks. Based on results, she began to wonder about other reasons girls did not play much with blocks.

---

## TEACHER RESEARCHER NOTEBOOK ENTRY #3

 As Dewey demonstrated with such profundity, true interest appears when the self identifies itself with ideas or objects, when it finds in them a means of expression and they become a necessary form of fuel for its activity.

(Piaget, 1970, pp. 158–159)

This chapter is all about you: your interests, passions, desires, wonderings, and puzzlements. Reflect on what you wonder (care) about. Then make a list of your wonderings. Start with:

I wonder…

After you have made a list of your wonderings, reflect on why things on the list are important to you. Then select one item from the list you are most passionate about. Finally turn it into a research question by rewriting it so that it could become the focus of a research study.

## Problems

Teacher research questions emerge from wonderings but may also come from what we perceive as a problem that needs to be solved. But before we can solve it, we need to research it—this is where teacher research comes into the picture. We are more apt to find workable solutions to problems if we tackle them systematically and with a doable plan.

For example, one early childhood teacher perceived lateness as a problem with her class. Several children were chronically late to school each day. She perceived this as a problem because these children consistently missed Morning Meeting (Kriete, 1999) group time. It was during Morning Meeting time that the teacher presented the activities for the day, conducted community building activities, and generally set the tone for the day. The children who were late had to be briefed individually by the teacher after they arrived. Some days she did not have time to do this and the late children missed out on what the group had done that morning.

The teacher perceived this as a problem of late children missing a large chunk of the day, missing important content, and missing those activities that enriched the classroom community. In addition, lateness of children had become a problem for the teacher who felt she didn't have time to redo Morning Meeting for each late child. Lateness was becoming so chronic that she felt she had to act to try to solve this problem. Rather than implementing a solution that may or may not work, she decided to do some research into the causes of lateness. She approached the problem with a systematic study including a parent survey, parent focus group, and discussion of lateness with children in her Morning Meeting group time. She analyzed the data she collected from these data sources for common themes. She reflected on what her data were telling her about the problem. Based on the results of her study, that she also shared with her children's parents, the situation improved. Parents took more responsibility for getting children to school on time and the teacher decided to rethink and adjust the time of the Morning Meeting.

## Interactions With Other Teachers

Interacting with other teachers can sometimes lead to ideas for teacher research studies. Discussing professional issues with colleagues can provide different perspectives on situations. Based on what others say and do, we may find our ideas change in how we address working with young children. In addition, there are times when interacting with others may lead to collaborative teacher research. Teachers may find they have common wonderings, interests, and problems that they can investigate together. And there are occasions when all teachers in a school decide to do collaborative teacher research.

For example, several teachers at one school found through getting together to discuss their teaching that they were all concerned with boys' lack of interest in writing. They decided it might be worthwhile to investigate reasons for this common problem. They solicited other teachers in the school and formed a teacher research collaborative group composed of one teacher from each grade level. They met regularly to plan the study, share findings, and discuss next steps based on results.

## Professional Literature

*I find that a great part of the information I have was acquired by looking up something and finding something else on the way.*

Franklin P. Adams (in Howe, 2003, p. 158)

It is helpful to read professional literature to keep updated on the most current thinking and practices in the field. Teachers read professional literature for many reasons, but usually to find out information that can enhance what they are already doing in their teaching. Professional literature can also be a source for teacher research questions. Reading about what others have done and learned can help us form questions for our own inquiry. Reading professional literature may affirm our ideas, stimulate our thinking about a classroom problem we may be experiencing, and provide guidance in how to go about doing teacher research.

The early childhood field has numerous outlets for professional literature including books, journals, magazines, and websites. Journals such as *Young Children, Early Childhood Research Quarterly, Childhood Education, Research in Childhood Education, Early Childhood Education Journal,* and *Dimensions of Early Childhood* provide a wealth of knowledge on research, teaching approaches, resources, policy issues, program descriptions, and current issues in the field. In addition, online sites such as the NAEYC online teacher research journal, *Voices of Practitioners* provide examples of what other early childhood teachers are doing to study their own professional work. For those who want to read more on a topic of interest, these professional publications provide the latest information on what is known on various topics.

For example, a teacher may desire to change the way children are assessed in his program. He may want to find out what other professionals are doing in assessment. Reading the journals, books, and other professional publications may give him some direction in the changes he wants to make in his program. He may decide to pilot the use of an assessment he has read about and study the extent to which he can identify children's learning from using the assessment. A systematic teacher research study may lead him to make improvements in his approach to assessment.

## Daily Experiences and Passions

Research questions can also pop up in other daily experiences beyond wonderings, problems, interactions with others, and reading professional literature. They can come to us anywhere and anytime including in the middle of the night when we are awakened by a thought that bubbles up into consciousness and makes us wide awake.

For example, one teacher who was also a parent of a 4 year old, noticed that her mornings in getting her child ready for school went more smoothly when she engaged her child in choosing and laying out what to wear to school the night before. She began to think about the role of choice in learning and ways to offer choice in her third grade classroom. Her research question was, What role does choice play in children's learning? She quickly realized her question was too broad to tackle in a reasonable way. She decided to narrow her question to focus on one learning activity resulting in revising her question to, Do children write more and learn more when they get to choose the topic for journal writing compared to when I assign a topic? She collected samples of children's writing in both conditions; when they chose the topic and when she chose the topic. She analyzed the writing samples for length, quality of writing, and ideas conveyed in the writing. She concluded that children wrote more when they chose the topic, but didn't necessarily improve the quality of the writing or the number of ideas conveyed in the writing compared to the teacher-assigned writing samples.

Questions may also come from our passions and interests. In early childhood education, the topic of children and play is of great interest to many teachers. Teachers may be interested in finding out how to incorporate play into the daily schedule or what the relationship of play to literacy development might be. Teachers with a passion for the importance of play may use their teacher research results to advocate for play in the curriculum or for retaining recess as part of the school day. Teachers' wonderings, passions, problems, interactions, readings, and daily experiences can all lead to questions for doing teacher research.

## The Purpose of Questioning

*That is the essence of science: ask an impertinent question, and you are on the way to a pertinent answer.*

Jacob Bronowski (in Howe, 2003, p. 169)

### Questions Point the Way

We question in order to find answers that help us understand our lives and improve what we do. The purpose of questioning in the process of teacher research is to find answers that help us improve not only our teaching but to improve our students' learning as well. Questions are like arrows that point the way. Without the direction that questions give us, we might never arrive at answers and might continue to make the same mistakes. Questions are also similar to a global positioning system that helps us get to our destination by guiding us each turn of the way.

From the perspective of chaos and complexity theory, we can look at questions as being two opposite things simultaneously (Kuhn, 1970). While this may sound contradictory, it gets at the purpose of questioning and the use of questions as research tools. To question something is to open yourself up to explore new perspectives in ways you might not have done before (van Manen, 1990). When we have a question, such as how to motivate students, the question itself opens up the possibilities of the many ways to think about the concept of motivation. We may consider motivation as intrinsic motivation, extrinsic motivation, reward systems, interest, and so on. The question points to many possibilities to consider in addressing the problem.

The opposite of opening up is narrowing. Questions can also help us to narrow our focus in order to be able to address a problem in a reasonable and doable fashion (Creswell, 2008). In the previous example of student motivation, we may find that the question of how to motivate students is too broad. When a topic or question is too broad, we may get discouraged by not knowing where to start to find answers. Narrowing the question may help to focus the research into a doable project. How might we narrow the question on student motivation?

**REFLECTIONS**

Before reading further, reflect on the preceding example and try to generate a teacher research question on student motivation that narrows the study into something that could be reasonably done. Write your research question in your Teacher Researcher Journal. How does your question compare to these examples of narrowing the question?

- In what ways do first grade students show their individual interests when given choice in journal writing?
- During kindergarten center time, which centers do children self-select and why?
- To what extent does working individually or in small groups influence third grade students' motivation to solve math problems?

By narrowing the question, we can obtain direction for planning the research and identifying appropriate data sources. To answer the first question about first grade students' writing, we may plan a study in which we collect samples of children's journal writing once a week for three weeks and analyze each sample for the interests that children write about such as sports, video games, or doing things with friends. A first grade teacher may find analyzing children's writing samples for interests to be no more time consuming than reading children's journal writing and possibly far more interesting and enlightening in learning about individual children's interests. Such knowledge may help the teacher get to know her children better and thus be able to improve their learning by incorporating their interests into learning activities.

## The Primacy of the Question

No one seems to be able to answer the old question about what comes first, the chicken or the egg? The same could be said for the question about what comes first in research, the question or the method? While most sources say the question comes first, the importance paid to methodology tends to downplay the role of the question. For example, if you analyze course offerings in colleges and universities, you will find a proliferation of courses on research methodology: quantitative methods, qualitative methods, mixed methods, ethnographic methods, to name a few. Research course offerings on questioning do not usually exist or rarely appear in the research curriculum. In education research, researchers have had a tendency to become methodologists wedded to one research methodology over others, such as quantitative over qualitative. This may be due to the history of educational research drawing heavily first from the research methods employed in the natural sciences and then from those in the social sciences (Creswell, 2008).

Much lip service is paid to the importance of the research question, but very little time or attention is given to the study of questioning in the research process. So many of the problems involved in research studies stem from poorly conceptualized research questions. Teacher researchers are known to have become very frustrated at the end of a study when they realize they didn't ask the questions they really wanted to get answered or when results do not fit the original questions asked.

In this chapter, tribute is paid to the primacy of the question. The research question rules the study and determines the direction it will take. The type of research question asked determines the type of study done including the methods that should be chosen to answer the question. Teacher research has a history of being focused on the lived experience of teaching and school life in an attempt to get answers that will improve the learning process. Teacher research in general has been more focused on the types of research questions being asked and answered than on the methods of doing research. Many of the questions asked in teacher research are questions of meaning that lead to deeper understanding of what it means to teach and what it means to learn. While teacher research has a history of being qualitative in nature, teacher research questions may lead to mixed methods studies including the use of qualitative and quantitative methods and can be of a quantitative nature as well. The next chapter on planning a teacher research study will address variations in research methodology.

## Formulating Research Questions

It may be helpful to read several teacher research studies to find out the types of research questions that others have "lived". The websites and journals mentioned in this book are sources for teacher research studies. For example, NAEYC's Gail Perry summarizes four early childhood teacher research studies from *Voices of Practitioners* (www.journal. naeyc.org/btj/vp) in an issue of *Young Children* (2008). The four different studies asked these questions:

- What strategies do preschool children use to gain access to other children's play without teacher assistance?
- What happens if first grade teachers focus on helping children write interesting stories before they have mastered spelling and grammar techniques?
- How can a teacher apply a critical literacy approach in teaching reading and writing and leading book discussions with the 5-year-olds in a kindergarten classroom?
- In what ways can an early childhood teacher support children's thinking so that they feel comfortable sharing their theories? (Perry, 2008, pp. 46–48)

Like these early childhood teachers, the first place to begin formulating research questions is to reflect on your interests, problems, and daily interactions with children and other teachers. Once you have a research topic in mind, peruse the professional literature on that topic to find out what is already known and to find out what others have done. Then practice writing a research question. You may have noticed the questions in this chapter tend to be what and how questions rather than why questions. What and how questions usually lead to more meaningful results that in turn impact teaching and learning than do why or yes/no questions (Lankshear & Knobel, 2004).

There are many guidelines for writing research questions. Hubbard and Power (1999, p. 28) offer four principles of refining a research question. They recommend to ask questions to which you don't already have the answers; to avoid asking yes/no questions; to eliminate jargon; and to avoid words that imply certain values such as best, excellent, or meaningful. Using their guidelines will help to prevent researcher preference or bias, studying what is already known, getting uninformative answers, and confusing readers with unfamiliar words or terms that may elicit a variety of definitions among different readers.

Hendricks (2009) suggests asking questions that are researchable given your limitations of resources and time and questions that can be answered with data. A good research question is clear, focused, of personal interest, doable, and not already answered (Lankshear & Knobel, 2004).

Using a conceptual web of the topic you wish to study is a technique for formulating a research question that is similar to one used by many teachers when planning projects with children. A kindergarten conceptual web of a project on the topic of Friendship generated these questions that children wanted to study:

- What is a friend?
- How can you be a friend?
- Why are some children friendly and some aren't?
- Do friends have to do everything together?
- Why do friends get mad at each other?
- Are friends like family?
- What if I don't want to be his friend?
- What does friendship look like? Sound like?
- What happens when you don't have any friends?
- How do you make friends with someone?

Children look for answers to their questions by reading books and stories on the topic, participating in class discussions about friendship, interviewing family members and other children, writing and illustrating stories about friendship, and role playing what it means to be a friend. They will learn much about friendship through these activities and through reflecting on their own experiences of having friends and being friends with others.

In the same way, you can make a conceptual web on a topic of interest to you that you would like to research. Start by generating a list of questions you have about the topic. Reflect on the questions you have generated and select the one or two that you are most interested in and could research. Then apply the guidelines from this chapter to refine your research question.

### From the Field

Sarah Sturzenbecker, a first grade teacher, is interested in doing a teacher research project on an aspect of the Responsive Classroom (Charney, Clayton, and Wood, 1996) approach that her school is implementing. Like many beginning teacher researchers, Sarah is trying to develop a research question to study the use of a classroom management technique similar to time out. Over the course of three months and with the help of a small group of her colleagues,

*Continued overleaf*

Sarah refines her research question to better fit what she is really interested in studying. Refining her question has taken three drafts with each draft followed by feedback from her colleagues and then revisions of her question. Reflect on the three drafts in terms of what changed in Sarah's focus. Then read her Final Reflections.

## Sarah's Draft 1

**Research Purpose:**
Recently I have been trained in the Responsive Classroom Technique. This technique teaches teachers how to work with students in different aspects. A few of them are; students rule making, behavior management, and academic choice time. One of the elements of behavior management is logical consequences for students. This consequence will vary depending on the student behavior. In my classroom in the past I felt like students who made poor choices constantly made the same choices over and over again. While attending this training it made me reflect on the reasons my students would make the same poor choices. I began to think it might have to do with the fact that all I did, every time regardless of the situation, was make students take a break and walk laps at recess. I did not really address the behavior in terms of what was done, should have been done, how to fix it and what an appropriate consequence for the behavior would be. The Responsive Classroom Technique really made me think about how I could adjust my consequences so that the student could make a connection to the problem and the solution.

**Research Question:**
In what ways do logical consequences affect future choices of students?

**Subquestions:**
1. What types of consequences did my students' previous teacher use?
2. To what extent are my consequences different from the parent's consequences?
3. In what ways have my students altered their behavior due to my teaching technique of logical consequences?

## Sarah's Draft 2

**Research Question:**
In what ways if any do logical consequences affect future choices of students?

**Subquestions:**
1. In what ways have my students altered their behavior due to my teaching technique of logical consequences?
2. What do parents think about how logical consequences affect their child's future choices?
3. What do my students think about the use of logical consequences as a way to solve problems in the classroom?

## Sarah's Draft 3

**Research Questions:**
What effects, if any, does "take a break" have in a first grade classrooom?
Subquestion 1: What effects, if any, does "take a break" have on students?
Subquestion 2: What effects, if any, does "take a break" have on teachers?
Subquestion 3: What effects, if any, does "take a break" have on parents?

## Sarah's Reflections

The more direct and clear I am with how to complete this project, the easier it will be for me to actually do this action research project in the future. In learning more about my own research plan I was reminded of how important it is in my teaching that I thoroughly go through the process of building the community with my students and addressing all aspects of the Responsive Classroom. This is the way that I feel the institution of the "take a break" method will succeed. I need to be consistent in setting up and enforcing the classroom rules that we collectively came up with. Specifically with addressing the "take a break" everything from the initial reaction to being told to "take a break" to how to come back to the class successfully needs to be modeled and practiced. It is imperative to also continually model and practice the thinking aloud of the break time. The break is simply about rules or procedures that have been broken. Therefore it is imperative that I model for my students what that process looks like within my head. As a class throughout the school year we will model and practice continually.

Feedback from colleagues at my school helped me make many revisions that were critical to improving my research plan. Originally I had a good main question, but struggled with subquestions. I knew the direction I wanted to go, but had a hard time articulating that in my draft. In my second draft, I improved my subquestions to better answer my main question, but then struggled to define logical consequences that could apply to every situation and coming up with a plan of attack for starting the research. Finally, I sat down with my group members individually and a few colleagues at separate times to explain what I wanted to do with this project and we talked through some ideas and came up with my better, more focused main question and subquestions in draft 3 that allowed me to still investigate what I am interested in researching just with more focus. It was really helpful that I was able to run ideas by the many supportive colleagues and discuss my plans for how to do this project. The best piece of advice I got was from a colleague that encouraged me to find something I'm passionate about and then set it up the best that I could so that I could actually do it. That is why I chose to research about the Responsive Classroom practice of "take a break" as a use of a positive time out in classroom management. I have always appreciated feedback, but through this project I truly got to appreciate talking about a topic I am passionate about and letting my conversation with a classmate or colleague guide me in a better direction for my research than I originally had. Sometimes, you just have to go with it, and I did.

**REFLECTIONS ON SARAH'S EXAMPLE**

What did you notice about the changes Sarah made across her three drafts? In what ways did her research change and become more focused on her interest in the study and on what she really wanted to learn? What role did collaboration with colleagues play in the development of her research focus?

## Protocols and Reflection to Formulate and Refine Questions

Chapter Eight discusses the use of **protocols** (structured conversations) in refining teacher research questions. Protocol discussions conducted in group settings help individual teacher researchers refine their research questions and also provide a place for the group to generate a common research question. Protocols can be very effective because they offer an opportunity for teacher researchers to benefit from the various perspectives of others within a supportive group. The Inquiry Circles protocol (Bisplinghoff, 2005) is particularly effective when used to generate and refine teacher research questions as demonstrated in Chapter Eight.

Individual teacher researchers do not always have the benefit of a supportive collaborative group to run questions by for valuable feedback. The use of **reflection** is an individual process for refining questions as in the example of Sarah's reflections that lead to the three drafts of her research questions. Reflection involves thinking deeply about something such as when we reflect on a topic and wonder what, why, how, who, where, when, and what would happen if. We take the topic apart and consider the aspects that make up the whole. We come up with tentative ideas to try out. We consider in our minds each idea carefully discarding the ones we deem as lacking merit. We connect what we know of our previous knowledge and experiences related to the topic. Reflection is helpful in teacher research when a direction emerges from the reflection that has potential to guide our study.

**REFLECTIONS**

Engage in the reflective steps to follow and then write an entry in your Teacher Researcher Journal about what the reflection has meant to you.

1. Think about a time in your life when you felt that you made a difference and felt good about it.
2. Think carefully about the experience and analyze each aspect of it in terms of what, why, how, who, where, when, and what would happen if.
3. Think about whether there is anything about the experience you would like to recreate or change.
4. Think about applying the aspects of this experience that you feel good about to your own teacher research in ways to make a positive difference.
5. Come up with a teacher research question based on your reflections.
6. Reflect on your question looking for values and themes that may carry forward into your teacher research.

**Explorations**

Review the guidelines in this chapter for formulating and refining research questions. Apply the guidelines to rewrite and improve the following questions:

1. How many 4 year olds in my program do not hear English being spoken at home?
2. Is NCLB leading to better phonemic awareness?
3. Does teaching for multiple intelligence work?
4. How can I show the other early childhood teachers that my literacy instruction gets better results than theirs?
5. Do my kindergarten children need more structure?
6. What impact does Morning Meeting have in my class?
7. Is the Smart Board good for teaching math?

Find an early childhood teacher research article from one of the websites or journals cited in this book such as the NAEYC online journal *Voices of Practitioners*. Read the article. Identify the research question/s the teacher researcher has asked. Use the guidelines in this chapter to analyze the question/s. What changes, if any, would you recommend for revising the question/s? Share your example and analysis with others.

# References

Bisplinghoff, B. (2005). Inquiry circles, a protocol for professional inquiry. National School Reform Faculty Harmony Education Center. Retrieved January 24, 2011, from www.nsrfharmony.org

Charney, R. S., Clayton, M. K., & Wood, C. (1996). *Guidelines for the Responsive Classroom, Training Manual*. Greenfield, MA: Northeast Foundation for Children.

Cresswell, J. W. (2008). *Educational research*. Columbus, OH: Pearson Merrill Prentice Hall.

Hendricks, C. (2009). *Improving schools through action research*. Columbus, OH: Pearson.

Howe, R. (Ed.) (2003). *The quotable teacher*. Guilford, CT: The Lyons Press.

Hubbard, R. S., & Power, B. M. (1999). *Living the questions*. York, ME: Stenhouse.

Kriete, R. (1999). *The morning meeting book*. Greenfield, MA: Northeast Foundation for Children.

Kuhn, T. S. (1970). *The structure of scientific revolutions* (2nd edition). Chicago: University of Chicago Press.

Lankshear, C., & Knobel, M. (2004). *A handbook for teacher research*. New York: Open University Press.

McDonald, J. P., Mohr, N., Dichter, A., & McDonald, E. C. (2003). *The power of protocols*. New York: Teachers College Press.

Perry, G. (2008). Voices of practitioners. *Young Children, 63*(6), 46–48.

Piaget, J. (1970). *Science of education and the psychology of the child*. New York: Orion Press.

Rogers, F. (2003). *The world according to Mister Rogers*. New York: Hyperion.

Stiekel, B. (Ed.) (2003). *The Nobel book of answers*. New York: Atheneum.

van Manen, M. (1990). *Researching lived experiences*. New York: State University of New York Press.

# four
# Why Plan?

*Imagining something may be the first step in making it happen, but it takes the real time and real efforts of real people to learn things, make things, turn thoughts into deeds or visions into inventions.*

Fred Rogers (2003, p. 99)

*You need to have a plan of sorts but don't become consumed by it. Winds change ...*
Joseph Ehrhard, Physics Teacher (cited in Howe, 2003, p. 134)

This chapter is about "turning your thoughts" into a "vision" of your own teacher research study. Your vision can be conceived of as a plan for doing your research. As with most plans, the final result may look different from the original plan due to unforeseen events that occur along the way. Therefore it is important to treat your research plan as a work in progress and be willing to make adjustments as they are needed and as "winds change." It is important to have a plan that can be modified and to have the flexibility to make changes as appropriate. This chapter is about planning a teacher research study once a question has been formulated and refined. Examples will be given showing the role of planning in teacher research studies. Ethical issues such as teacher researcher responsibilities to the young child, coercion, confidentiality, child and parental consent, and working with human subject review boards will be addressed.

## The Importance of a Research Plan

A research plan maximizes the chances that you will actually do the research. While most teacher researchers can generate many interesting questions about their work any of which might become the focus of a study, it is much easier to question than to turn the question into a well-developed teacher research study. As Chapter Three emphasizes, questioning is very important and necessary but not sufficient for doing teacher research. Planning the various aspects of the study is important to insure that all aspects of the study get completed, data gets gathered and analyzed, and results lead to action and better understanding of the topic of research all within a well-developed timeline that is reasonable and doable.

In addition to helping insure the study gets done, a research plan outlines what needs to be done and why, how it will be done, when and where it will be done, who will do it, who will participate in it including issues of consent and confidentiality, who will help, and how results will be used. Some teacher researchers describe the research plan as the back-bone or skeleton of the study (Hubbard & Power, 1999) or the overview or clear picture of the study (Stringer, 2008). I like to think of it as the roadmap for the study showing the various destinations, routes, and alternative routes that might be taken. Teacher research can be compared to a journey that has been carefully planned with a timeline for certain destinations or events and a sequence for each phase of the trip acknowledging that deviations may occur. The research plan helps us reach our destination in a reasonable fashion and with memories of grand vistas experienced along the way.

Finally, a research plan helps the teacher researcher to decide if the study is doable. Charting a timeline for the research and planning how to integrate it into the classroom routine and schedule help a teacher see the possible need to scale down the study into one that can be done within the constraints at hand. It helps identify modifications that may need to be made such as the possible need to enlist an assistant to help collect data. It encourages the teacher researcher to consider each aspect of the study and what support will be needed for each. For example, in considering when to collect data, a research plan helps the teacher researcher to schedule time to first gather the appropriate approvals and permissions to do the research so that data collection can begin on time.

Making a research plan helps a teacher to decide the scope of the study and whether to do the study in one month, one year, or two years. Such planning helps prevent frustrations and helps keep the teacher researcher on track. Ideally a teacher research plan and preparation for the study are done during summer break or during a period of time in which the teacher researcher can reflect on how to proceed and what needs to be done before the study actually begins. Planning during a break allows the study to begin at the start of the program and possibly continue for an entire year if necessary. However, some teacher researchers want to get to know their students before planning a study. Either approach is appropriate as long as time is taken to plan the details of the study. The following template shows an outline of a teacher research plan that is commonly used to plan teacher research studies (Hubbard & Power, 1999; Lankshear & Knobel, 2004). Please note that while there are many ways to plan a teacher research study, the template below is an example of one way to plan that reflects the basic elements involved. The template gives a preview of each aspect that goes into a plan. Later in this chapter details and examples will be given of each aspect of the plan below.

## Template for a Teacher Research Plan

Purpose of the research

Research questions

Literature review

Methodology: Data collection and data analysis

Support for research

Ethical issues

Permissions

Sharing results

Reflections before study begins

Timeline.

---

**REFLECTIONS ON PLANNING AN EVENT**

Think of a time you were involved in planning an event such as a party, a field trip, a wedding, or an outing of some sort. In the first phase of planning, thoughts of the event can be very exhilarating. But soon the reality of all that needs to be done to make it happen sets in. Think about the event you planned. What was the reason or purpose for the event? Was it a celebration, a new experience such as a ski trip, or a formal affair? Who did you invite or involve and why? What arrangements did you have to make such as ordering food, scheduling a room, or making decorations? How did you accomplish what needed to be done? Did you enlist the help of others or do everything yourself? How did you determine a timeline for necessary tasks leading up to the event? Are your reflections of what happened positive or do you look back at it with frustrations? How might you share what you learned from planning the event with others so that they might benefit from your experiences?

Planning a teacher research study may be somewhat similar to planning an event such as a party. Many decisions must be made along the way at certain times so that when the time comes for the party to begin everything is in place to insure an enjoyable experience for you and your guests that you will want to repeat in the future. Planning any event takes time, work, and preparation. The work may feel burdensome at times. But any job worth doing brings a sense of accomplishment and satisfaction when the work is completed. When a teacher research study is completed, it also brings results that help the teacher researcher address the initial problem, improve the situation under study, and better understand the situation.

---

## Teacher Research Design

The decisions made about each aspect of the research plan are influenced by a teacher's worldview including his beliefs about teaching and learning. All of us have assumptions about what children are like and how best to teach them. In the history of educational research, various worldviews or paradigms for teaching and doing research are evident. An education **paradigm** is a worldview with a loose set of assumptions about the goals of education, how learning occurs, what teaching is most likely to lead to student learning, and what methods are most useful for studying educational problems. A **behaviorist** paradigm dominated educational research throughout the first two-thirds of the twentieth century resulting in scientific method and experimental research as the most accepted research design. In this view the use of statistical procedures for demonstrating significant results and the use of **randomization** including random assignment of subjects to research conditions or groups and the use of randomized trials in experimental studies became the gold standard for judging the quality of the research (see Chapter Six for additional information). The behaviorist worldview holds that truth exists "out there" in the world to be discovered through experimental research and that all behavior is caused or controlled by certain variables that can be predicted and determined by highly controlled experimental studies (Cozby, 2007). For example, from a behavioristic perspective, to find out the best way to teach reading, you would need to design an experiment that controlled for type of teaching approach and attributes of students such as age, gender, ethnicity, and baseline reading performance level. Such a study would involve random assignment of subjects into treatment groups with each group getting a different approach to the teaching of reading and whose reading achievement test scores could then be compared to the reading achievement of a control group (no treatment; status quo teaching approach). It could then be concluded that the teaching approach used with the group that showed the most reading achievement demonstrated by statistical tests for significance of results was indeed the best approach. Such studies are considered to be highly objective because any bias about effective teaching methods held by the researcher could be controlled and mostly eliminated through experimental controls and procedures. Behaviors and performance are the focus of behaviorist research, not thoughts, perceptions, feelings, and understandings of those involved in the educational process, the teachers and students, and the context in which education occurs. Due to this limitation other paradigms emerged to consider and study these things.

About halfway through the twentieth century, other paradigms for considering educational problems and doing research came to prominence, particularly the **interpretist paradigm** came into acceptance as a legitimate form of educational thought and research (Lincoln & Denzin, 2003). An interpretist worldview holds that truth does not exist externally outside to be discovered, but rather is internally constructed by each individual. All understanding and truth is interpreted. Educational research must consider the context in which students and teachers work, that interpretations of reality are highly subjective, and that subjectivity (considered by behaviorist researchers as bias) can be a powerful research tool for studying educational problems and interpreting results (deMarrais & Lapan, 2004).

Examples of an interpretist approach to research include narrative research, autobiographical research, ethnography, and naturalistic inquiry to name a few. The interpretist paradigm has long held sway in the field of early childhood education exemplified by the common application of constructivist theory to teaching young children. Constructivist theory contends that reality of the world can't be given or taught to someone but rather is interpreted by each individual. **Constructivism** views children as active constructors of knowledge rather than passive recipients of knowledge handed down by the teacher. A constructivist approach to research is focused on what it means to construct knowledge and how teachers can play a role in helping the knowledge construction process of their students. Much constructivist research is on how children construct their ideas about various content areas such as mathematics (Kamii, 1985/2000), literacy (Ferreiro & Teberosky, 1979/1982) and science (Chaille, 2008). Teacher research done from a constructivist perspective is focused primarily on teaching and learning for understanding (DeVries & Zan, 1994; DeVries, Zan, Hildebrandt, Edmiaston, & Sales, 2002).

Each paradigm in educational research has called for certain research designs that reflect the worldviews of the paradigms. For example, behaviorism has employed primarily scientific method and experimental design. The interpretist paradigm has used grounded theory, ethnography, narrative, and naturalistic, qualitative research designs.

There are numerous research designs that can be found in educational research including experimental, correlational, survey, grounded theory, ethnography, narrative, and mixed methods designs among others (Creswell, 2008). Most published teacher research found in professional literature is primarily qualitative but also reflects a mixed methods design in which both quantitative and qualitative data are gathered in order to make sense of the research problem. You will read more about these methods of data collection and analysis in Chapters Five and Six.

The teacher research design you choose should be based on the purpose of the study, the research questions asked, your beliefs about teaching, learning, and research, and the experiences you have had with research. Much teacher research is **qualitative** coming from a naturalistic approach to research focused on gaining insights into teaching and learning in a naturalistic setting for students which is where they spend a great deal of time such as in the classroom and school setting. Such research involves a teacher identifying issues or topics she needs to explore through collecting and analyzing data available in the classroom and generated by the educational process in order to improve the learning situation for students. Teacher research may also involve **quantitative** data that can be counted or measured. Teacher research may involve both qualitative and quantitative aspects and result in a **mixed methods** research design because teachers may need as many kinds of data as are available and both types (quantitative and qualitative) of information are more likely to give rich results than one alone.

For example, a third grade teacher researcher studying the effects of using pair reading (two students reading to each other) to increase reading comprehension and fluency may collect student scores on reading performance measures of comprehension and fluency (quantitative data) as well as interviews with students about their experiences with pair reading (qualitative data) in order to get a robust picture of the usefulness of pair reading to students' reading success and satisfaction. Such a study would employ mixed methods. Chapter Six also addresses the topic of research design in terms of giving more details about data analysis from the standpoints of various designs, but it is just as important to consider research designs when deciding on a research plan. What follows is a brief, not exhaustive, discussion of some of the types of research designs available to teacher researchers.

## Experimental Design

Historically educational research employed experimental design in the systematic study of cause and effect relationships involved in an educational problem, such as the study of the relationship of motivation to performance (Creswell, 2008). In using experimental design to study something, a researcher attempts to control as many factors or variables as possible in order to find out how a certain variable or treatment (**independent variable**) might affect the variable (**dependent variable**) of most interest to the researcher. For example, a researcher may use a measure to identify motivation in students (independent variable), group students in terms of high, medium, and low motivation, and then compare the groups in terms of their performance (dependent variable) on a certain task such as doing a mathematical computation controlled by the researcher. The researcher would control for age, gender and other variables so that students in each motivation group in the study had the same or equivalent composition in terms of these variables as the other groups to show that these factors themselves were not affecting performance. This would be necessary in order to attribute differences in performance to motivation and not to something else such as age.

Such highly controlled studies are rarely possible for teachers to conduct with their students. Teachers may not be able to control who is assigned to their class much less the grouping of students into highly controlled attribute groups for making comparisons. Such experimental studies usually require random assignment of large numbers of participants into groups that can be compared statistically using **inferential statistics** that have the power to show significant results are not due to chance. Such random assignment and control of variables is rarely possible in teacher research. While the scientific method and such experimental studies are useful for contributing to the knowledge base in the field, they are usually carried out with students in more than one classroom by outside researchers who are not themselves involved in teaching the students of focus in the study. While it is possible to use experimental design in teacher research, such as when all or many teachers in a school collaborate on researching a topic that affects all students in the school and can satisfy the requirements for randomization and experimental control, it is more the exception than the rule of doing teacher research.

## Correlational Design

**Correlational studies** designed to show the degree to which a relationship exists between two attributes, such as the relationship between number of sight words and level of reading comprehension, are not very typical of teacher research. While correlational studies can demonstrate that one attribute is associated with another, correlations do not demonstrate causality, that one attribute causes another. Correlational studies are used in education research but are not typical of teacher research, given the constraints of a classroom. For example, it may be suspected that there is a correlational relationship between the level of reading comprehension and number of sight words a reader knows, where the higher the number of sight words a student knows, the higher the student's level of reading comprehension. However, due to the too limited number of students within a class, it's not always possible to meet the research requirements to statistically show such a relationship.

## Ethnography

**Ethnography** is a type of design common in the social sciences including anthropology and sociology. It involves the study of certain groups or cultures (such as schools and classrooms) to ascertain how the group functions, the language and rituals typical of the group, and all the written and unwritten rules and codes for social behavior that exist and regulate the group. Most ethnographic studies occur over a lengthy period of time, such as a year, during which a researcher immerses herself into the culture being studied and may become a **participant observer** of the culture. The researcher then writes a highly detailed narrative of findings using thick, rich description of the entire situation. An example of an ethnographic study in education might be the study of a school culture or single classroom culture. For example, teachers Joni Chancer and Gina Rester-Zodrow (1997) wrote a rich description about a long term, ethnographic study they did with their elementary students. Due to children's interests and questions, the teachers facilitated their students' interests in a study of the moon. The study deeply engaged children in writing about the moon, creating artwork and doing inquiry into the science of the moon. The teachers wrote a book about this long-term inquiry. The book gives details and describes how their students began the study and all aspects of the study including child artifacts of drawings, journal entries, poems, and anthologies. The teachers wrote, "What started as a question ended in a journey into writing, art, science, nature—into life. It began quite simply when Joni and her students made a place for the moon in their lives." (Chancer & Rester-Zodrow, 1997, p. 3) Ethnographic teacher research, although rare, can be found in the teacher research professional literature.

## Narrative Inquiry

**Narrative inquiry** is a form of research design that is sometimes used in teacher research. It involves the study of the lives of students and teachers as perceived by the teacher researcher as stories told by the lived experiences of those studied. A teacher researcher using a narrative approach might try to capture daily happenings in general or focused on a certain topic such as children's sharing and write up results in terms of a narrative that tells a story about the everyday activities of classroom life in which children shared with each other. An example of narrative inquiry in teacher research is the work of Vivian Gussin Paley who studied her kindergarten students' experiences as narratives of their lives. In her books such as *Wally's Stories* (1981), she expertly describes her own teacher story of working with children and the stories of the children themselves. She highlights the power of narrative in helping children grow socially and intellectually as they act out together the stories in their lives that have meaning for them. She created a classroom environment where story is encouraged and valued and in which she could study the role of children's storytelling in their sociomoral development. In her book *The boy who would be a helicopter: The uses of storytelling in the classroom*, she says, "For me the questions are: How can each day's priorities and attachments be used to further an environment in which children tell us what they think? And what happens to those who remain on the outside?" (1970, p. 11) Her numerous books focus on storytelling as a means to achieve community in the classroom by including the teacher and all children in the process.

Another type of education research focused on narrative is the area of teacher stories, teacher lore, also called teacher narrative (Jalongo & Isenberg, 1995; Schwarz & Alberts, 1998). "Stories ... invite us to remember that we are in the business of teaching, learning, and researching to improve the human condition" (Witherell & Noddings, 1991, p. 280). Teacher narratives often spring from a problem or issue a teacher experiences with students. Through writing a narrative of the situation, a teacher may come to new insights and understandings of how best to address the situation. For example, teacher Joanne Bergbom studied the use of student and teacher journal writing as a means for her troubled students to feel special about themselves as people and as writers. Reflecting on her study, she wrote:

> Writing becomes my opportunity to examine and clarify. In a reflection on my periodic need to confront the issue of journal writing in my classroom, I realize it is very much about my need for meaningful connections with my students.
>
> (Joanne Bergbom as cited in Schwarz & Alberts, 1998, pp. 57–58)

Teacher narrative can be an evocative and powerful form of documenting the trials and joys of teaching while providing lessons to help readers with similar situations. While teacher narrative is an important genre in the field of education and may serve as a springboard into a teacher research study, it is not characteristic of typical teacher research.

## Quantitative, Qualitative, and Mixed Methods

Most teacher research studies fall into one of three common research approaches: quantitative, qualitative, or mixed methods involving both quantitative and qualitative data. In determining which design to choose, ask yourself these three questions and then take a close look at the research questions of most interest to you:

"Do I believe that what I want to study exists out there and I can study how much of it exists or is important to learning including how I might control it?" If so then consider a **quantitative** study in which you can measure what you study.

"Do I believe that meaning and understanding are most important in education and the study of what the learning situation means to students is worth pursuing?" If so then consider a **qualitative** study focused on elements of meaning, understanding, and the interpretation of lived experiences.

"Does my topic of interest have both quantitative (measureable) and qualitative aspects (meaning and understanding) I want to know more about?" If so then consider a **mixed methods** study. Much teacher research employs both quantitative and qualitative methods.

---

**TEACHER RESEARCHER NOTEBOOK ENTRY #4:**

Reflect on your beliefs about teaching and learning. Compare your beliefs to the various research paradigms and approaches to doing research. Record your beliefs and comparisons in your Teacher Researcher Notebook and write an entry in which you discuss which paradigm or approach best fits your beliefs at this point in your professional life.

---

## Explorations

Examine each teacher research question below and determine what type of design would best fit the question: quantitative, qualitative, or mixed methods.

1. Math Talk: To what extent do children talk about math in their daily classroom interactions and what meaning does math have to them in their communications?

*Continued overleaf*

2. Self-assessment: What strategies do children use in assessing their written work?
3. Writing: How often do children use writing to accomplish a goal in the course of a typical day?

The first question could probably be best addressed with mixed methods. The number of times children talk about math can be quantified or counted and the meaning of math can be ascertained through a qualitative analysis of what children say about math. The second question lends itself to a qualitative analysis of the strategies children use to assess their work. The researcher can classify each strategy within a qualitative framework such as a constructivist framework. The third question calls for a quantitative approach of conducting a frequency count of the number of times children write each day. Chapter Five gives more examples of data types and Chapter Six provides methods for the analysis of quantitative and qualitative data.

## Examples of Teacher Research Plans

To plan your own teacher research study, you can use the template given previously in this chapter. Descriptions of each aspect in the template follow.

### Template for a Teacher Research Plan

#### *Purpose of the research*

The statement of research purpose is about what you want to study, why it is important to you, and why others may also find it important. When presenting a purpose, it is also common to tell what is significant about doing such a study, why it is significant, who might find it significant, and how doing the study may lead to improvements or changes in a specific situation you are addressing with the study. This is also the place for presenting a problem statement in which you discuss the problem or issue that lead you to want to do a study about it. Why is the situation a problem for you and for other teachers? How might the study help you to eventually address the problem or reach a deeper understanding of the situation?

For example, a first grade teacher wanted to study her teaching of measurement and children's learning of measurement. The purpose of her study was to analyze her teaching of measurement and what children were learning about measurement. This topic was important to her because she felt she could be doing more to help children learn about measurement. She felt measurement was a curriculum objective that she had merely skimmed the surface of what children needed to know. She wanted to improve the way she was teaching it. Studying her teaching of measurement would help her to better understand what exactly she was teaching about it, how she was teaching about it, how much she was teaching, and how children were affected by the measurement activities she planned for them.

From interactions with other teachers, she knew that other teachers were also concerned about how to teach measurement for student learning. Standardized test results for their school showed that children in third grade did well on all aspects of mathematics as measured by the test except for the area of measurement in which they scored below the state average. Teachers were concerned because their students typically scored above the state average in all parts of the mathematics test. Pressure was on teachers to improve test scores, specifically in the area of measurement. The school principal told teachers to get the scores up by the next testing period. The first grade teacher wondered what she could do in first grade to prevent poor scores by her children when they reached third grade and took the tests. She felt that such a study would help her improve her teaching and children's learning and help them do better on future tests. She was prepared to share her results with other teachers so that they could all address this issue informed by the research.

## Research questions

Most teacher research studies are guided by a primary research question or umbrella question that is the main thing to be studied and several secondary or subquestions that help to answer the main, umbrella question. Chapter Three describes the role of research questions, where they come from, and how to generate them. The number of research questions asked in any study varies from study to study. Only one research question may be asked or a multitude of questions may be asked. Typically teacher research studies have one main question and three or four sub questions. In the example of the first grade teacher studying teaching and learning about measurement, the research questions were:

**Main Question**: What is the nature of teaching and learning about measurement in a first grade classroom?

**Subquestion 1**: How does my current teaching about measurement influence children's learning about measurement?

**Subquestion 2**: What is the meaning that measurement holds for children in terms of their understanding of the concept, their need to measure, and how subsequent learning builds on their understanding?

**Subquestion 3**: What do I need to change, if anything, about how I teach measurement so that children will increase in their understanding of it?

## Literature review

Reviewing what has been written about the research topic or problem and reading the most recent research done on the topic informs and guides the research. It is not uncommon for a teacher who begins to read professional literature on a topic to find that someone has done a similar study that helps answer her research question without having to conduct a study herself. Also reading the professional literature on a topic may help a teacher to either change focus or refine or modify the research she plans to do based on the experiences and results of other educators. It contributes to the information and knowledge a teacher has about the topic and informs the teacher of what others have done so that she can build on, not duplicate what has already been done and thus make a contribution to the field through her research efforts. Probably the greatest benefit from conducting and writing a literature review is to convince yourself and others that you are knowledgeable of the topic and have done your homework on what is current and up to date in the field.

Professional literature and summaries of research studies can be found in professional books, journals, and reports that are housed in libraries, professional development sites, and internet sites of journals and professional associations such as NAEYC (see Chapter Three for a listing of resources). The NAEYC website houses the early childhood teacher research journal, *Voices of Practitioners*, as well as numerous journal articles and position statements on a great variety of topics important to the early childhood community. A professional literature search can now be easily conducted online through the search engines that tap into the major databases in the field including the major professional journals in the field. For example, the Educational Resources Information Center (ERIC, http://www.eric.ed.gov/) contains a wealth of information from the professional literature in early childhood education.

Taking some time to explore and read the most current (within five years) professional literature on a topic is time well spent that will help you conduct your study. It also shows who are the people who have explored your topic or might be interested in what you plan to do. While there is no magic number for how many sources are enough for a literature review, it is suggested that you read several primary sources (written by the researchers themselves) as well as several secondary sources (written by those summarizing the research of others) in order to get a balanced reading on the topic. Once you feel you have a good understanding of what has been done on your topic and the issues yet to be addressed, it is time to write a narrative of your review that builds a case for the importance of your study based on previous research. Professional literature can also help you frame your study within a broader theoretical view showing where your study might fit with what has been done on the topic.

For example, the first grade teacher wanting to research measurement read about the most current thinking and research on the topic in professional journals and online at the National Council of Teachers of Mathematics (NCTM) website. She also found an NCTM yearbook with numerous articles and professional recommendations on the teaching of measurement. She used these resources to frame her study.

## Methodology: Data collection and data analysis

Your research plan should provide details about how you plan to collect and analyze data relevant to your study. All data you gather should directly relate to one of your research questions and thus help to answer the question. Many data collection methods exist to choose from, but typically may include: your own teacher journal, student artifacts such as their writing, drawing, and performance, surveys and interviews of students on the topic of interest to you, and recorded observations of students. Chapter Five provides numerous examples of data collection. Similarly, data analysis methods are numerous and related to the type of data collected. Frequency counts and computations can be made of quantitative data. Theme analysis and textual analysis can be made of qualitative data. Chapter Six gives many examples of data analysis methods.

## Support for research

Time, other people, and funding are helpful resources that can support teacher research. It is very important to consider and plan for the support you will need to complete your study. Think about what you will need in order to collect data, analyze data, and share results of your study. You may need others to assist in doing classroom observations or making transcripts of audio/video segments of classroom activities. Consider what support you might need from other teachers to collaborate with you in the research or just serve as a sounding board with whom you can discuss ideas. You may want to consider who might be a trusted friend or colleague who could give you emotional encouragement through the process of doing the study.

You may need funds to purchase a digital or video camera to record data. Look for grant funding possibilities to tap for expenses. Some school systems have foundations that fund teacher research projects. You might consider writing a grant to a foundation to get the funds you need such as the National Foundation for the Improvement of Education (NFIE) or the Teachers Network Leadership Institute (TNLI). Consider time as a resource that requires support and think of ways to utilize existing time so that how you currently spend time becomes integrated with data collection. In other words, plan to use as data sources the activities you would normally do in the course of teaching. And finally, enlist the support of your principal, director, or supervisor by informing and involving them in what you plan to do. They may be able to offer support you hadn't considered was available.

## Ethical issues

Teacher researchers have a professional and ethical responsibility to insure no harm is done to their students or anyone else through the research. Since most teacher research is done on what would normally take place in an educational program and does not include anything beyond the regular classroom program, a teacher researcher would adhere to existing professional norms and standards for teaching young children. Professional codes of ethics are adopted by many professional associations such as NAEYC and provide guidelines for ethical practice. In addition to these codes, teacher researchers must make sure that other ethical considerations are practiced as well. These include informing all those involved in the research of the purpose of the research, the procedures, what is required of research participants including the time involved, the rights of participants including the right to withdraw their consent without penalty, how results will be used, and any benefits they might receive from participation. Also involved is getting appropriate consents and permissions to do the research.

The ethical issue of coercion is one that all teacher researchers must consider and account for. Since teachers are viewed as authority figures, and in most cases children don't have a choice of participating in the program, teachers have power over the lives of their students. Such power carries with it the responsibility to do no harm including coercing students to participate in the research. The younger the child, the more easily they can be coerced. One way to address the issue of coercion is to conduct research on the existing program in which children would normally participate. Another way is to make sure that you are sensitive to the issue and inform parents and children that participation is voluntary and refusing to participate carries no penalties including effects on grades.

## Permissions

Parental consent to participate in research is required for children under the age of eighteen. Child assent (a child gives permission to participate) is required and can be obtained in written form by children who can sign their names or verbally by those who can't. Most teacher research does not need to ask for permission to participate in the normal classroom routine or program activities since these are already required and part of the educational program. But permission is needed in order for the teacher to use data from required classroom activities, such as student artifacts, for research purposes and to share data and findings in a public forum such as at a teachers' meeting, workshop, or conference. Teacher researchers must obtain permission from parents and children for participation in the study as well as for use of child artifacts in subsequent professional presentations and publications. Permission is obtained prior to beginning the research study.

In addition to parental and child consent/assent, permission to conduct research is usually required by the program, school, and district. Most districts have human research committees that approve research proposals. In addition, if the teacher researcher is involved in her own educational program at a college or university, she would need to get written approval by the human subjects review board at that college or university. It is important to plan enough time to obtain permissions from the appropriate groups because it can take several weeks to get a study approved.

## Sharing results

Planning for how and when results will be shared helps define the timeframe for the study by giving the teacher specific dates as goals for study completion. For example, if you know that you would like to share results at a teacher workshop scheduled for the month of May, then you should aim to be completed by May. Results can be shared with individual teachers, groups, the community, and other professionals. Results can be shared verbally and in written form. Consider who may benefit from results and plan ahead to share results with that audience. Chapter Seven offers many suggestions for how to share results.

## Reflections before study begins

It helps to do a final reflection before the study begins in order to finalize plans and anticipate beginning steps in the research process. Final reflections before beginning the research help to reinforce why you want to do the study and its significance to you. It also helps you to get organized for what is to come.

## Timeline

A timeline for the study is very important and provides benchmarks to chart progress. A timeline is best done on a weekly basis detailing what is to be done each week of the study, similar to a lesson plan. It helps to keep the teacher researcher organized and thinking ahead to the next week and what needs to be done.

### From the Field: Example of a Teacher Research Plan

Second grade teacher Joy Modenbach works in a classroom with several children diagnosed with autism. She is concerned about their lack of verbal communication and decides to study ways to increase their level of verbal communication. Below is her tentative research plan.

## Purpose of the Research

Communication skills are an integral part of the society in which we live. Some individuals with autism are nonverbal and thus have no way to verbally communicate their needs. As a teacher in a classroom with nonverbal students I am interested in determining how I can help my students express themselves. The students in my class do not have hearing problems. Determining the basic needs of students in my classroom is currently a guess. I often wonder if they are upset because something hurts or they do not want to work on the assignment. Some of my students will pull me to something to show me what they want but I cannot help but wonder if there is a better method. The purpose of this teacher research project is to determine successful methods to help my students who are autistic and nonverbal to learn to communicate their needs.

## Research Questions

### Main Question

What is the nature of the communication process of children with autism in a self-contained multi-age (6–8 years) classroom?

### Sub Questions

What types of strategies do students with autism use to learn communication skills?

To what extent if any do symbols or pictures help nonverbal students with communication problems learn a mode of communication?

What types of pictures/symbols are most helpful to communication?

In what ways might technology help students with autism who are nonverbal communicate their needs?

## Preliminary Literature Review

I have done some reading about communication patterns of children with autism that has guided my research. I found one article of suggested teaching practices for working with children with communication difficulties that has been helpful. I found an article on the use of pictures with nonverbal children that I thought would help me to develop picture/symbol cards. I plan to continue

*Continued overleaf*

to read the professional literature primarily the special education journals that focus on autism such as *The Journal of Early Intervention*, *Teaching Exceptional Children*, *The Journal of Autism and Developmental Disorders*, and *Focus on Autistic Behavior*. The websites of the Division of Autism and Developmental Disabilities and the Division for Early Childhood of the Council for Exceptional Children have given me listings of articles and professional resources that I plan to continue to tap.

## Methodology: Data Collection and Data Analysis

### Data Collection
Multiple data sources will be used including child artifacts, teacher observation of communications of children with autism recorded in a teacher journal, and interviews with one veteran special education teacher trained in multiple modes of communication and with one speech pathologist who specializes in working with students who have communication delays.

### Data Analysis
All data will be converted to text for analysis. A selective highlighting theme analysis of the textual data will be made to identify themes of successful communication strategies.

## Support for Research

Some financial support will be needed to purchase materials consisting of sign and symbol cards ($225) and one piece of assistive technology ($450). I plan to write a grant request to our district professional development foundation for funds. I will ask for peer support from one of my colleagues who also teaches second grade and with whom I can discuss aspects of the study. I will need support from my principal as well.

## Ethical Issues

To insure ethical guidelines are followed, I will review existing teacher research ethical codes and the information on ethics posted on the local university website of their Institutional Review Board. I will take the online ethics of research training. I will contact the district office for the Assistant Superintendant of Elementary Curriculum for additional information on ethical requirements for research in my district. I will consult the district handbook on this topic.

Student confidentiality and anonymity will be protected throughout the study. I will communicate using a letter to parents (see below) of children in my classroom detailing my plan and asking for consent to use data generated by their child in my study and in reporting results. I will aggregate results when possible and will not reveal the names or identities of the children in the study.

Due to the nature of the lack of communication skills among students in the study, who may not be able to give verbal or written assent to participate in the study, I plan to use a series of signs and symbols to elicit their assent and when they are able, to ask for their verbal assent.

Parents and children will be able to withdraw from the study at any time without penalty.

## Permissions

District and building level permission will be obtained through the established procedures outlined in the teacher handbook for my district. Parent/guardian and teacher written consent will be obtained prior to beginning the study.

## Sharing Results

I plan to share results with educators at my school and in my district. I plan to share results with parents interested in the study. I would like to present my findings at our annual professional development workshop sessions and submit my final report to a teacher research or special education professional journal for publication.

## Reflections Before Study Begins

I am very enthusiastic to begin collecting data. I know much work is involved, but I think it will be worth the effort. I plan to meet weekly with my second grade colleague discussing the study with her and getting her suggestions. I know my principal's support and the support of the parents will be very important to the success of my study.

## Timeline

February 1–6: Reflect on classroom practices and teaching

February 7–28: Conduct literature review

March 1–7: Contact assistant superintendant and building principal to request permission to conduct study

March 8–15: Conduct parent informational meeting and obtain parent/guardian permission. When parent written consent is given, obtain child assent.

March 16–30: Collect baseline data on modes of communication.

April 1–7: Conduct individual interviews with veteran special education teacher and with speech language pathologist; implement sign/symbol and assistive technology activities to facilitate children's modes of communication

April 8–15: Conduct selective highlighting theme analysis on interview data

April 16–May 31: Observe and make field notes in teacher journal of children's modes of communication; collect child artifacts representative of their communications

June 1–30: Convert all data to text and analyze using selective highlighting theme analysis looking for emerging themes of communication

July 1–15: Write results in report; communicate results

August: Conduct workshop sharing results of study; submit manuscript to journal.

The following are the documents I used to obtain informed consent for participation in the research program.

### Informed Consent Letter for Authorization for a Minor to Serve as a Research Participant

Dear Parent/Guardian:

I will be conducting a study in our classroom to determine effective modes of communication. I am writing to ask your permission to use the data I collect from your child in the form of classroom observations and your child's work on assignments and activities in the study. Please note that your child will participate in the regular classroom program as usual. I am only asking for permission to use the data I gather from regular classroom activities for research purposes and to share with other education professionals. Your child's identity will be protected and not disclosed. No real names will be used to report results. My principal has approved this study.

The purpose of this study is to determine ways that students communicate their needs to others. The study will begin when all permissions are obtained and will continue until the end of the school year. The final report will be completed during the summer and will be mailed to you upon request. During the study your child will learn about different types of communication methods including signs, symbols, and assistive technology.

Benefits for participating in this study may include the learning of communication modes that your child may use to communicate with others. There are no known risks beyond what is encountered during a regular school day. Only the teacher conducting the study will have access to the data which will be kept in her locked file cabinet in the classroom.

Use of data from your child in this study is voluntary. Your child will be asked to give permission to use work produced and any classroom activities resulting in artifacts produced. Either you or your child may withdraw permission at any time with no penalty. Your child's performance record will not be affected in any way by either participation or withdrawal from the study.

You may contact me by email, joy.modenbach@school.edu or by phone at XXX-XXX-XXXX with any questions you might have.

Please check the appropriate line below, sign and date, keep a copy, and return a signed/dated copy to me no later than February 1. Thank you for your consideration.

_____ I give consent for my child's data to be used in this study. I understand that I will receive a signed copy of this consent form. I have read and understand it.

_____ I do not give consent for my child's data to be included in this study.

_____         _____
Student's name                                      Parent's signature

Date _____

## Informed Consent Form for Teacher Participants

### Project Title
The Study of Communication Modes of Children with Autism.

### Purpose
The purpose of this study is to determine ways that students communicate their needs to others.

### Procedures
You are asked to participate in an individual interview for about 45 minutes on the topic of communication modes of children with autism. You will be asked to share your knowledge and experiences of this topic with the teacher researcher. The location of the interview will be at your convenience at the school, local coffee shop, or other location you designate. The interview will not be recorded. The teacher researcher will take notes on your responses to interview questions.

### Risks of Participation
There are no known risks associated with this project which are greater than those ordinarily encountered in daily life.

### Benefits
Benefits from the study may include better understanding of the communication modes of children with autism that may improve the way they are taught.

### Confidentiality
The interview data will be kept in the teacher researcher's locked file cabinet in her classroom. She is the only person with access to the data. The data will be destroyed upon completion of the written report. Your identity and real name will be protected and not revealed in any written reports of the study.

It is possible that the consent process and data collection will be observed by research oversight staff responsible for safeguarding the rights and well-being of people who participate in research.

### Compensation
There is no compensation for participation in this study.

### Contacts
If you have questions about this study please contact me, joy.modenbach@school.edu or at XXX-XXX-XXXX. If you have questions about your rights as a research volunteer, you may contact Dr. Harry Smith, Superintendant, at XXX-XXX-XXXX.

**Participant's Rights**

Participation in this study is voluntary. You may withdraw from this study at any time without penalty.

I have read and fully understand the consent form. I sign it freely and voluntarily. A copy of this form has been given to me.

_____          _____

Signature of participant                                Date

I certify that I have personally explained this document before requesting that the participant sign it.

_____          _____

Signature of teacher researcher                   Date

For additional samples of permission forms and letters and other information on planning teacher research projects go to the Teachers Network website http://teachersnetwork.org.

---

**REFLECTIONS**

Reflect on the example of the second grade teacher's research plan. Why do you think written informed consent is crucial to doing research? Why is child assent important? What happens if the parents give consent but the child does not? What should the teacher researcher do in that case? What would you do? It is very important to consider and prepare for ethical issues involved in teacher research.

## Ethics of Teacher Research

Some define being ethical as doing the right thing (Mills, 2007). Mertler (2009) defines research ethics as the "moral aspects of research, including such values as caring, honesty, fairness, and openness" (p. 248). Mills (2007) says that a researcher's ethical perspective should be very close to their personal ethical position. Ethical guidelines assist in defining what are right and good ways to treat others. In teacher research, this means respecting child participants, doing no harm, reducing/eliminating the threat of coercion, maximizing the benefits of the research, obtaining informed consent, and instituting anonymity and confidentiality.

One of the main reasons for ethical guidelines is due to those researchers in the past who have done harm to participants, primarily physical harm but also emotional harm and even death. Historically this problem can be seen in the harmful experimentation by Nazis on unwilling subjects during World War II and chronicled in the Nuremberg Trails of Nazi war crimes including medical experiments on Jewish prisoners against their will (Punch, 1994). In this country, there is also a history of harmful research. In the 1930s a study with harmful effects was done of African American men in Georgia for forty years who were given placebos for syphilis and not offered the cure of penicillin when it became available. In the 1950s in a study of the effects of hallucinogenic drugs, American army soldiers were given LSD and were not told what it was until twenty years later after suffering adverse effects. In the 1960s, inmates in Ohio were injected with live cancer cells without their consent in order for researchers to study their immune responses. And in the 1990s some breast cancer patients died after being given harmful drugs being tested for safe use in chemotherapy.

The **Belmont Report** (1979), created by the National Commission for the Protection of Human Subjects of Biomedical and Behavioral Research under the direction of the Department of Health and Human Services, gives three ethical principles for human subjects research: "respect for persons, beneficence, and justice" (Nolen & Putten, 2007, p. 401). Beneficence refers to the benefits that may come from the research and justice refers to equity issues such as including representation of all population groups in the participant samples and not discriminating against certain groups. The Belmont Report has lead to the creation of human subjects review boards that apply ethical principles to proposed research. In universities and some schools, those who want to do research must first pass a research tutorial and exam covering ethical issues to insure the public that researchers are knowledgeable of the ethics of doing research.

Today safeguards for research participation have been put in place including human subject review boards that review proposed research for its potential to do harm. Most universities have Institutional Review Boards (IRBs) whose approval is required for faculty and student research studies involving human participants. It is important to note that not all IRBs will consider an application for a teacher research study primarily due to the issue of coercion. In the case of some IRBs it is useless to even apply for approval of a teacher research study. Some IRBs assume that teachers by the nature of their authority position in the classroom, should not do research on their own students because it would be considered a coercion of students who perceive they are not free to refuse to participate. Teacher researchers may appeal and advocate for consideration of teacher research in the IRB process. This usually involves educating IRB members about teacher research as a legitimate form of educational research. The more informed IRBs do recognize teacher research and understand that most teacher research is done on existing programs that students are already required to participate in. Also certain conditions can reduce the potential of coercion, such as having another teacher or adult explain the research and administer the consent form reassuring students that there is no penalty for refusing to participate and that their refusal is not of participation in the educational program, but only a refusal to allow the teacher researcher to use the student's data in the reporting of results. It is important to find out the procedures and requirements for getting approval of research in your own program and make sure that you meet the approval criteria before beginning the research (Brown, 2010).

Dunn (1995) outlines five safeguards to protect research participants in studies involving children, parents, and early childhood programs:

All aspects of the research must be explained to participants.

Consent of participants must be obtained before research begins.

Participation is completely voluntary.

All data gathered must be confidential.

All risks and benefits must be explained to participants.

(p. 4)

## Guidelines

The following are ethical guidelines for early childhood teacher researchers.

### Do not coerce or harm research participants physically, emotionally, academically, or in any way

The younger the child, the more easily this guideline can be violated because young children are very trusting of adults, especially their teachers. Young children are vulnerable and subject to adult coercion.

### The early childhood teacher researchers' primary responsibility is to their students

Teacher researchers wear the two hats of both teacher and researcher. When it comes to child safety and well-being, the teacher hat or role is foremost. Teacher researchers are teachers first, then researchers.

### Obtain informed consent of parents and students

Before the study begins tell parents and students what you plan to do, why, what you will do with results, what they are consenting to, and that participation is voluntary and they may withdraw without penalty at any time. Continue to keep parents and students informed of progress of the study.

### Maintain confidentiality and anonymity

Confidentiality refers to protecting the data in order not to identify participants so that participants remain anonymous and not named either by given name or descriptive details that might identify them. Researchers must protect data for example by securing it in a locked file or password protected computer file.

### Treat students and colleagues with respect and care

Show respect through maintaining confidentiality and anonymity and respecting their desire to stop participating in the study. Thank students and show appreciation for their participation. Give credit to colleagues for their research contributions that influence your research. In written reports of research, cite them for their contributions.

## Establish ownership of the data before beginning the research

Make it clear to students who owns the data, such as their work and artifacts they have produced. Tell them that you will return their work at the conclusion of the research or research presentation, if this is what you intend to do. If you intend to keep their work, then tell them so in the informed consent message including what you intend to do with it.

### Template for Typical IRB Informed Consent Form

Title of study

Listing of all teacher researchers with contact information (email/phone number)

Purpose of research

Research procedures including what participants will be asked to do

Risk to participants or statement to the effect that there are no known risks associated with the research which are greater than those ordinarily encountered in daily classroom life

Benefits to participants

Confidentiality protections

Participant right to withdraw permission at any time without penalty

Date and parental signature and/or signature of minor child

Researcher signature and date.

The teacher researcher provides a copy of the signed consent form to the participant or consenting parent.

## Codes of Ethics of Professional Associations

Check with the professional association of which you are a member for adopted codes of ethics. One of the first codes of ethics was adopted in 1975 by the National Education Association. NAEYC has a well-established Code of Ethical Conduct and Statement of Commitment (http://www.naeyc.org/positionstatements/ethical_conduct) to guide early childhood professionals. It is important to study the code in your field and reflect on what it means for you as a professional. The American Educational Research Association (AERA) has adopted ethical standards for educational researchers including teacher researchers. Under the leadership of Marian M. Mohr, the Teacher Research Special Interest Group (SIG) of the American Educational Research Association drafted a Statement of Ethics for teacher researchers:

> **The Teacher-Researcher Role:** Teacher-researchers are teachers first. They respect those with whom they work, openly sharing information about their research. While they seek knowledge, they also nurture the well-being of others, both students and professional colleagues.

**Research Plans:** Teacher-researchers consult with teaching colleagues and appropriate supervisors to review the plans for their studies. They explain their research questions and methods of data collection and update their plans as the research progresses.

**Data Collection:** Teacher-researchers use data from observations, discussions, interviewing, and writing that is collected during the normal process of teaching and learning. They secure the principal's permission for broader surveys or letters to solicit data. They also secure permission to use data already gathered by the school to which they would ordinarily have access as part of their teaching responsibilities (such as standardized tests) or for school information that is not related to their assigned responsibilities (such as protected student records).

**Research Results:** Teacher-researchers may present the results of their research to colleagues in their school districts and at other professional meetings. When they plan to share their conclusions and findings in presentations outside the school or district, they consult with the appropriate supervisors. They are honest in their conclusions and sensitive to the effects of their research findings on others.

**Publication:** Teacher-researchers may publish their reports. Before publishing, teacher-researchers obtain written releases from the individuals involved in the research, both teachers and students, and parental permission for students eighteen or younger. The confidentiality of the people involved in the research is protected.

(Hubbard & Power, 1999, p. 64)

---

## Explorations

1. Visit the NAEYC website, locate the Code of Ethics, read it, and explore ways to apply it to your own professional life. What is the number one primary principle in the Code? Why is the principle so important? In what ways do you honor the code? Interview an early childhood professional about their knowledge of the code and the extent to which they know about and apply it to their professional situations.
2. Use the template in this chapter to plan your own teacher research study. Then discuss your plan with a mentor and get feedback from this person.
3. In a small group of trusted friends, discuss the following ethical dilemmas and what you would do in each situation:

   (a) A teacher in your research group gives you an idea that greatly impacts your study.
   (b) A parent contacts you to find out the results of your study on the children in your class.
   (c) A student wants to know the results of your study.
   (d) Your study has produced unflattering information about certain teachers at your school.

(e) Your study has produced results indicating great dissatisfaction with some of the new policies of your principal.

(f) One parent has not given consent for videotaping of her child.

(g) In interviewing one child for your research, he discloses that he is abused by his parent.

(h) A student artifact is one of the critical pieces of data in your research. The student decides not to allow you to use it.

## Additional Resources

### Ethical Issues

Christensen, P., & James, A. (2000). *Research with children: Perspectives and practices*. London: Falmer Press.

Flinders, D. J. (1992). In search of ethical guidance: Constructing a basis for dialogue. *Qualitative Studies in Education, 5*(2), 101–115.

Graue, M. E., & Walsh, D. J. (1998). *Studying children in context: Theories, methods, and ethics*. Thousand Oaks, CA: Sage.

Hammack, F. M. (1997). Ethical issues in teacher research. *Teachers College Record, 99*, 247–265.

MacLean, M. S., & Mohr, M. M. (1999). *Teacher-researchers at work*. Berkeley, CA: National Writing Project.

Miller, S. K. (2001). Lessons from Tony: Betrayal and trust in teacher research. *The Quarterly of the National Writing Project, 23*(2).

National Association for the Education of Young Children (NAEYC) Code of Ethical Conduct and Statement of Commitment. Retrieved January 24, 2011, from http://www.naeyc.org/positionstatements/ethical_conduct.

Pritchard, I. A. (2002). Travelers and trolls: Practitioner research and institutional review boards. *Educational Researcher, 31*(3), 3–13.

Zeni, J. (Ed.) (2001). *Ethical issues in practitioner research*. New York: Teachers College Press.

### Narrative

Paley, V. G. (1979). *White teacher*. Cambridge, MA: Harvard University Press.

Paley, V. G. (1981). *Wally's stories*. Cambridge, MA: Harvard University Press.

Paley, V. G. (1990). *The boy who would be a helicopter: The uses of storytelling in the classroom*. Cambridge, MA: Harvard University Press.

Paley, V. G. (1992). *You can't say you can't play*. Cambridge, MA: Harvard University Press.

Paley, V. G. (1999). *The kindness of children*. Cambridge, MA: Harvard University Press.

### Planning Teacher Research

Teachers Network: http://teachersnetwork.org.

# References

Brown, P. U. (2010). Teacher research and university institutional review boards. *Journal of Early Childhood Teacher Education, 31*(3), 276–283.

Chaille, C. (2008). *Constructivism across the curriculum in early childhood classrooms*. Boston: Pearson Allyn & Bacon.

Chancer, J., & Rester-Zodrow, G. (1997). *Moon journals: Writing, art, and inquiry through focused nature study*. Portsmouth, NH: Heinemann.

Cozby, P. C. (2007). *Methods in behavioral research* (9th edition). New York: McGraw Hill.

Creswell, J. W. (2008). *Educational research*. Columbus, Ohio: Pearson Merrill Prentice Hall.

deMarrais, K., & Lapan, S. D. (2004). *Foundations for research: Methods of inquiry in education and the social sciences.* Mahwah, NJ: Lawrence Erlbaum Associates.

DeVries, R., & Zan, B. (1994). *Moral classrooms, moral children.* New York: Teachers College Press.

DeVries, R., Zan, B., Hildebrandt, C., Edmiaston, R., & Sales, C. (2002). *Developing constructivist early childhood curriculum.* New York: Teachers College Press.

Dunn, L. (1995). The rights of children, parents, and early childhood programs participating in research. Oklahoma City, OK: Early Childhood Association of Oklahoma Newsletter, pp. 4–5.

Ferreiro, E., & Teberosky, A. (1979/1982). *Literacy before schooling.* Portsmouth, NH: Heinemann.

Howe, R. (Ed.) (2003). *The quotable teacher.* Guilford, CT: The Lyons Press.

Hubbard, R. S., & Power, B. M. (1999). *Living the questions.* York, MN: Stenhouse.

Jalongo, M. R., & Isenberg, J. P. (1995). *Teachers' Stories.* San Francisco, CA: Jossey-Bass.

Kamii, C. (1985/2000). *Young children reinvent arithmetic.* New York: Teachers College Press.

Lankshear, C., & Knobel, M. (2004). *A handbook for teacher research.* New York: Open University Press.

Lincoln, Y. S., & Denzin, N. K. (2003). *Turning points in qualitative research.* New York: AltaMira Rowman & Littlefield.

Mertler, C. A. (2009). *Action research* (2nd edition). Los Angeles: Sage.

Mills, G. E. (2007). *Action research: A guide for the teacher researcher* (3rd edition). Upper Saddle River, NJ: Merrill/Prentice Hall.

Nolen, A. L., & Putten, J. V. (2007). Action research in education: Addressing gaps in ethical principles. *Educational Researcher, 36*(7), 401–407.

Paley, V. G. (1981). *Wally's stories.* Cambridge, MA: Harvard University Press.

Paley, V. G. (1990). *The boy who would be a helicopter: The uses of storytelling in the classroom.* Cambridge, MA: Harvard University Press.

Punch, M. (1994). Politics and ethics in qualitative research. In N. Denzin, & Y. Lincoln (Eds.), *Handbook of qualitative research.* Thousand Oaks, CA: Sage.

Rogers, F. (2003). *The world according to Mister Rogers.* New York: Hyperion.

Schwarz, G., & Alberts, J. (1998). *Teacher lore and professional development for school reform.* Westport, CT: Bergin & Garvey.

Stringer, E. (2008). *Action research in education* (2nd edition). Columbus, OH: Pearson Merrill Prentice Hall.

Witherell, C., & Noddings, N. (Eds.) (1991). *Stories lives tell.* New York: Teachers College Press.

# five
# Data, Data, Who Has the Data?

*You can observe a lot by watching.*

Yogi Berra

This chapter explores what data are and the purpose they serve. It gives examples of appropriate data sources for early childhood teacher research including teacher journals, observations, child artifacts, surveys, interviews, and documents. The relationship of each research question and its connection to a data source will be emphasized. The main point of this chapter is to show that data come from the everyday life and activities of the classroom.

## Defining Data

In teacher research, the word data is used often to refer to the bits of information we collect to help us answer research questions. The word data is from the Latin and is the plural of the word datum (Merriam-Webster, 2010), a word you do not often see in professional literature. The word data can be used in two ways, sometimes as a plural noun and sometimes as a singular noun. It is a plural noun when it refers to more than one bit of information or to multiple bits of information. It is also used as a singular collective noun or mass noun when it means "information" in a singular way. For example: "Data are shown in Table 1" is the plural version while "Data from the research literature on motivation shows that interest plays a major role" is the singular version. In speaking and writing about data in teacher research, the word is most often plural because we most often use the word to refer to the multiple bits of information we have collected or analyzed. Whether you use the word in a singular or plural way, it refers to all the facts and pieces of information that we gather in order to make sense of our research questions. While research questions are helpful in pointing to the data sources we need, data are helpful too in providing the material we need to analyze for meaningful findings ultimately leading to deeper understanding of the situation we are researching.

Most data do not exist out there in the world to be gathered, although we tend to speak of data gathering as if data were out there waiting to be collected. Data are actively constructed in order to make meaningful connections between research questions and the activities of classroom life. Data are constructed by the teacher researcher because it is the teacher researcher who decides what will be considered data in a study. She may construct data in the form of observations, field notes, and the journal she keeps. The teacher researcher also constructs data by interpreting them. Data only carry meaning when interpreted.

## Purpose of Data

The purpose of data is to serve as the representation or embodiment of what it is we are studying. In a study of children's responses to poetry, data may be any number of things such as children's own poetry written or spoken, children's drawings inspired by poetry, children's desire for additional examples of poetry as evidenced by their requests for more poetry books, and/or children's performances and dramatic play enacting poems they have heard. We use data by analyzing it in order to answer our research questions.

The person conducting the research is in the position of asking the research questions and then deciding which forms of data to collect and analyze in order to answer the questions. The teacher researcher decides which data sources are most likely to lead to meaningful information. She may decide that several data sources are appropriate to address the study. When several data sources are used to show findings, the study is more believable than when only one data source is used as evidence. The process of using and analyzing multiple data sources to produce credible results is called **triangulation** and provides more **trustworthiness** in results than when only one source has been used (Mertler, 2009). The process of triangulation will be discussed in Chapter Six. Teacher research studies using multiple data sources may be more believable or trustworthy than those that use a single source.

---

**TEACHER RESEARCHER NOTEBOOK ENTRY #5**

Do you ever wonder how you might use everyday data to study how you spend your time? Think about the examples of data you generate daily such as hours slept each night, calories eaten per meal, text messages received and sent, sports statistics monitored, type and amount of reading done, type of leisure activities engaged in, quality of work done, miles traveled, etc. How might you use these data to find out how you spend your time on a daily basis? Before reading further, make a list of as many types of data you generate within a typical day as you can think of. As described in Chapter Four, these data may be of a quantitative nature that means they can be counted and measured or of a qualitative nature that means they can be reflected upon for the meaning they convey.

Once you have made a list, then reflect on your list. What does your list tell you about how you spend your day? Is there anything in the list you would like to change? If so, select this piece of data and write about what you might like to change. Then write a question that would help you study this change. For example, if you chose from your list an item such as what you read daily because you don't read much for fun, your research question might be, "How can I read more for leisure?" You may decide to keep a log for a week of the amount and type of reading you do. At the end of the week, analyze the data in your log. Then use your analysis to plan changes in the amount and type of reading you do for leisure.

---

The same can be done to analyze data generated in your professional life as well. Think of all the examples of data that early childhood teachers encounter in working with children. In your journal, make a new list of all the examples you can think of that would be data found in an early childhood setting. Then compare your list with the list below.

## Data That May Be Found in Early Childhood Classrooms

- **Written Data:** stories, songs, poetry, letters, dictation, labels/captions, journal entries, reports, project work
- **Spoken Data:** conversations, talk during group time/center time/dramatic play, interviews, directives, "silly talk" or nonsense words, and audio/video recordings of what is spoken
- **Child Constructed Artifacts:** murals, block constructions, collages, sand structures, games, performances, and photographs of children's work
- **Observations of:** individual activities, group activities, children's choices of activities, indoor/outdoor play, and interactions
- **Assessment Documentation and Records:** checklists, anecdotal records, report cards, rating scales, test/performance scores, and other documents such as curriculum guides and brochures describing the mission of the program or school.

How does your list compare to the one above?

## Identifying Data That Already Exist

It should be clear by now that there is no limit to the amount and type of data that can be found in an early childhood setting. You may recall from Chapter Three that the data chosen to be used in a teacher research study are determined by the research questions asked. The questions point to the data sources that will help the teacher researcher to explore the question. For example, if you want to study what children choose to read in an early childhood setting, there are many data sources that you may record as a matter of course: observations of what children choose to read when given time for choice reading; quantity and type of books selected by children from the library; and interviews of individual children about their reading choices. The list of an individual child's reading record shown in Figure 5.1, was made by a second grade teacher who routinely recorded the reading materials of all children in her class. She can then use these records to answer research questions about the types of books children like to read, the relationship of number of books read to level of reading ability, or other questions that require records of children's reading over time.

It is helpful to consider what types of data currently exist in an early childhood setting that may be useful to a teacher engaged in teacher research. In general, teachers keep track of children's learning in many ways in order to chart children's progress, assess what children are learning, show which required skills children have accomplished, and share documentation of progress with parents, other teachers, directors, and administrators. Before creating new data sources to inform teacher research, it is helpful to

**BOOKS I CAN READ**     NAME: Christian

| DATE | TITLE | PRACTICE LEVEL * | PARENT/TEACHER COMMENT |
|------|-------|------------------|------------------------|
| 9/8 | Cat Games | E | Christian read it several times to me. He read it quickly & easily |
| 9-9 | Seven Blind Mice | Ch | Christian read it several times. The long words were a challenge. He loves that book! |
| 9-13 | Go Dog. Go! | E | He read it quickly & easily. |
| 9-14 | Surprise Soup | E | He picked this one! |
| 9-14 | Frog and Toad are Friends | Between R + Ch | I suggested that he read a story a night! |
| | | | Christian read a lot of the words quickly & easily, but had to sound several words out. He enjoyed the story & laughed many times. |
| 9-24 | Frog and Toad All Year | Between R + Ch | He's asking me for help less and less. Risk taking with words seems to be getting easier! |
| | | | I really have the same comment as I made last time—he reads most of the words quickly & easily but has to sound some words out. He seems to sound them out quicker |
| 10/2+3 | Henry + Mudge Under the Yellow Moon | R | He has to sound out a few words, but |
| 10/5 | Frog + Toad Together | R | in a majority of the 2 books he reads it quickly & easily. |
| 10/8 | Dogs With Frog + Toad | R | I see such an improvement in his reading skills + confidence |
| 10/19 | Danger The Dog Yard Cat | Between R + Ch | Wonderful! This is exciting... It seems to really be "clicking" for him! |
| | | | Many words he reads quickly, several he had to sound out. Several were very large words |
| 10/21 | Henry + Mudge in the Green Time | R | I am so proud of how well he is doing! |

*Practice level

E = Easy; R = Just Right; Ch = Challenging; H = Too Hard

FIGURE 5.1  Books I Can Read

Source: Courtesy of Kristi Dickey

consider what data are currently available to draw from. In this way teacher research is integrated into what teachers already do and not an additional task to add onto the teacher's workload. For example if the research question is focused on children's learning, then already existing records may be all that are necessary to explore the question. Existing records may include performance and progress assessments, rubric assessments, scores on assignments and tests, and anecdotal notes of children's accomplishments. For example one kindergarten teacher kept a file for each child throughout the year in which she recorded the new words each child used in their journals. She used the files to show parents how many new words children learned through the course of a year. She could use the existing files to help answer a research question about the extent to which children incorporate new words into their writing. It is always a good idea to consider existing data in order to reduce the time and effort required to create new data sources or new situations for data collection. Considering existing data may also result in a more efficient research design.

For example, Chuck, a second grade teacher researcher, wanted to study the extent to which his students were achieving state mandated learning skills through the inquiry approach to science that he was using for the first time. As required by his principal, he was keeping skill achievement records for each child in tables where he recorded notations using a rubric with categories from skill not observed (score of 0) to skill achieved (score of 3) as in Table 5.1. He correlated his inquiry science activities with the required skills. For each inquiry science unit, he identified which required skills were to be learned. For example, he correlated the activities from his inquiry unit on "What do plants need to grow?" with state mandated learning skills. In Table 5.1 the skills are in the shaded boxes and the unit activities that correlate with the skills are italicized. The evaluation key he used assigned a skill score of 0 to the category Not observed; 1 to the category Area of concern; 2 to the category Working toward; and 3 to the category Achieved. In the example in Table 5.1, one student, Shawn, achieved three of the mandated skills and is working toward one. Chuck also recorded a concern about Shawn's use of a ruler to measure plant growth. Chuck can tally Shawn's total score as 12 for this unit. Chuck can do this for all students. This data would begin to help him answer his research question about the extent to which his students are achieving state mandated learning skills.

**TABLE 5.1  Rubric for Achieved Outcomes**

| SHAWN 3-4-10 | Not Observed | Area of Concern | Working Toward | Achieved |
|---|---|---|---|---|
| Pose an inquiry question | | | | |
| Pose a question about plant growth | | | | 3 |
| Observe events | | | | |
| Observe plant growth | | | | 3 |
| Describe events | | | | |
| Describe and illustrate plant growth in journal | | | | 3 |
| Classify objects | | | | |
| Classify 4 plantings by growth | | | 2 | |
| Use simple tools to gather info: magnifier, ruler | | | | |
| Use magnifier to observe and describe; use ruler to measure height of plants | | 1 doesn't use base line on ruler yet | | |

In addition, Chuck kept anecdotal notes in his journal recording children's conversations during inquiry science activities. He also used as a data source the science journals children wrote to record their activities during inquiry science. He then had three data sources: skill learning records, teacher journal, and children's inquiry science journals. The data from the three sources were both quantitative (rubric scores) and qualitative (learning themes from textual analysis of teacher and children's journals). The three data sources represented already existing records. Rather than developing and recording other data sources, he could then put his efforts into analyzing the data he already had.

## Additional Data Sources

The previous section showed how existing data can be used to help answer research questions. It is always more efficient to begin with the existing data at hand and then add additional data sources as needed to answer research questions. Data can be gathered and recorded from many different sources such as teacher journals, observations, interviews, surveys, child artifacts, and documents. The teacher researcher reflects on each research question and decides which data sources to draw from in order to answer the questions. In early childhood teacher research, the most frequently used data collection devices tend to be observations of children recorded as anecdotal records and field notes in a teacher research journal. While interviews and surveys are possible data sources, they tend to be used more frequently in research with older children. Surveys and interviews of very young children may be impractical and not always appropriate, especially when young children are not yet reading and writing, and may have difficulty understanding instructions and even the purpose of what is being asked of them. Teacher researchers must consider children's capabilities in the selection of data sources and select those data sources most appropriate in representing what children can do.

### Teacher Journal

A teacher journal is a recording of thoughts, observations, feelings, and insights that teachers have. A teacher journal may take various physical forms. It can be kept on pieces of paper, sticky notes, or note cards. More often it is kept in a notebook either spiral or loose leaf. Or it may take a digital form and be kept in a computer file or on a digital personal assistant. Teachers write in their teacher journals whenever they like. They may write once a day, once a week, or at those times when they feel the need to put their thoughts in written form. While it may seem that scheduling time to write in a journal is difficult due to all the other obligations of teaching, it can actually be a time saver in the long term. A teacher journal provides a way for teachers to think and write about what went well and what needs to be changed. The writing involves reflecting on what happened and next steps that lead to planning and implementing plans. Writing about these things gives teachers directions for what to do next time and may decrease the time teachers may need to spend making lesson plans.

Keeping a teacher journal also provides quiet moments for teachers to debrief from all the activity of the day and can be cathartic. Scheduling 10 or 15 minutes before children arrive or right after they leave to write in a journal can help teachers organize. Some teachers like to illustrate their journals as well. Periodically reviewing what one has written in a journal helps teachers discover patterns in their teaching and programs and provides insights into the extent to which they are meeting their professional goals.

### Example of Teacher Journal Entry

What a day! Nothing went the way I planned it. I wanted my supervisor to see how the children could carry on a respectful discussion during Morning Meeting but it was just the opposite. Jarrett's dad walked in carrying his guitar. When the children saw him, it was pandemonium. I tried to get them back with a finger play, but it didn't work that well. My supervisor practically took over while I talked with Mr. Johnson. Not my best day. (Maybe next time I will ask the children to welcome the parent into the group.)

Teacher journals can be meaningful reflective devices. Reading journal entries at a later point in time can help teachers look for patterns in their teaching and in what is important to them. Reflecting on journal entries can help teachers think about what changes they might make. In one sense, a teacher journal can chart a teacher's professional development. It is interesting to review a journal one has written from a previous year to see how far one has come in professional development.

When a teacher keeps a journal for teacher research purposes, it is kept systematically on a regular schedule. A journal should always be kept secure such as in a locked file cabinet so that confidentiality of information is maintained. The purpose of a research journal may go beyond recording daily thoughts and events. A specific purpose may be assigned to the journal such as recording notes about children's storytelling using a white board. This would be an example of using a teacher journal to record **field notes** that describe what a teacher sees children doing in an activity that is the focus of her research. Field notes can be written spontaneously when a teacher notices something or they can have a specific focus based on what a teacher is studying. Field notes are usually written in the middle of activities when a teacher notices something that is significant to her research that she wants to record. Teacher researchers often make field notes dividing the notepaper into two large side-by-side columns (Hubbard & Power, 1999). The left hand column is used to record notes (raw notes). At a later time, such as at the end of the day, the right hand column is used to record thoughts and insights after analyzing what has been written in the left hand notes (see Figure 5.2). Hubbard and Power call this approach "cooking the notes" (p. 129).

### Observations

Data gained through observations can be the most important data in a teacher research study because it may help a teacher determine whether or not a new approach being studied is successful or unsuccessful (Hendricks, 2009). Observations can be done in many ways. Teachers may record their observations of activities they find significant as field notes in their teacher journal. These types of observations tend to be done informally and as a teacher feels the need to record them. In some cases teachers may want to take an ethnographic approach to observations by observing as much as possible of classroom activity and recording as much as possible of what has been observed (Short, 1991). Such an approach may serve to help a teacher reflect on the big picture of classroom life in order later to narrow a research focus. For example after reflecting on her

| Raw Notes | Cooked Notes |
|---|---|
| *5-5-10 10:15-10:30*<br>*Storytelling with the*<br>*Smart Board: Marissa,*<br>*Chantelle, Jeff, & Logan are*<br>*retelling The 3 Little Pigs.* | This group usually works well together. |
| *Marissa takes control of*<br>*choosing a setting of an*<br>*amusement park. She brings*<br>*it up on the Smart board*<br>*and the children talk about*<br>*where to put the pigs.* | Marissa seems to need to be in control when she is in a group.<br><br>Interesting idea! I wonder where it came from? I need to ask her. |
| *Logan doesn't like the idea*<br>*and tries to take the marker*<br>*pen from Marissa. Chantelle*<br>*supports Marissa, and*<br>*Logan lets Marissa create the*<br>*setting. Jeff stands by just*<br>*looking, seeming to be*<br>*uninvolved.* | I'm surprised that Logan gave in so easily to Marissa.<br><br>I need to look into Jeff's behavior. I wonder if he is upset about something or just not interested |

**FIGURE 5.2  Example of Cooked Field Notes.**

ethnographic notes, she may decide to study interactions in the dramatic play area because it is a popular area for children and rich in examples of a variety of types of play. An example of a detailed ethnographic description of the physical set up of a first grade classroom can be found in Appendix A Ethnographic Description of a First Grade Classroom.

In teacher research, observations may also be done systematically and for specific purposes. For example, teachers may use a time sampling technique to record classroom activities at a designated interval such as at 60 second intervals, a standard interval in observational research. A teacher may want to study children's interactions in a systematic way. She may decide to use a 60 second interval to record what interactions are taking place each minute. A time interval provides a rigorous form of reliability in data gathering because if the activity is significant and consistent, then it will show up in the time interval data. Later the teacher can analyze the data for types of interactions that were observed and recorded. The following is an example of using a 60 second time sampling technique to record child-to-child interactions of a child, Seth, in a preschool setting.

### Example of 60 Second Time Interval Samples of Child-to-Child Interactions

1. Seth stacks a block on top of another block
2. Seth stacks blocks
3. Marissa bumps Seth's construction and it falls
4. Seth looks at Marissa

5. Marissa helps restack Seth's blocks
6. Seth wanders over to easel watching Jennifer paint
7. Seth watches Joseph, Brinton, and Shaney trying on hats in dramatic play
8. Seth watches
9. Seth watches
10. Seth wanders to woodworking area where Will asks him if he wants to hammer
11. Seth hammers with Will
12. Will asks Seth what he wants to make
13. Seth and Will hammer
14. Seth and Will hammer
15. Seth wanders to computer desk.

This example shows Seth's child-to-child interactions over a 15 minute period. Seth's teacher can analyze this data for the frequency and types of interactions Seth has with his classmates. In this example, there appear to be two examples of Seth interacting with other children. His teacher may conclude that Seth does not often initiate interactions with other children. In the two child-to-child interactions in this example, the other child has initiated the interaction. Although Seth does not avoid other children or react to them in anger, he seems to do more observing of their behavior with no overtures toward them. There is no evidence of Seth's expressive language in this data set. The teacher may want to do additional time samplings listening for Seth's verbal expressions and looking for evidence of initiation of interactions before drawing any final conclusions about Seth's behavior.

Another approach the teacher might have used instead of a time sampling technique is to record every interaction as it happens. If she is interested only in analyzing child-to-child interactions, she may decide to record only when she observes an interaction occurring. While the time sampling technique is a more rigorous method, recording interactions as they occur may give her a more complete picture of Seth's interactions with other children.

Teachers may want to use observation record forms such as tally sheets and checklists. Instead of using a time interval to record activities, a tally sheet that lists all categories of the activities the teacher is focused on can be used to tally an activity as the teacher observes it. Checklists can be very helpful observation recording devices. If a teacher wants to observe which children engage in certain activities, she can use a list of children's names in the left hand column with the activity categories in a row across the top. Each time she observes a child engaging in an activity on the list, she can check it off on the observation form.

In the example below, a kindergarten teacher wants to find out which children are playing which math games during free choice time. The teacher has incorporated into her math center some of the games suggested by Kamii (2000) for promoting children's construction of number relationships (see Table 5.2). The teacher has kept track of game playing for one week using the checklist in the table. She can analyze the data for frequency and type of game playing. She can also look for patterns in the data. In this example the most frequently played game for girls is a tie between Go Fish and Tic Tac Toe. For boys it is the card game War. Such a checklist provides evidence of game playing that she could use to answer her research question about the extent to which children play math games in her program.

**TABLE 5.2 Weekly Game Playing**

| Names | War | Go Fish | Concentration | Tic Tac Toe |
|---|---|---|---|---|
| Ella | | ✓ | ✓ | |
| Brandy | ✓ | ✓ | ✓ | |
| Clarissa | | | | ✓ |
| Michelle | ✓ | ✓ | ✓ | ✓ |
| Kim | | ✓ | | ✓ |
| Janelle | | | | ✓ |
| Trisha | | ✓ | | ✓ |
| Holden | ✓ | | | |
| Sammy | ✓ | | ✓ | |
| Jonathan | ✓ | | | ✓ |
| Lance | ✓ | ✓ | ✓ | ✓ |
| Alexander | | | | |
| Martin | ✓ | | | ✓ |
| Jordan | | ✓ | | |
| Dameron | | | | ✓ |
| Jeff | ✓ | ✓ | ✓ | ✓ |
| Lance | | | ✓ | |

Another way of recording observations is to use a log to record events chronologically such as using a daily log to record which toddlers take naps and the duration of their naps (see Figure 5.3). This nap log can be posted for parents to read as they pick up their children.

| Child | Date/Time | Comments |
|---|---|---|
| Sawyer | 3/1/10 9:30-10:15 | Slept soundly |
| Elizabeth | 3/1/10 9:45-12:00 | Fussed before falling asleep |
| Solomon | 3/1/10 10:20-11:05 | Slept with his blanket |
| Gracie | 3/1/10 12:30-1:15 | Fitful sleep; tossed and turned |
| Brandon | 3/1/10 12:30-1:30 | Wanted book during nap |
| Sawyer | 3/1/10 1:45-2:30 | Needed more nap time today |

**FIGURE 5.3 Daily Nap Log**

Teachers can keep logs of activities, such as nap time, to help answer questions. For example a daily log may help answer which children may benefit more from taking naps, children's soothing behaviors before, during, and after nap time, and the relationship of naps to children's play behaviors. Teachers can also keep logs similar to the following one kept on 14-month-old Brian that documents developmental accomplishments

### Example: Brian's Log

2-10 Brian was watching Ms. Stacey yawn today. He opened his mouth wide and pretended to yawn too (imitation of other's behavior).

2-11 Brian patted a crying toddler's head (response to others' feelings with empathy)

2-12 Ms. Stacey sang Itsy Bitsy Spider. Brian walked to books and found Itsy Bitsy Spider book and said, "Look! Spider!" (enjoys books).

2-19 Brian held hand mirror to face and looked at self in mirror and touched mirror with hand. At lunch he used spoon to feed himself (understands how objects can be used).

2-20 Brian played at water table with Myra (plays with other children).

2-25 I asked where his hair was and he touched his hair. Same for his nose when I asked (receptive language).

2-27 Brian drew lines and scribbles on paper with crayons (fine motor coordination).

When teachers want to study how children move through the classroom, where they go, which areas are most utilized, or traffic congestion in the classroom, they may make a map of the classroom floor plan that contains the centers, areas, and tables. The floor plan can then be used to chart children's movements during various activities such as center time. A teacher can observe, mark areas on the plan, and learn which areas get the most use and which areas need reorganization to alleviate traffic jams. Figure 5.4 shows a floor plan of a primary classroom.

## Observing the Big Picture

Teachers may feel that with all the demands of teaching, they don't have time to teach, observe, and record observations simultaneously. They may decide to ask for help from others who can come to the classroom, observe, record, and then share recorded observations with the teacher. This will also provide a wide-angle view of classroom activities. There may be another adult in the classroom or program who can help with observations. Or ask a teacher, teacher assistant, or volunteer to observe. If you're doing teacher research with someone from a nearby university such as a university faculty member, it might be this person who can help conduct classroom observations.

Another option for observing the classroom without taking time out of the day is to use recording devices such as audio recorders and video cameras that can be set up in the classroom. The advantage to these devices is that they provide a record of observations that objectively captures what happened in such a way that the recordings can be reviewed as many times as necessary during the data analysis. Some difficulties with

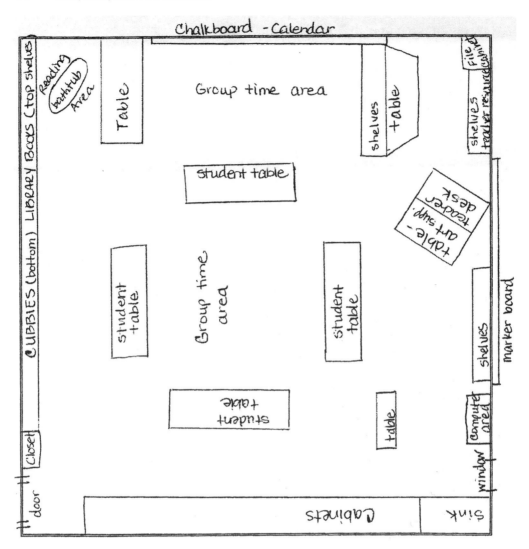

**FIGURE 5.4 Classroom Floor Plan**
Source: Courtesy of Krisi Dickey

using tape recorders and cameras can be equipment failures in the middle of observations, problems with positioning equipment to get the best recording, and the novelty effect of children playing to the camera or wanting to use the camera. To prevent problems teachers can practice with the equipment for a period of time that allows children to become so familiar with it that the novelty wears off and they don't notice it as much.

Teachers working toward National Board Certification (2010 Guide to National Board Certification) are asked to submit video entries of their lessons. Teachers can choose what to video within the parameters given. They analyze the video, reflect on what happened during the lesson, and write reflective entries in which they discuss the purpose of the lesson, what happened in the video, insights they come to, and any changes they might make for the future. This process is similar to analyzing video recordings for teacher research purposes.

## Example of National Board Video Reflection

A second grade teacher, Kristi Dickey, videotaped a class discussion to explore if the current class schedule of reading activities was still meeting children's individual needs. The reading schedule of 45 minutes called for silent reading first followed by choice time among listening centers, science observations, math games, puzzles, and partner reading. Kristi found that children were doing partner reading during silent reading time and assessed that the schedule was not giving them enough time for partner reading, a choice among other choices. She also noticed that children were confused when some began partner reading during silent reading time thinking that silent reading time was over and choice time had begun. Kristi decided to videotape a class discussion of this problem in order for children to express their opinions about which activities should be included in the morning schedule. The following is Kristi's reflection on the video taped class discussion. Please see Appendix B Reflection on National Board Video of Class Discussion for the full transcript of Kristi's reflection.

> My overall objective in involving my students in decision making processes is to contribute to our atmosphere of mutual respect (DeVries & Zan, 1994). From the video, I observed that my class is comfortable sharing ideas and listening to each other. I became more aware that children were able to disagree in an agreeable way. When one person suggested that we change writer's workshop from its own separate time to be included as a choice along with silent reading and partner reading, Samantha stated, "I think that would be too much at once. Some people might want to do all three and just not have time."
>
> Time and again the conversation among the children returned to this solution: silent reading and partner reading would take place during the same block of time, with a choice of which one to do. I saw evidence of children respecting others when a few children made a comment that it would be important to partner read with soft voices to respect those people who were choosing to read silently. I asked the children if this was the solution that they would like to try. Henry felt comfortable sharing his concern that he was afraid we weren't going to have choice time. Once I assured him that having silent reading and partner reading in the same block would allow time in our schedule for choice time, he enthusiastically agreed to this solution. We ended the discussion with the decision to try this solution the next school day, then to get back together to discuss its success.
>
> Later, after trying the solution, I asked the children if it was working for them and they all agreed that it was. The solution we agreed upon is still working in our classroom.

## Interviews

Interviews can be a data source for teacher research. Teachers may decide to interview children, their parents, other teachers, administrators, or community members. Interviews are done in teacher research when a teacher needs to get ideas and perceptions of others about the research problem and when interview responses can be used to help answer the research question. Interviews can be done informally or formally. An example of an informal interview is the conversational interview (Mills, 2011). For example, a teacher may do research on what children write in their journals. He may engage individual children in a conversation about what they have written in a certain journal entry. He may first ask a child about the topic of the entry. Based on the child's response he may ask another question, ask for clarification, or end the conversation.

It is more comfortable for children when interviewed by people they know and trust such as their teacher. When interviewing children it is important to be in a familiar, quiet setting with few distractions. Some privacy helps so that a child doesn't think others are listening to the interview. If a child gives simple one-word or brief responses, it may help to provide encouragement or offer an example. But it is best to end the interview if a child is not interested or forthcoming in responding.

## Example of Conversational Interview on Journal Entries

### Key: T = Teacher, C = Child

T: I would really like to hear about what you wrote in your journal today. Can you tell me about it?

C: Well, I wrote about the earthquake in Haiti. I wrote that it was a big quake and lots of people were killed.

T: How did you decide to write about the earthquake?

C: It was on the news and my mom was talking about it.

T: Would you read me some things you wrote?

C: Sure. The earthquake in Haiti was a big one. Many people were killed. People have no homes and are living in tents. They have no water or food. Some people are going there to help them. Kids lost their parents. Schools fell down on top of kids.

T: You seem to know a lot about what happened there. Tell me about the schools falling down.

C: Well, it was very scary. The floors fell down on top of kids and they were hurt. I hope that doesn't ever happen to our school.

T: Me too. Thanks for sharing your journal with me. I noticed that last week you wrote about a major snowstorm in Washington DC. Do you like to write about things happening in the news?

C: I guess so.

In this example, the teacher was studying children's interests as reflected in their free choice journal writing. This teacher learned that the child he interviewed consistently wrote about news events. After interviewing all children in the program, the teacher can analyze the interview data by identifying categories of topics such as news events. Based on his results he should achieve a better understanding of his children. He can learn if children in the program have common interests in what they write in their journals. He may also decide to try to stretch children by asking them to write on certain topics they don't normally write about.

In some interview studies it is better to ask the same interview questions of all participants. For example a teacher may want to find out how other teachers in the program use the outdoor classroom. She may decide to create a set of structured interview questions and ask each teacher the same set of questions in order to make comparisons. She may schedule individual interviews with teachers and record their responses.

### Example of Structured Interview on Use of the Outdoor Classroom

Thanks so much for letting me interview you about the ways in which you use the outdoor classroom at our school. I have a set of questions to ask and I will record your answer for each question. Please don't feel like you have to answer all questions. This interview shouldn't take longer than about 15 minutes.

1. Do you ever take your class to the outdoor classroom? (If the teacher says no, then ask why. Thank the teacher and end the interview.)
2. When (what times of the year) do you take your class to the outdoor classroom?
3. What units, projects, or assignments do you have your students do in the outdoor classroom?
4. In what ways if any do the activities you have students do in the outdoor classroom help you achieve the required learning outcomes for your grade level?
5. How have your students reacted to the outdoor classroom?
6. Are there any things students can only learn in the outdoor classroom that would not be possible in the regular classroom?
7. What are any safety issues around the outdoor classroom?
8. What do you do to keep students safe there?
9. Do you ever join with other classes in the outdoor classroom? If so, then for what purposes?
10. Is there anything you would like to change about the outdoor classroom?
11. Is there anything else you would like to tell me about the outdoor classroom?

Thanks so much for your help with this interview. You are welcome to the results of the research when it is completed.

Notice that the final question in the structured interview was open-ended allowing the person interviewed to respond with additional information that the researcher might not have thought to ask. It is always a good idea to incorporate such a "catch all" question into an interview so that you capture as much relevant information as possible and don't miss something important. The structured interview is similar to the questionnaire. The major difference is that interviews, both informal and structured, are usually conducted in person and individually. Questionnaires can be sent to participants who complete them on their own then return them to the sender. If a teacher wants feedback from a great number of other teachers, such as all teachers within the district, then she may choose to send a questionnaire to all. Questionnaires can be returned through school mail, regular mail, or email.

## Surveys

In addition to questionnaires, teachers may use surveys to collect responses from participants. Surveys may be similar to questionnaires in the types of questions asked. The major difference between a survey and a questionnaire is that surveys are used more often to get information from a larger group. Questionnaires are most often used with smaller groups or given individually. Surveys are used when the teacher researcher wants to throw a wide net and survey a large number of participants who may be at a distance. Surveys, like questionnaires, may be mailed, emailed, or conducted online through survey sites such as Surveymonkey.com. Most surveys provide a choice of responses along a continuum. A typical continuum found often in survey research is the **Likert scale** where response choices range from strongly agree to strongly disagree (Mertler, 2009). A numeric value is usually associated with each response choice where 1=strongly disagree, 2=disagree, 3=no opinion, 4=agree, and 5=strongly agree. Some researchers discourage the use of a neutral choice (3) because respondents may then default to it without giving much thought to the question asked. Others recommend including it because it provides an option that may reflect the respondent's true feelings about not having an opinion or feeling neutral about the question. A variation of the Likert scale is the Likert-type scale in which there is a continuum but not one that measures agreement. It may instead measure something else such as a continuum from "always" to "never" or "very satisfied" to "very dissatisfied". Surveys may also be constructed asking for specific information that can be counted or measured or qualitatively analyzed.

The following survey was sent to early childhood teacher educators to survey their participation in teacher research. Questions asked for specific responses in terms of their experiences with teacher research. Notice that the survey includes a place for open-ended comments ("other") in order to "catch" information that might otherwise be missed.

### Example Teacher Research Survey of Early Childhood Teacher Educators:

Please check all that apply and add any comments to clarify your selections.

1. How many teacher research studies have you done? Please respond to all that apply.
_____As an individual teacher researcher (please specify or estimate a number here)
_____As the lead teacher researcher with others (please specify or estimate a number here)
_____As a co-teacher researcher with others (please specify or estimate a number here)
_____Uncertain (please specify)

2. Are you currently engaged in a teacher research study?
_____Yes, as an individual teacher researcher (please specify)
_____Yes, as the lead teacher researcher with others (please specify)
_____Yes, as a co-teacher researcher with others (please specify)
_____I am not currently engaged in a teacher research study. (please specify)
_____Uncertain (please specify)

3. Where have you reported the results of your teacher research? Please check all that apply.

_____Faculty meetings
_____Professional conferences
_____Newsletters
_____Online sites
_____Written Reports
_____Professional journals
_____Books
_____I have not reported results.
_____Other (please specify)

4. Please check all areas where you teach about teacher research.
_____Undergraduate program (please specify)
_____Graduate program (please specify)
_____Professional development workshops (please specify)
_____Conference presentations (please specify)
_____Online (please specify)
_____Other (please specify)
_____I don't teach about teacher research.

5. Do you work with other teacher education faculty members in doing teacher research?
_____Yes (please specify)
_____No (please specify)
_____Uncertain (please specify)
_____Other (please specify)

6. Do you work with early childhood teachers in doing teacher research?
_____Yes (please specify)
_____No (please specify)
_____Uncertain (please specify)
_____Other (please specify)

7. Do you supervise students who are assigned by your program to do teacher research?
_____I supervise undergraduate students doing teacher research (please specify)
_____I supervise graduate students doing teacher research (please specify)
_____I do not supervise students doing teacher research (please specify)
_____Other (please specify)

8. Are you a member of a teacher research community or group interested in teacher research? If so, please describe.
_____Yes (please describe)
_____No (please specify)
_____Uncertain (please specify)
_____Other (please specify)

It is possible to give surveys to very young children when the surveys are constructed with simple words and illustrations. Sometimes surveys can be given with the teacher reading each item and providing simple instructions for how to respond. Surveys should be brief with consistent response choices and simple text and illustrations. For example, a teacher researcher of 4-year-old children was interested in studying their preferences for pets. She gave the survey shown in Figure 5.5.

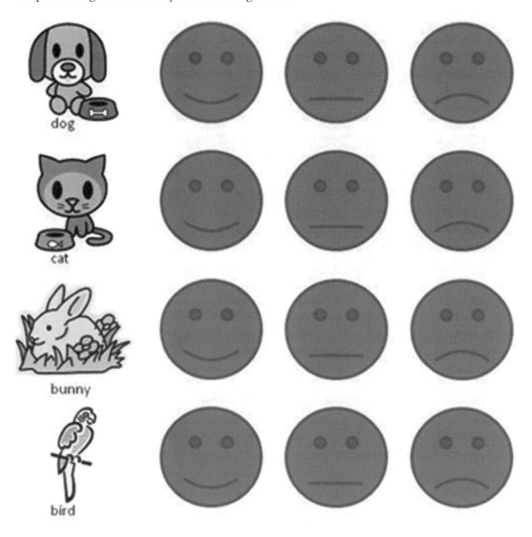

**FIGURE 5.5 Favourite Pet Survey**

## Artifacts from Children's Activities

One of the most meaningful examples of data in early childhood teacher research is an artifact that represents what a child has done or learned. An artifact is an embodiment of the activity for a child. Child artifacts can be anything the child completes or produces. Child artifacts are used to demonstrate learning, performance, skill mastery, creativity, and progress over a period of time such as writing samples across a nine-month period. Examples of artifacts include children's writing such as journal entries, authored books, drawings and illustrations, object constructions, block constructions, sand constructions, collages, art products, and photographs of children's activities such as photos of their block constructions. Figures 5.6, 5.7, and 5.8 show artifacts of one child's art over a period of months. A teacher may analyze the artifacts for developmental progress. Or a teacher may use the artifacts to answer a research question about the extent to which a child incorporates alphabet letters and words into drawings.

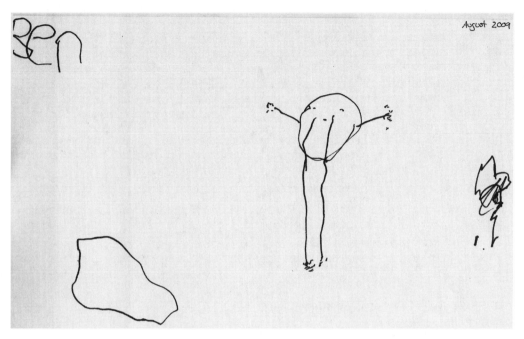

**FIGURE 5.6 Ben's Drawing in August**
Source: Courtesy of Holly Schuler

**FIGURE 5.7 Ben's Drawing in October**
Source: Courtesy of Holly Schuler

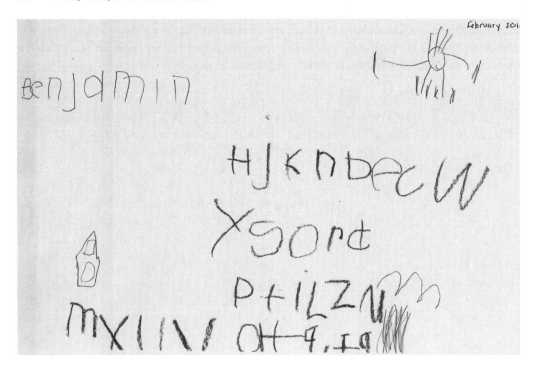

**FIGURE 5.8 Ben's Drawing in February**

Source: Courtesy of Holly Schuler

Children can be asked to keep journals on a variety of topics such as free choice, math, writing, and science. Teachers can analyze children's journal entry data to help answer research questions and to better understand children's thoughts and perceptions. The example shown in Figure 5.9 is from a third grade child's free choice journal. He wrote about his thoughts about being in the third grade.

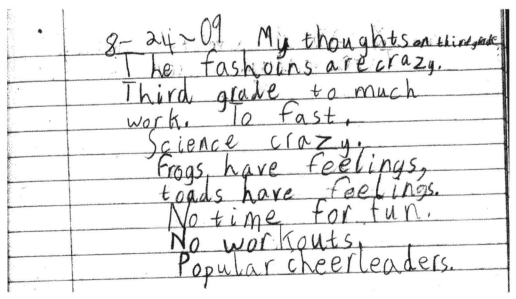

**FIGURE 5.0 Child's Journal Entry Artifact: My Thoughts on Third Grade**

Source: Courtesy of Rhonda Hover

The newsletter artifact shown in Figure 5.10 was produced by second graders and analyzed by a teacher researcher, Lori Beasley, who was studying child autonomy (self-regulation). Children engaged in various activities on the day of and the days following the Oklahoma City bombing in 1996. The teacher researcher's question was to what extent do children exercise autonomy (self-regulation) in a second grade classroom? The teacher researcher found many examples of child autonomy or self-regulation in this class (Castle, Beasley, and Skinner, 1996 ). Children took control of their feelings about the bombing by producing a classroom newsletter, recording stories and making drawings for hospitalized children injured by the blast, writing thank you letters to the numerous rescue workers, and making booties for the rescue dogs among other activities (see Figure 5.10).

**FIGURE 5.10 Example of Daily News Artifact**

Source: Courtesy of Lori Beasley

In an attempt to find out what children learn from inventing their own games and comparing that to required learner outcomes, a second grade teacher implemented an invented games project. Her research question was to what extent mandated learner outcomes were evident in project work such as in inventing games. First she allowed time in the daily schedule for game playing because she felt it helped children learn mathematical relationships such as addition, subtraction, and multiplication. After two weeks of game playing, she supplied the Invention Center with a variety of materials such as index cards, poster boards, empty containers, plastic toys, balls, and a variety of beautiful junk or discards found around the house such as cereal boxes, paper towel rolls, plastic toys, etc. (Castle, 1998). She encouraged children to invent games and then to use the materials to put their invented game plan into a game made from available materials. Over the course of several weeks, children invented games and shared them in "Inventor's Chair" getting feedback from other children similar to children sharing their written stories using an author's chair approach. Children taught their games to each other. The teacher planned a game day and invited the third grade class to play the second graders' invented games.

The teacher analyzed each child's invented game for type of learning children engaged in to make and play the game. She compared what children learned from the games to the state mandated learner outcomes. She found evidence of achievement of all state mandated learner outcomes with the exception of the outcomes related to music. Children did not invent any musical games. What follows is an example of a child's invented game artifact and the teacher's assessments of the game (see Figure 5.11).

## Example of Children's Invented Games Artifacts and Teacher Analysis

### The Garden Game by Lora, Second Grade Girl
The inventor of the Garden Game drew a first draft of the game and invented some rules, as shown in Figure 5.11.

**FIGURE 5.11 The Garden Game Rules**

Then she used the first draft to construct the game board, as shown in Figure 5.12.

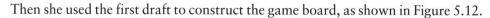
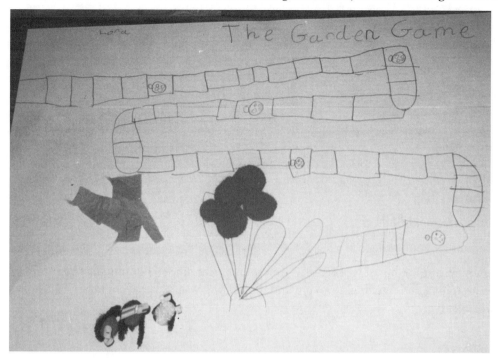

**FIGURE 5.12 The Garden Game Board**

## Teacher's Analysis of the Garden Game

Written rules for the Garden Game:

1. try to get to the carrot
2. try to get to the carrot without getting caught
3. for 3 players
4. the ladybugs can eat you and if they do you have to go back to start.

Literacy outcomes achieved

Use of functional print (e.g., directions) to accomplish tasks.

Demonstration of an understanding of concepts of print (understand directionality of print, the function of letters, words and spaces and that print is talk written down).

Can retell and draw pictures of beginnings, middles, and endings.

Demonstration of awareness of characters, settings, and events.

Effective expression of ideas in oral and written modes for a variety of purposes and audiences.

Organization of ideas into chronological or logical sequence (e.g., $1^{st}$, $2^{nd}$, $3^{rd}$; sequence of events).

## Analysis of Learner Outcomes Reflected in Second Grade Invented Games

Problem solving

Divergent/convergent thinking

Classification

Ordering

Sequencing

Making relationships

Creativity

Organizational skills

Communication skills

Literacy: authorship of work, use of functional print, understanding of concepts of print, telling and retelling, drawing and illustrating work, use of character, setting, and events.

## Documents

In teacher research, already existing documents may be used as data sources. A good question for a teacher researcher to ask is what documents are currently available that might be analyzed to help answer the research question. Examples of existing documents are those items that teachers are required to keep such as grade records, performance charts, report cards, attendance records, curriculum guides, program descriptions and brochures, handbooks, meeting minutes, portfolios of children's work, and lesson plans. For example, a teacher conducting a study on communication and mathematics curriculum may analyze the curriculum guide document for recommendations on teaching mathematics as communication. She may also compare the curriculum guide document to recommendations in other documents such as the National Council of Teachers of Mathematics (NCTM) standards or the National Association for the Education of Young Children (NAEYC) document, *Developmentally Appropriate Practice in Early Childhood Programs Serving Children from Birth through Age 8* (3rd edition, Copple & Bredekamp, 2009).

## Data Collection

Data from data sources are very important in doing teacher research. In order to answer research questions, data are required. However data and data sources are not enough. Teacher researchers have to plan procedures for how and when data will be collected. Depending on the research questions asked, data may be collected in one day, in one setting, or over a longer period of time such as several months, a year, or even multiple years. Teacher research data collection typically occurs over the course of a few months. A thoughtful plan for data collection will ensure that the data needed will actually be collected in a reasonable manner. Chapter Four provides suggestions for making a timeline for the research including when and at what intervals data will be collected. In addition to carefully planning a timeline for data collection, it is also important to formulate a plan for how data will be collected. Time for data collection and procedures for getting appropriate permissions from parents and administrators for certain types of data should be included in the timeline and in how data will be gathered. It helps to plan for more time than is actually needed in case delays occur.

## Plan for Data Collection

■ Consider each research question and think of data sources appropriate to answer each question.
■ Connect each question to one or more data sources (1 to 3 data sources per question).
■ Revise any research questions that do not point to data sources.
■ Consider use of data sources that already exist. If none exists then determine what data sources might be planned.
■ Schedule time in the daily routine for data collection and analysis.
■ Collect data systematically, label each piece of data, and secure data in appropriate files including digital files.

The first step in data collection is deciding what data are necessary to answering the research questions. Examine each research question beginning with your main question then each subquestion asking what data source or sources would be most appropriate to help answer each question. Matching the research question to the needed data to be gathered will prevent you from collecting unnecessary data that would take time away from collecting the data you need. You don't want to find yourself swimming in data and not knowing which data to analyze. If a question does not point to a logical data source, then reconsider whether that question will benefit your study. A common problem in teacher research is asking questions that are too broad and not specifically focused enough on the data sources at hand (Hendricks, 2009).

The next step in data collection is to make sure that you include time for data collection in your daily schedule. For example scheduling just 15 minutes at the end of each day for writing in your teacher journal, reviewing responses to interview questions, or collecting child artifacts will go a long way in working toward completion of the study. One kindergarten teacher made time for writing in her journal during each lunch period. She said not only did it keep her on track for completing her study, but it gave her some quiet alone time to regenerate her energy in anticipation of the afternoon session.

Next it is always recommended to engage another person in your ideas for planning data collection. The other person can be a colleague, university professor, friend, or classroom volunteer, knowledgeable about the program's policies and procedures. Having another adult to actually help with the data collection is also important. It may be easier to enlist other adults in the data collection process than in the data analysis. Having another person to sound out ideas helps to consider what you are doing from different perspectives. The other person may help you discover things you hadn't yet considered.

### From the Field: Iditarod Research

Third grade teacher Jamie Norris introduced her children to the Iditarod dog sled race with a story about Balto, the lead dog who helped transport diptheria medication to Nome during an epidemic in 1925. She showed them a map and pointed out the location of Alaska. She compared the journey then to the commemorative Iditarod race from Anchorage to Nome that is held each year in March. The children were very interested in the story and asked many questions:

How many years has it been since Balto took the medicine to Nome?

How many miles did Balto run to get the medicine there?

How many miles do dog sled teams run today in the Iditarod?

Who won the race last year?

If a dog's paw is injured, what happens then?

Do they replace a dog that is taken out of the race?

How many days does the race last?

How do dogs know where to go to get to the end?

How many dogs run in the Iditarod?

Do the dogs wear special socks?

Do the racers ever get to sleep? What about the dogs?

Children showed so much interest and had so many questions that Jamie decided to conduct a class inquiry on the Iditarod. She also decided to do her own teacher research study on what third graders learn through their research of the Iditarod because their interest level was high and she felt that required learner outcomes in literacy, mathematics, and social studies might be addressed in such a study. She collected data to answer her research question simultaneously with the children as they researched their own questions about the Iditarod. First the children reflected on what they knew.

### What We Already Know About the Iditarod:

1. It is a dog sled race with mushers.
2. It commemorates the medicine run to Nome.
3. Iditarod is a town in Alaska.
4. The race is over 1,000 miles long.
5. There are 2 routes.
6. It takes several days.
7. It happens in March.

## What We Want to Learn:

1. Who are the people called mushers and why are they called mushers?
2. What do dogs and mushers eat?
3. How do they camp?
4. Are there any requirements to enter the race?
5. How do they care for animals?
6. How are the race routes determined?
7. How fast do they go?
8. How often do they rest?
9. Do they go alone or in teams?
10. How cold does it get?
11. Does anyone check on them?
12. Does weather alter the race?
13. What kinds of jobs are involved? Are emergency people employed?
14. How does the race affect the Alaskan culture?
15. What happens if a dog is injured?
16. How many dogs can you race with?
17. When they finish the race, do the mushers ride all the way back to where they started the race?
18. Why would anyone want to do the race?

Children gathered data and engaged in numerous activities including drawing, dramatic play, writing stories and news items, recording data and documenting findings, visiting the website http://www.iditarod.com, and interviewing class visitors who had been to the Iditarod. They were very interested in the information that the Iditarod Teacher provided online. One class visitor brought a dog that had run in two Iditarod races. Each child selected questions to research and presented a report to the class. The project was so successful that Jamie planned an Iditarod night for children to share with their families the artifacts and reports that children created.

Jamie kept a journal recording what she observed of children's activities. She analyzed the artifacts and reports to help answer her own teacher research question. She concluded that when children are very interested in a topic such as the Iditarod, they become so engaged in their activities they sometimes don't want to go to recess or to other activities. She found evidence in the artifacts and reports that children were achieving mandated learning objectives. She concluded that in the future she would try to identify those topics of most interest to children to explore.

## REFLECTIONS

In reflecting on Jamie Norris's inquiry, what data sources do you think were most helpful to her in answering her own teacher research question?

Reflect on the data sources presented in this chapter. Which ones do you think would yield the most meaningful results for teacher research? Give a rationale for your choices.

Now that you have thought about doing your own teacher research study, what data sources do you think you would need to answer your research questions? Use Table 5.3 to connect your research questions to data sources.

**TABLE 5.3  Connecting Data Sources to Questions**

|  | Data Source | Data Source | Data Source |
|---|---|---|---|
| Main Question |  |  |  |
| Subquestion 1 |  |  |  |
| Subquestion 2 |  |  |  |
| Subquestion 3 |  |  |  |

## Explorations

Choose one of the websites below to explore for ideas about data collection in teacher research. Find at least 10 top tips for data collection that you can share with others.

http://gse.gmu.edu/research/tr/
http://oldweb.madison.k12.wi.us/sod/car/carhomepage.html

## References

2010 Guide to National Board Certification. Retrieved March 15, 2010, from http://www.nbpts.org/resources /publications.

Berra, Y., & Kaplan, D. (2011). *You can observe a lot by watching.* Retrieved January 29, 2011, from http://www.yogiberra.com.

Castle, K. (1998). *Cool junk.* Danbury, CT: Creative Thinkers.

Castle, K., Beasley, L., & Skinner, L. (1996). Children of the heartland. *Childhood Education, 72*(4), 226–231.

Copple, C., & Bredekamp, S. (Eds.) (2009). *Developmentally appropriate practice in early childhood programs serving children from birth through age 8* (3rd edition). Washington, DC: National Association for the Education of Young Children.

DeVries, R. & Zan, B. (1994). *Moral classrooms moral children.* New York: Teachers College Press.

Hendricks, C. (2009). *Improving schools through action research*. Columbus, OH: Pearson.

Hubbard, R. S., & Power, B. M. (1999). *Living the questions*. York, MN: Stenhouse.

Kamii, C., with Housman, B. (2000). *Young children reinvent arithmetic* (2nd edition). New York: Teachers College Press.

*Merriam-Webster Online Dictionary*. Retrieved March 4, 2010, from http://www.merriam-webster.com/dictionary/data

Mertler, C. A. (2009). *Action research* (2nd edition). Los Angeles: Sage.

Mills, G. E. (2011). *Action research* (4th edition). Boston: Pearson.

*Principles and standards for school mathematics*. (2000). Reston, VA: National Council of Teachers of Mathematics.

Short, E. C. (1991). *Forms of curriculum inquiry*. New York: State University of New York Press.

# six
# What Do Data Reveal?

*The true nature of things is seen to lie not in the things themselves but in the relationships which we construct and then perceive among them.*

Max van Manen (1990, p. 185)

The primary purpose of this chapter is to provide examples of how to analyze and interpret data. **Analysis** means breaking something down into its parts, organizing the parts into relevant categories, and then interpreting or making sense of the parts, the categories, and the relationships among them to reach a deeper understanding of the problem under study. This process often involves reducing data down into smaller units of meaning, sometimes called **unitizing the data,** examining the parts, and then making holistic sense of the parts. The data analysis methods presented in this chapter include quantitative, qualitative, and mixed methods. Ways to address rigor in research and the demonstration of validity, reliability, trustworthiness, and triangulation are also presented. Chapter Four described several teacher research designs. Chapter Five presented various types of data sources. This chapter presents several common types of data analysis methods and when to apply each to make sense of collected data.

## Swimming in Data

A common problem in teacher research is collecting more data than you really need. You can find yourself swimming in data and overwhelmed by the task of making sense of it all. As mentioned in Chapter Five, it is always a good idea to collect only the data you need to answer your research questions. In an attempt to be thorough, teacher researchers tend to err on the side of collecting too much rather than too little data, and then may not know what to do with all of it. It helps to maintain focus on the purpose of your study and not panic due to the high volume of data you feel you must analyze. Please note that you don't have to use all the data you collect, and that you, the teacher researcher, are the one who gets to decide which data are meaningful and likely to lead to answering research questions and which data are tangential to the research and can be discarded or saved for later use. You don't have to use every piece of data you collect.

Because in their everyday activities early childhood teacher researchers commonly collect student work and conduct performance assessments, they tend to know what types of data to collect and how to collect it, but not necessarily how to analyze it. In published teacher research articles and reports, it is common to find more description about data collection and less given to data analysis. It is frustrating to readers of teacher research studies when they can't find enough information about how the data were analyzed in order to be able to judge the credibility of the study and/or to replicate the study. Data analysis tends to be the most daunting task of the teacher researcher. It can also be quite time consuming, especially if left to do after the data collection process has ended. But it need not be. In this chapter you will find suggestions not only for data analysis but also for how to keep from drowning in data. The key to preparing for data analysis is to get organized.

Data analysis and interpretation are usually the most revealing phase of doing teacher research because through data analysis and interpretation, you find the answers you need to your most pressing problems of teaching and learning. Teacher researchers use the insights gained from data analysis and interpretation to make sense of their situations and to make needed changes in what they do. Just like anything else, data analysis gets better with practice. With practice, teacher researchers learn to be discerning in terms of data collection and continuous data analysis. This chapter will give you the preliminary data analysis tools you need to make data analysis decisions.

## Tips for Getting Organized for Data Analysis

Organizing for data analysis involves selecting data sources based on research questions, labeling data, organizing and securing the storage of data, making ongoing data summaries, using or developing coding systems, and asking relevant questions.

### Select Data Sources Based on Research Questions

In Chapter Five several types of data were described with examples given of each. There is a wide range of data sources to choose from when planning a study. The study will be more meaningful and productive if the data sources you select are based on the research questions you ask. In getting organized to do research, consider each of your research questions—both main question/s and subquestions—and ask yourself, what data would help answer this question? You may decide that one data source will be enough to answer one question. Or you may decide that each research question calls for a couple of data sources to give a comprehensive picture of the study. One suggestion for determining how many and which data sources to use is to begin data analysis along with data collection. If through data analysis you find a similar pattern across data sources that helps answer the research question, then further data collection may not be necessary. Deciding on how many data sources to use is up to the judgment of the researcher. The following example shows the connection of each research question to appropriate data sources for answering each question. Some questions require a single source while others require multiple sources. The key to how many sources you use is a function of getting the research questions answered. If questions can be answered with one data source, then you don't need to use other sources, even if you have planned to use them.

## Example of Connection of Each Research Question to Appropriate Data Sources

**Research Question 1:** To what extent do children participate in group time?

**One Data Source:** Frequency count of the number of times each child verbally expresses his/her ideas during a 20 minute group discussion.

**Research Question 2:** In what ways do children express their knowledge of numerical relationships?

**Three Data Sources:** Children's math journals; children's game playing; and children's responses to teacher initiated numerical problem solving activities.

Once you have tied each research question to a data source/s, you will be less likely to collect data you don't need.

## Label Data

Make sure as you collect data, to label it in such a way that you can easily access it for analysis and for categorization. Labels might include the following:

- Date when the data were collected
- The activity taking place when the data were collected, such as observations taken during outdoor play
- Information to identify which child the data belongs to, such as a child's initials, a fictitious name, or a number assigned to each child to differentiate that child's data piece from another child's data piece.

Disguising a child's identity in data collection and analysis is a way to maintain anonymity and protect the identities of children participating in the study. For example, in labeling several drawings for Andrea Becker, you might label and date the first 10/2 AB #1 and the second one 11/4 AB #2, and so on.

## Organize and Secure Storage of Data

Organizational techniques such as filing all data according to data source help maintain easy access to data for analysis. Depending on your preference, you may want to store and secure data in a locked filing cabinet to which only you have access. This will keep data in a place where you always know the location and the security of the data. You might make a labeled file for each data source such as observations, interviews, surveys, child artifacts, etc. Or you may prefer to file data electronically on a password protected computer so that you are the only one who has access to the data. In filing data electronically, it is a good idea to back up your files to prevent loss due to possible computer malfunctions.

## Ongoing Data Summaries

At the conclusion of each data collection event—such as recording observations of children's activities one afternoon—plan time to write a brief summary of the data collected. File the summary with the data. The summary should be a short synopsis of what data were collected, who was involved, when, where, under what context, and include any unique situations that may have occurred during the data collection such as an interruption, accident, or unforeseen occurrence. For example, one teacher who was videotaping a group discussion became distracted by a child who was not in her class, but who barged through the classroom door sent by another teacher to ask her a question. Shortly following the videotaped group discussion, the teacher wrote a brief note to file with the videotape that explained her behavior due to the interruption. It is important to record such notes to jog your memory so that you can address the context to better understand what was happening and to share the context in any reports of the study.

## Coding Systems

Data can be coded while it is being collected by using an existing coding sheet or list of codes to record data as they are collected. For example, in studying young children's social interactions as data, a checklist or list of codes can be used to sort observations of children's interactions. Examples of such codes might be recording the letter (see bolded letters) that represents each event of social interaction as an **I**, **R**, **A**, or **C** as described below:

**I**nitiates an interaction with another child

**R**esponds to an initiated interaction of another child

Displays **A**ggressive behavior toward another child

Displays **C**ooperative behavior toward another child.

Recorded coding of 5 social interactions of one child might look like this:

1- R

2- A

3- A

4- I

5- I

Codes for analyzing data may be assigned *before* data are analyzed or *during* the process of data analysis as the researcher reads for meaning and creates codes that fit the data. Data may be coded after they have been gathered with either an existing coding system or the researcher may read the data for meaning and derive a set of codes as data are being interpreted for meaning. The researcher can then use the derived codes from the initial reading to code data in subsequent readings. This approach is especially appropriate for coding textual data such as children's narrative stories.

Before data analysis begins, it is important to decide on a coding system for the data. A coding system is a way to unitize or break the data down into manageable units or pieces for analysis. Teacher researchers may choose to use existing coding systems (such as coding using Bloom's taxonomy or Howard Gardner's multiple intelligences), develop a new coding system that best fits the research questions, or plan to identify codes that emerge from the data during multiple readings of the data and interpretations of the readings. It is important to begin coding data as soon after collecting them as possible while the experience is fresh on your mind (Altrichter, Feldman, Posch, & Somekh, 2008).

## Important Questions to Ask During Data Analysis

When analyzing data, especially data that require some researcher interpretation, such as qualitative data (written text, journal entries, interview responses, etc.) it is important to continuously ask, What are the data telling me? What are they saying about the research questions? What sense can I make of the data? Similar questions have been identified by Phillips and Carr (2010):

> What seems to be happening in this data?
>
> What is *not* happening in this data?
>
> What is repeated in this data (words, behaviors, attitudes, occurrences)?
>
> What is surprising, perplexing, disturbing in the data?
>
> What information seems to be missing from the data?
>
> (p. 106)

Asking such questions will help make sense of the data and provide the focus you need for data interpretation.

## Quantitative Data Analysis

**Quantitative data** is numerical data representing events that have been measured or counted in some way, such as the frequency of books read by children in a first grade classroom. Quantitative data reflects regularities that exist in classroom life. Quantitative research studies are most typical of an experimental design approach to educational research. While experimental design may be appropriate for some teacher research studies, most don't use it. However, even when not using an experimental research design, it is very common for teacher researchers to gather quantitative data. Quantitative data analysis can be used in any teacher research design that includes quantitative data. Quantitative data analysis reflects a continuum from simply counting events and presenting frequencies of occurrence of those events through a range all the way to using **inferential statistical tests** to show causal relationships exist between and among variables. Although quantitative data analysis is used in teacher research, most teacher research studies do not use quantitative data analysis to show causal relationships or to demonstrate statistical significance of results. But it is not uncommon for teacher researchers to employ quantitative analysis when they have gathered measurable data. Chapter 4 presents a more detailed account of the role of research design in planning teacher research. This section will provide examples of the most commonly used quantitative data analysis techniques employed in teacher research.

Typical quantitative data includes:

- Frequency counts of events recorded in observation notes, field notes, teacher journals, documents, or other data sources such as student writing.
- Scores on assignments, teacher made tests, standardized tests, benchmark assessments, report cards, or surveys.
- Performance ratings on scaled rubrics or checklists.

## Frequency Counts in Observation Data

Observations of classroom life, children's activities, and teachers' activities are typical data sources for early childhood teacher research. Analysis of observation data for **frequency of occurrence** of specified events can be done in several ways. The teacher researcher who has made field notes during observations can analyze notes by counting the number of times an event has been recorded in the notes. Or in recording observations the teacher researcher may choose to record only those events under study and not try to record anything else except those events. A numbered recording sheet with categories or codes for events facilitates the recording and counting of the events. An additional analysis technique is a **time sampling approach** that involves timing the observation period in increments such as recording at 60 second intervals. The teacher researcher may record with a code what is happening at each interval. Time sampling can be a more rigorous approach to data collection because it will show whether or not the events under study are actually occurring and to what extent within the time period studied. The following example is a sample observation recording sheet divided into twenty 60 second time intervals over which events of play behavior were recorded for one child whose initials are RPA. The codes for the play behavior in the example are modifications of Parten's (1932) types of play behavior. Onlooker play is coded when a child is merely observing the play behavior of other children, but not participating in it. Solitary play is coded when a child is playing alone. Pair play involves a child playing with another child. Small group play occurs when a child is playing with a few other children such as 3 to 5 children playing together. A teacher research question about social interaction may be, In what ways do children's social interactions show a need for social interaction intervention to help children develop social interaction skills?

### Example Showing Time Sampling of Play Behavior

Codes: O (onlooker) S (solitary) P (pair) SG (small group)
Child's Initials: <u>RPA</u>  Date/Start Time: <u>10:10 a.m.</u>
Observation Context: <u>Center Time</u>
1. <u>O</u>
2. <u>O</u>
3. <u>O</u>
4. <u>S</u>
5. <u>S</u>

6. <u>S</u>
7. <u>S</u>
8. <u>S</u>
9. <u>P w/ RAS</u>
10. <u>P w/RAS</u>
11. <u>S</u>
12. <u>S</u>
13. <u>S</u>
14. <u>P w/MSP</u>
15. <u>P w/MSP</u>
16. <u>S</u>
17. <u>S</u>
18. <u>S</u>
19. <u>S</u>
20. <u>S</u>
Totals: 3 Os; 13 Ss; 4 Ps

## Teacher Research Interpretation

These data confirm my hunch that RPA is not very engaged in play with other children. Although he does pair up with two different children, their play behaviors are brief with each of the other children quickly leaving RPA to play with others. RPA may need some help with how to appropriately initiate play with others. I plan to try an intervention in which I model for him behaviors and words to say to other children in order to enter their play.

**TABLE 6.1 Frequency of Kindergarten Play Behaviors During 30 Minute Center Time**

| Play<br><br>Child | O (onlooker) | S (solitary) | P (pair) | SG (small group) |
|---|---|---|---|---|
| RPA | **7** | **19** | 3 | 1 |
| NHG | 1 | 3 | 11 | 5 |
| MSP | 0 | 1 | 5 | **24** |
| RAS | 0 | 4 | **22** | 4 |
| KJC | 3 | 2 | 17 | 8 |
| DBA | 2 | 6 | 2 | **20** |
| ADP | 4 | 4 | 7 | 15 |
| APC | 0 | 0 | 14 | 16 |
| JRH | 0 | 0 | 15 | 15 |
| JLM | 1 | 5 | **21** | 3 |
| PUB | 0 | 0 | 0 | 30 |
| KJR | 0 | 0 | 7 | 23 |
| LSR | **6** | 8 | 12 | 4 |
| MIE | **11** | **17** | 2 | 0 |
| GRN | 2 | 3 | 12 | 13 |
| PON | 3 | 8 | 11 | 8 |
| CPA | **7** | 7 | 8 | 8 |
| TOTAL | 47 | 87 | 169 | **197** |

Regardless of which of the three approaches you use (recording all events; recording specific events; recording with time sampling), all involve counting the frequency of events. Once the frequency counts have been made, the data can be graphically represented typically in frequency tables such as in Table 6.1 in which frequency counts are presented of play behaviors in a kindergarten class during center time in which children moved freely among activity centers.

---

## REFLECTIONS

Reflect on the data presented in Table 6.1. What is your interpretation of the data? Who are the children who interact least/most in their play behavior? Based on the data, what would you do, if anything, as the teacher of this class?

---

## TEACHER RESEARCHER'S INTERPRETATION

The teacher researcher has bolded the cells in Table 6.1 that load the heaviest. In interpreting the data in the table, she may conclude that the play behaviors in her class parallel what one would expect from the professional literature on play behavior for this age group (Fromberg, 2002; Frost, Wortham, & Reifel, 2008) with a progression of increasing social behavior across the categories from onlooker with the least frequency total to small group with the most. The bolded numbers are in the cells that load the most for that category. In the on-looker category, four children (RPA, LSR, MIE, and CPA) engage in more frequent onlooker behavior than the other children with MIE showing the most at almost twice the frequency as the other three. In the small group category, four children (MSP, DBA, PUB and KJR) engage in the most frequent small group play with one child, PUB, engaging in nothing but small group play. Based on her interpretation of the data, the teacher researcher may decide to plan an intervention for those children who engage the least in small group play (RPA, JLM, and MIE) in order to help them develop some strategies for social interactions with others. Please note that although CPA has a high frequency of onlooker play, this child's onlooker frequency plus the frequencies in the other three categories show a more balanced engagement in all categories that may not call for an intervention to increase social play.

Collecting and analyzing frequency data can give the teacher a broad view of the whole class in terms of the events being studied as well as individual child profiles. This data may be used to help answer the teacher researcher's question about whether or not children may need intervention from the teacher to develop social interaction skills. The data may also lead to a new research question focusing only on small group play in order to find out children's existing social interaction skills demonstrated in small group play that can be identified and modeled for children who might need help with these skills. Such data can help the teacher decide what to do: whether to make changes, continue what she is currently doing, or do further research on the topic of study.

## Scores on Assignments: Descriptive Statistics and Measures of Central Tendency and Dispersion

In order to organize, summarize, and make sense of quantitative data from a whole class or several classes in large data sets such as scores on assignments, tests, or surveys it is helpful to use **descriptive statistics and measures of central tendency and dispersion**. Descriptive statistics and measures of central tendency and dispersion indicate general tendencies or trends in the data such as the **mean, mode, median** and the spread of a set of scores (Creswell, 2008):

- **The mean** is the numeric average of a set of scores. To calculate the mean, take the total sum of the scores in the data set and divide it by the number of scores in the set.
- **The mode** is the score in the data set that occurs most frequently and indicates the most common score in the set of scores. The mode tells what score is most represented in the group.
- **The median** is the score that splits the data set in half. It is the middle score of all the scores around where 50% of the scores fall above the median and 50% of the scores fall below it.

To find the median, all scores are put in rank order from lowest to highest scores. The score that is in the middle of the ranked scores is the median. If the data set has an odd number of scores, the median is the score in the middle that divides the set in half. If there is an even number of scores in the set, then the median is found by locating the two scores in the middle of the set and taking the average of the two scores. Calculations may be done by hand or by any number of software packages such as Microsoft Excel that tabulates data and calculates measures of central tendency and dispersion.

**Measures of dispersion** include the **range** and the **standard deviation** of a set of scores and tell how much spread or diversity exists in a set of scores (Mertler, 2009):

- **The range** is found by subtracting the lowest score in the data set from the highest score.
- **The standard deviation** is the average distance of scores away from the mean. A high standard deviation usually indicates a wide spread among scores. Scores at the extremes of the data set are called **outliers** and can impact the range to a large extent and the standard deviation to a lesser extent because the standard deviation consists of averages.

In analyzing a data set, it is important to be alert for extreme scores that may skew the measures of central tendency and dispersion. One extreme score can distort how the group as a whole looks in terms of performance.

### Explorations

In the following example, compare your calculations and interpretations to those of the teacher researcher.

The teacher researcher, a third grade teacher, has asked a research question about the extent to which children learn about chemical reactions doing investigations in project work on plants. The teacher researcher decided to collect data from three data sources: observing and recording children's investigations, keeping a teacher journal, and giving an assignment on chemical reactions that is used to measure children's learning. The assignment is a set of questions that children answered based on what they learned from their investigations. The teacher evaluated each child's assignment with scores that can range from 0 (no items correct) to 50 (all items correct). The scores of the assignments of 22 students are listed in Table 6.2.

Find the mean, median, mode, and range of the set of scores. Then interpret the data for results that may help answer the research question.

**TABLE 6.2 Scores on Chemical Reaction Assignment**

| Student | Score |
| --- | --- |
| 1 | 32 |
| 2 | 37 |
| 3 | 45 |
| 4 | 38 |
| 5 | 23 |
| 6 | 45 |
| 7 | 36 |
| 8 | 47 |
| 9 | 29 |
| 10 | 40 |
| 11 | 33 |
| 12 | 41 |
| 13 | 49 |
| 14 | 40 |
| 15 | 45 |
| 16 | 43 |
| 17 | 30 |
| 18 | 39 |
| 19 | 42 |
| 20 | 37 |
| 21 | 38 |
| 22 | 27 |

## Teacher Researcher's Analysis and Interpretation

The teacher researcher may conclude that 5 students scored correctly 90% or more of the items on the assignment; 5 students scored correctly 80–89% of the items; 6 students scored correctly 70–79% of the items; 3 students scored correctly 60–69% of the items; 2 students scored correctly 50–59% of the items; and one student scored correctly less than 50% of the items. He may conclude that 16 students did satisfactory or above and 6 students did unsatisfactory in their learning about chemical reactions based on the assignment. He may compare how students did on the assignment to what he has recorded in his observations of children's investigations and his teacher journal. If the comparisons show similar results, he may decide to engage the 6 students who scored unsatisfactory with additional learning activities. He may conclude that in general the majority of children did learn about chemical reactions but several need additional help based on the assignment and his observation and journal notes. He may also decide in order to promote satisfactory learning in all his students, to revise the original assignment by adding several new activities and then to research how well children learn based on the revised assignment.

Compare your calculations to those of the teacher researcher:

Mean = 38
Median = 38.5
Mode = 45
Range = 26

Now recalculate these measures by substituting a new score of 0 for student number 4. How would this score of 0 affect the measures? How might you interpret the dispersion of scores? What would you conclude about this outlier score? In what ways might the teacher researcher interpretation of the data change?

## Performance Ratings on Scaled Rubrics or Checklists

Early childhood teachers often use **rubrics** to assess children's performance of developmental milestones, learning outcomes, and mandated benchmarks. A rubric is usually presented in a matrix that describes a set of criteria for various levels of performance on an assignment or learning outcome from low to medium to high levels (Shea, Murray, and Harlin, 2005). Rubrics can be used for both **formative assessment** (to show progress) and **summative assessment** (to make a final evaluation). Rubrics are sometimes used to record progress on report cards that may include a space to record the date of the accomplishment of each level of performance. For example, developmental milestones may be charted with rubrics that indicate the dates at which a child's performance began to emerge, was developing, was accomplished, and was proficient. Teacher researchers may use rubrics to collect and analyze data.

### Example Demonstrating Use of Rubric to Collect Data

In this example, a pre-kindergarten (pre-k) teacher wanted to research social/emotional development in her class of 3-year-old children. She wanted to find out if children made progress in their interpersonal skills following a unit on friendship. She developed a rubric to collect data for each child on several levels of interpersonal skill development (see Table 6.3).

She also used the rubric to compare all children's skills before and after implementation of the unit (see Table 6.4).

**TABLE 6.3 Pre-K Interpersonal Skills Pre Data N=1**

Child #1 Female; 3 years 4 months old; Pre Unit Date: 9/14

Score of 1 Emerging: skill is demonstrated for the first time

Score of 2 Developing: skill is demonstrated occasionally but not always appropriately

Score of 3 Demonstrating: skill is demonstrated routinely and appropriately

Score of 4 Proficient: skill is demonstrated consistently taking into consideration the feelings of others

|  | Score of 4 Proficient | Score of 3 Demonstrating | Score of 2 Developing | Score of 1 Emerging |
|---|---|---|---|---|
| Greets others on arrival |  | X |  |  |
| Initiates conversations |  |  | X |  |
| Listens and responds to others |  | X |  |  |
| Helps others | X |  |  |  |
| Shares materials | X |  |  |  |
| Knows what "friend" means |  | X |  |  |
| Repairs ruptures in relationships |  |  |  | X |

## Teacher's Comments

This child interacts mostly with two other girls. She waits for them to arrive and rushes to them to get them involved in play. She is willing to share materials and take her turn when it is time. When conflicts occur, she tends to fall apart; she cries and becomes agitated. She goes to her cubby to be alone and usually does not recover quickly unless encouraged by a teacher.

The teacher researcher consolidates data from the pre and post rubrics for all 12 children in her class in Table 6.4.

## Analysis of data in Table 6.4

The numbers in the table indicate general class improvement in all interpersonal skills from pre to post scores. The post scores show that the majority of children are functioning with interpersonal skills at the Demonstrating (3) and Proficient (4) levels with one exception: *Listens and responds to others*. The post measure shows half the class (6 children) functioning at the Developing (2) level in *Listens and responds to others* while the other half is at levels 3 and 4 for that skill. In general the class is most proficient in *Knows what "friend" means* and least proficient in *Listens and responds to others*. The teacher may conclude that the friendship unit contributed to children's development of interpersonal skills. She may also decide to plan additional activities to promote active listening and responding to others.

**TABLE 6.4 Pre-K Interpersonal Skills Pre/Post Data N = 12**
**Pre Date: 9/14 Post Date: 5/7**

| | Score of 4 Proficient Pre/Post | Score of 3 Demonstrating Pre/Post | Score of 2 Developing Pre/Post | Score of 1 Emerging Pre/Post |
|---|---|---|---|---|
| Greets others on arrival | 0/5 | 1/5 | 1/1 | 10/1 |
| Initiates conversations | 1/4 | 3/7 | 5/1 | 3/0 |
| Listens and responds to others | 0/3 | 2/3 | 8/6 | 2/0 |
| Helps others | 0/5 | 4/5 | 4/2 | 4/0 |
| Shares materials | 1/5 | 0/2 | 8/3 | 3/2 |
| Knows what "friend" means | 0/11 | 1/1 | 5/0 | 6/0 |
| Repairs ruptures in relationships | 0/6 | 0/4 | 0/0 | 12/2 |

## Displaying Data to Show Results

In order to interpret and report research results, it is helpful to display data in appropriate ways that best convey what the data mean. Data can be displayed graphically and in a narrative format. Quantitative data are usually displayed graphically especially when there is a large amount of data to report. Tables such as Table 6.2, graphs, and charts including bar graphs and pie charts are ways data can be displayed. The purpose of the graphic representation of data is to organize data in a simple and concise way to show results in a visual format that allows for identifying patterns in the data. Presenting quantitative data in narrative form may be cumbersome to report and to read. Data from the same study can be displayed using several methods. It is best to select the method (table, chart, or graph) that most accurately and easily shows the data in a way that can be readily interpreted. A teacher researcher who displays data can use the display to help interpret what the data mean in terms of the study. Graphic representations are then both a means for interpreting data as well as a method for reporting data.

For example, in a study of third graders' library book selections, the teacher researcher was interested in finding out the types of book selections children make when checking out books from the library. He recorded the number and type of books that were checked out by his students during a two-month period. In order to determine the best way to represent his data, he first made pie charts of the data and then bar graphs (see Figures 6.1 and 6.2).

## Library Book Selection

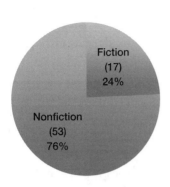

## Nonfiction Book Topics

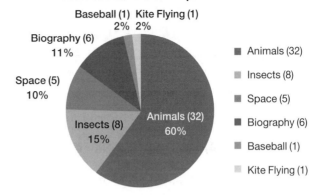

**FIGURE 6.1  Pie Charts**

## Library Book Selection

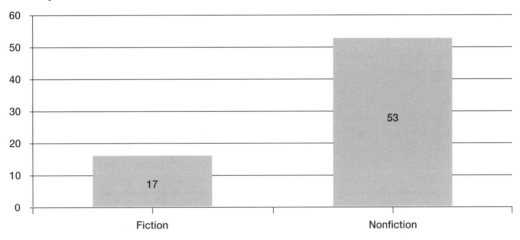

## Nonfiction Book Topics

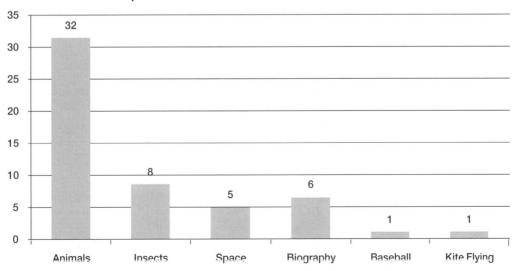

**FIGURE 6.2  Bar Graphs**

---

**REFLECTIONS**

Which graphic representation (Figure 6.1 Pie Charts or Figure 6.2 Bar Graphs) do you think most clearly and accurately shows the data and why?

---

**TEACHER RESEARCHER NOTEBOOK ENTRY #6**

Read the description of the following study. Reflect on the best way to represent the data in the study. Then write a notebook entry in which you describe how the data should be represented graphically and why.

A kindergarten teacher researcher studying emergent writing conducted a mid-year assessment of the 18 children in his class. He collected three samples from each child's writing journal to assess their achievement of seven criteria. He analyzed each child's journal to determine whether or not each had achieved each of the seven criteria.

N=18
Assessment criteria (number of children who achieved criteria): draws pictures to write (18); supplements pictures with scribbles (18); uses scribbles or symbols as writing (16); makes isolated letters (13); writes first name (9); copies displayed words (4); writes words from memory (2).

---

## Inferential Statistics

A section on quantitative data analysis would not be complete without mentioning the role of inferential statistics in the process. Descriptive statistics enable a teacher researcher to summarize data in such a way to shed light on the topic under study or to describe what is happening in the data. Descriptive statistics are usually all that are needed to analyze data in a teacher research study. However, when teacher researchers need to compare groups or draw inferences from data from a smaller group of students representative of a larger population beyond the students participating in the study, then inferential statistics are called for to test hypotheses and answer research questions.

For example, a teacher researcher may want to know which of two approaches to teaching reading comprehension in her district is the most effective as demonstrated by statistically significant results. She may want to compare two groups of second grade students and their performance on a reading comprehension test. One group gets teaching approach #1 and the other group gets teaching approach #2. She may collect performance scores from both groups and use a statistical formula to compare the groups for significant differences in performance scores. Such statistical tests for significant differences employ **inferential statistics** to allow researchers to draw generalizations from a sample of students to a larger population of students (Creswell, 2008).

Research **hypotheses** or predictions comparing groups or predicting relationships among variables, such as the relationship between gender and play preferences, can be tested for statistically significant differences using inferential statistical tests. Variables are characteristics of students that can be studied such as performance level, achievement level, attitude, etc. **Independent variables** are manipulated by the researcher such as in the example of studying two different teaching approaches where teaching approach is the independent variable. The **dependent variable** is the variable under study such as performance level that may be affected by the independent variable or teaching approach. Researchers using inferential statistics attempt to show that certain relationships exist between and among variables such as between performance level and attitude toward school. Significance of results as determined by a high level of probability can be shown with inferential statistics. Typical research designs that use inferential statistics include experimental design, quasi-experimental design, correlational, and causal-comparative studies. In order to be able to show that statistically significant results exist and to generalize results to the population at large, experimental studies are highly controlled and usually involve large numbers of student participants. In experimental studies it is important to control all variables, or as many as possible, except the one of interest.

When doing group comparisons, a researcher may designate a **treatment group** and a **control group**. The treatment group is given the treatment, intervention, instructional approach, or program whose effectiveness is being studied. The control group does not get the treatment, intervention, or program under study so that comparisons can be made between the two groups to ascertain the effectiveness of the treatment. Comparisons across multiple groups can also be made when studying more than one intervention or various levels of the intervention. Experimental design calls for **randomization** in assignment of participants to the groups, in that participants in the study must be representative of the larger population to which results are to be generalized. For example, in a study of reading comprehension approaches in second grade classrooms, the second graders in the treatment and control groups should include characteristics in the same proportion that they exist in the population of all second graders to which results will be applied. If boys make up 50% of the population of all second graders, then each group studied should maintain that ratio. This holds for all other variables such as age, performance level, socioeconomic background, ethnicity, etc. Otherwise results will not be generalizable to the larger population.

There are many reasons teacher researchers do not typically conduct experimental design research. One reason is that descriptive statistics may be enough to answer research questions. Experimental studies can be expensive in terms of cost and time expended to do them. They may require sophisticated statistical tests and analysis. In order to conduct statistical tests and to generalize results to a population beyond students in a classroom or school, large numbers of student participants are required to do the study. Probably the most important reasons have to do with situations beyond the control of most classroom teachers. It is usually not possible to randomly assign students to groups; students in the classroom may not be representative of the larger population of students; and treatments, interventions, approaches, and programs may not be able to be withheld from some groups for control group comparisons.

You may be familiar with the term randomized trials, particularly in the medical field where they are used for testing the effectiveness of certain drugs in order to eventually recommend them for use with the population as a whole. Such randomized trials are not usually possible in teacher research. Teachers usually have little control of which students are assigned to their classrooms or over resources necessary to conduct large scale experimental studies. It is important for teacher researchers to know about the different types of research designs including experimental design in order to choose the most appropriate design for a study. Although experimental design is not often used in teacher research, there may be teacher research studies that call for it.

Types of inferential statistical tests to determine significant differences and establish relationships among variables include independent-measures *t* test, repeated-measures *t* test, analysis of variance, and chi-square test (Mertler, 2009). The **independent-measures *t* test** is used to test for statistically significant differences in the means of measures when comparing a treatment or intervention group with a control group. A **statistically significant difference** between groups shows that the effect studied (dependent variable) is not likely due to chance. The test indicates a **p-value** or numerical probability value of the difference between groups occurring by chance. The p-value is compared to the **alpha level** set in educational research as 0.05. A p-value at an alpha level of 0.05 or less indicates the difference would be due to chance only 5% or less of the time. If the p-value is greater than 0.05 then the difference would not be considered statistically significant.

In research studies in which a group of students is given a pre-test followed by a treatment or intervention followed by a post-test, a **repeated-measures *t* test** can be used to test for significant differences among the same individuals due to the intervention. When multiple groups are involved in the pre-post design then an **analysis of variance (ANOVA) test** can be done to determine significant differences among groups. A **chi-square test** may be used to determine statistical significance when frequency data within categories has been collected (Mertler, 2009). Additional inferential statistical tests include multiple regression analysis and factor analysis. **Multiple regression analysis** is used to find the combined relationship of multiple independent variables on a single dependent variable. **Factor analysis** is used to determine which factors or which independent variables affect the dependent variable under study both separately and in combination (Gay, Mills, and Airasian, 2009). For more detailed information and examples of inferential statistics see Gay, Mills, and Airasian (2009), Creswell (2008), and Kirk (1995).

## Qualitative Data Analysis

**Qualitative data** are diverse and can include information recorded in field notes, observations, narratives, interviews, open ended responses to surveys and questionnaires, documents, audiovisuals, photographs, performances, child artifacts such as drawings, paintings, written work, work samples, constructions, etc. There is a broad range of possible qualitative data that can be gathered in a study. The determination of what constitutes qualitative data to be collected is a function of the research questions asked, the time and resources available to collect data, and the teacher researcher's judgment of what data would best answer the research questions. In general, qualitative data is data that can be turned into text or written narrative such as interview data that can be made into written transcripts that can be analyzed qualitatively. It can also be data such as child artifacts including drawings, constructions, and performances that can be analyzed for qualitative characteristics identified by the researcher that contribute to understanding of the research question or problem. For example in the previously mentioned study of kindergarten children's emergent writing, artifacts of children's drawings can be analyzed for ways in which children use pictures they create to "write" or tell a story. Drawings can be analyzed for evidence of character, plot, sequence, and theme of what is being portrayed by a drawing, and how a child uses a drawing to narrate an event or experience.

Qualitative analysis is basically making sense of the data. It is a subjective process dependent on the knowledge, experiences, and thoughtful interpretations the researcher brings to the analysis. The researcher becomes, to a certain extent, the research instrument. Qualitative analysis of data looks for the qualities, characteristics, concepts, and meanings that it holds. It is time consuming and repetitive due to the multiple readings necessary in order to make sense and interpret data. It is getting close to the data and knowing it so well that you can use it to tell a story or write a narrative about the research problem. The most important tool in qualitative data analysis is the researcher who brings her knowledge, experiences, intuition, wisdom, ability to conceptualize, open-mindedness, and perseverance to the task. Qualitative research includes an analysis of the context in which the data were collected and often attempts to provide a holistic view of the study. Anyone who thinks it is easier to do qualitative research than quantitative has probably never done qualitative research.

Typical qualitative data analysis techniques in early childhood teacher research involve organizing and unitizing the data, doing multiple readings of the data, categorizing and coding the data, conducting theme analysis, and reconceptualizing the data in light of the research questions. It is very important in qualitative analysis for the researcher to keep an open mind for content in the data that may be surprising, disconfirming of preconceptions of the problem, or that is missing or not evident in the data. It is important to continually be open to the data and to ask what are the data telling me? The following sections describe several approaches to qualitative data analysis.

## Organizing Data

Teacher researchers who have gathered data from several data sources are often faced with the formidable task of where to begin in analyzing all of it. Organization is the key to overcoming the apprehension of where to begin. One form of organization is charting the research questions with the data sources identified for each question. Such a chart helps the researcher to see which data sources can be used to answer which research question/s. It can be appropriate for data sources to be used to answer more than one research question. The chart could therefore include space for results to be listed for each question and data source/s. When completed the chart will give an organizational outline of the study that the researcher can use to determine what comes next in the data analysis process. The organizational chart in Table 6.5 provides an outline of a second grade teacher research study of what children learned about slavery, history, and artistic expression during a project on the Underground Railroad. The outline indicates that the teacher has yet to analyze group discussions.

Data from the various data sources used in a study also need to be organized. Such organization may involve cataloging data in chronological order or by type of data collected: observation field notes, interviews, survey data, documents, artifacts, etc. Then each data type can be further organized by date or by student. The organizational approach should be chosen based on its relevance and usefulness to the researcher.

**Table 6.5  Organizational Chart for Teacher Research on 2nd Grade Underground Railroad Project**

| Questions | Data Sources | Findings |
| --- | --- | --- |
| 1. What will children learn about the role of the Underground Railroad in the escape of slaves? | Children's journals<br>Teacher journal & field notes<br>Group discussions | Journals show understanding of slave life and hardships. Teacher journal documents learning including role play at recess.<br>*Need to analyze group discussions.* |
| 2. How do children incorporate historical learning about significant events and people during the time of the underground Railroad into their work? | Children's journals<br>Children's drawings | Maps show factual knowledge about Underground Railroad such as routes and dangers. Drawings and journals depict knowledge of slave life. |
| 3. In what ways will children artistically express their learning of the Underground Railroad? | Children's drawings<br>Children's created maps<br>Children's created quilts | Drawings depict slave auction, safe houses, routes to freedom, and use of symbols in quilts and maps.<br>Class play (not an original data source) reveals learning through drama and song. |

A common approach to organizing qualitative data is to convert all data to text or narrative format. To convert observations to text, a researcher may produce a textual **transcript** or narrative of field notes taken to record observations. Or a researcher may review videotaped observations constructing a narrative of what is observed as the video is viewed. Leaving margins in the transcribed text that is developed from the data allows space for making notes while categorizing text. The researcher may produce a script tape of what is happening in the observations or a written summary of what has been observed. Both will provide text for analysis. The researcher may also apply a checklist or rubric to analyze observations classifying each observation using the checklist or rubric.

The following is an example of a teacher's journal with field notes of observations converted to textual narrative made by a second grade teacher studying what children learn through a project on the Underground Railroad (see Figure 6.3). She has read the text at least three times. The first time she read for understanding, the second to make margin notes and ask questions (memos) about elements of the text she thought were important, and the third time to highlight significant phrases (see bolded phrases). The next step in analysis would be to reflect on what is highlighted (bolded) and begin to categorize the highlighted phrases. And finally she would reflect on the categories and identify emerging themes from them. In this example, common themes emerging from this data center around what leads to learning: questions, interest, dismay, and writing prompts that require taking a slave perspective. In addition the teacher is wondering

| Observations: | Comments: |
|---|---|
| 9/10 I read *Who Owns the Sun?* and *Barefoot: Escape on the Underground Railroad.* Students wrote in journals from a first person account from a slave's perspective. They took a lot of time to get started writing in their journals. They asked many questions about why slaves were slaves in the first place and what they were expected to do as slaves. They talked to each other about the books I read and indicated much dismay about the lives of slaves. Their first writing attempts were scanty and tentative. BeLinda asked if children were also slaves and I answered yes. Caleb wondered if slaves had no shoes how they protected their feet. We discussed barefeet and foot toughening. Kasidy seemed to have trouble focusing and sat for a long time playing with his pencil. I talked privately with him about how he might start his journal. | *I'm wondering from their questions if they know much at all about slavery or when it occurred?* |
|  | *They seemed most interested in the books and the stories about slave life.* |
|  | *I wonder if some journal prompts would help their writing?* |
| 9/13 Today I read *Sweet Clara and the Freedom Quilt* and *Follow the Drinking Gourd.* We discussed what the Underground Railroad was and when it was used by slaves to get to freedom. Children asked many questions. Kody wanted to know why there were no trains on the railroad. Hannah asked about the significance of using quilts to plot the route to freedom. Braden asked how the slaves found food along the way. They wrote in their journals with my prompt from the perspective of a slave about planning their trip to the north to freedom. They quickly began to write and to tell each other about their ideas for the trip. Several illustrated their journals with drawings of quilts and symbols slaves used to read the quilts as maps. We had a share time before getting ready to go home. Dakotah told the class that some names for slaves were very bad and not to say them. | *I'm beginning to see more interest in finding out about slave life.* |
|  | *They are interested in the idea that a quilt could be a map. The journal prompt really helped them get started more quickly.* |
|  | *I am excited to see them use symbols in their illustrations.* |
|  | *I wonder how far to take this? It is such a touchy topic.* |

**FIGURE 6.3 Field Notes**

how to handle the comments of one child about "bad names" and whether to attempt to turn that comment into a learning experience.

Transcripts can be made of all interview data as well. Producing transcripts of each interview is time consuming and generally takes about 4 hours to produce a transcript for every hour of recorded interview (Creswell, 2008). If interviews have not been taped but rather recorded in notes the researcher has made during an interview, the notes can be used to write a narrative or text of the interview. Computer programs and technology assistance exist for interview transcriptions that have simplified the process. More advanced technology is on the horizon to make possible automatic transcriptions by feeding digital interview information into the computer. But until that technology becomes accurate and readily available, making transcriptions can be time consuming. When appropriate, others may be called upon to help with the process.

## Multiple Readings of Data

Once data have been converted to text, multiple readings of the text will help the researcher determine what the text is saying and interpret the text by bringing meaning to it. Multiple readings of the text involve not just reading and rereading but bringing to bear on each reading the knowledge and discernment of the researcher, what is known from professional literature on the topic, the research questions being asked, and the tentative researcher interpretations of the text that continue to develop during the process. The researcher reads and rereads for patterns in key concepts reflected in the data. Interpretation of data means to create understanding of it. Multiple readings help the researcher to glean the most meaning from the text. It is not an attempt to find ultimate truth but rather to find some insights that can be used to address the research questions. It is not unusual for interpretation to result in new questions about the study that may then direct future studies. It is important to note that two or more researchers reading and interpreting the same text may create different interpretations of the data.

In order to determine how many readings to do, a researcher continues to read until no new patterns, themes, insights, or interpretations emerge. When no new themes are found in the data, the researcher can do one more reading for what is missing (missing or absent themes) in the data that one might expect to find. This process is sometimes called saturation when multiple readings of the data for meaning yield no new themes (Krathwohl, 1998).

## Unitizing, Categorizing and Coding Data

One approach to organizing data is to **unitize** the data and to assign units of data to fit various categories the researcher creates to make sense of the data. Unitizing is similar to assigning codes to segments of textual data in a way that reflects the interpretation of the data by the researcher. This process involves breaking down the data from the text into units or the smallest units of meaning relevant to the topic of the research question or problem such as words, phrases, or sentences. Breaking data down into units is a way to narrow the analytic focus to those concepts or units of meaning that are relevant to answering the research questions. In this way the researcher searches the text to find those segments that communicate to the researcher what the text means in terms of answering the research questions. For example, if the study is focused on children's attitudes toward school, then data collected such as interviews can be broken down into individual text segments that contain statements about liking or disliking various aspects of the schooling process. Unitizing data may involve cutting up the data into small segments of the text that reflect specific meanings. This can be done manually or with computer assistance. Each segment represents the smallest unit of meaning. Segments may be cut and pasted onto index cards or catalogued in a computer program for organizing databases. Once the data have been broken down into small parts, the parts can be moved around and categorized and recategorized as the researcher interprets them to make best sense of the data and provide evidence for drawing conclusions.

The example below is the same interview from Chapter Five in which a teacher researcher has conducted a conversational interview with a child in his class. The teacher researcher is studying what children write about in their journals when given free choice. In this example the teacher researcher has made a transcript of the interview, highlighted (see bolded words) or unitized phrases that reflect topics in the child's journal, and then categorized (dark gray) the phrases into broader concepts or themes (see Figure 6.4). Teacher researchers often use colored markers to highlight significant words or phrases. He could also analyze the categories for an emerging theme about journal topics such as the topic of news items on natural disasters. The analysis process involves researcher interpretation of the data that makes sense to the researcher in terms of its relevance to the research questions. The researcher also interprets the connections across units to identify major categories or concepts that may repeat across data sets.

In this example, the researcher has done multiple readings of the data highlighting key concepts or ideas and then categorizing them into larger themes. He determines that the data set is saturated when he continues to do multiple readings of the data but does not find any additional categories. At this point the researcher reads for what is missing from the data in terms of missing themes that one might have predicted would be in the data but are not. In this example the teacher might have expected the child to have written about superheroes because he knows that superheroes is a common interest and writing topic for children in his class and in this age group. But the topic of superheroes is missing from this writing sample. The researcher may suspend judgment about superheroes as a missing theme until additional writing samples have been analyzed.

**Categorizing** and **coding** textual data is similar to unitizing the data in the sense that you are breaking down the data into meaningful bits and labeling the bits in a way that makes sense considering the patterns in the data. Categorizing and coding data is a way to break it down to identify themes in it. Themes are then used to build meaning and sense from the data and to provide a holistic view of what is in the data in order to adequately describe it. Computer software programs can be used to code data based on repetitions of certain words and patterns in the data. Such programs are helpful when you have large quantities of data to code. In most teacher research, coding is done by the researcher who is in the best position to decide which words, phrases, sentences, and meanings bring understanding to the study.

This process involves the researcher having a reflective conversation with the text (Altrichter et al., 2008) in which researcher and text interact about the research questions. Begin to categorize and code data by doing several readings of the text and highlighting or underlining phrases that seem important to the study and the research questions. It is also helpful to write in the margins any ideas or questions that come to mind as you read. Then reread the text and ascribe meanings or categories to the

T: I would really like to hear about what you wrote in your journal today. Can you tell me about it?

C: Well, I wrote about the **earthquake in Haiti**. I wrote that it was a big quake and lots of **people were killed**. *Category: natural disasters*

T: How did you decide to write about the earthquake?

C: It was on the **news** and my **mom was talking** about it. *Category: news topic discussed at home*

T: Would you read me some things you wrote?

C: Sure. The earthquake in Haiti was a big one. Many people were killed. People have **no homes and are living in tents**. They have **no water or food**. Some **people are going there to help them. Kids lost their parents. Schools fell down** on top of kids. *Category: disasters lead to bad things happening to people*

T: You seem to know a lot about what happened there. Tell me about the schools falling down.

C: Well, it was **very scary**. The floors fell down on top of kids and they were hurt. I hope that doesn't ever happen to our school. *Category: concern for self and others if disasters happen in his world*

T: Me too. Thanks for sharing your journal with me. I noticed that last week you wrote about a major snowstorm in Washington D.C. Do you like to write about **things happening in the news**? *Category: news topics, specifically natural disasters*

C: **I guess so**.

**FIGURE 6.4 Conversational Interview**

highlighted passages. The categories can then be coded simply and codes then applied to the analysis of textual data. The following example consists of excerpts taken from observation notes converted to narrative text. The teacher researcher is studying what it means for a teacher to be physically present to young children and has observed a first grade teacher over a period of several months. The teacher researcher searches the text made from the observations for examples of the observed teacher's bodily movements that indicate she is tuned into the children in her class. The researcher looks for text that describes the teacher's movements, gestures, bodily stance, and posture that indicate this teacher's bodily focus on children. The teacher researcher has done multiple readings of the text, highlighted (bolded phrases) significant phrases of meaning (units) to the study, categorized (darker gray) the phrases, and developed codes that can be applied to analyze additional text (see Figure 6.5).

**1/12  8:00 a.m.** Before Children Arrive: Kay (first grade teacher) made preparations for various activities. She **accessed** the computer and **typed** "My Dream for the World", **printed** the page, **trimmed** the title and **taped** it to a sheet titled "January Journal". She took this page to the workroom and **made a copy** for each student. This was to be a journal prompt. She returned and started **reading and writing** in a book. She said she was **preparing** weekly learning centers. She **found** two poster board maps of the United States and **placed** the posters at an activity center with a bucket containing puzzle pieces of the states. She **glanced** at the clock and **returned** to her desk. She **wrote** a note. She **went** to the cabinet, **took out** a large container with a sign **taped** to the side that read "How Many". She **put** crayons in the container and **placed** it on a shelf with a large piece of paper. This was to be an activity for estimating with the students writing their estimations on the large paper. She **opened** a package of paper, **glanced** at the clock, and said, "I have eight minutes, and I still have things to copy." Next Kay **went** around the room **organizing** the work tables. She **put** writing folders and markers away. She **checked** the supply trays for crayons, scissors, pencils, and glue. She **went** to the office and **made copies** of a paper before children began to arrive.

Category: activity through movement of body including hands and eyes in

preparation of children's arrival                    *Continued overleaf*

**FIGURE 6.5  Teacher Researcher Observations of a First Grade Teacher**
Source: Courtesy of Caren Feuerhelm

**1/13 8:30 a.m.** Children begin to arrive: Kay's interactions with children begin at about 8:30 each morning. As each one enters, Kay **acknowledges** them by **calling** their names and **saying**, "Good morning." A parent enters the room, talks briefly with Kay, then leaves. Although Kay is **talking with an adult**, she **never misses** a child's arrival. She **remains bodily turned** and **constantly glances** toward the door. She **maneuvers** herself and others so that she **has a clear view** of the door. She **shifts** her weight slightly and **takes a few steps**.

Category: communication with children and adults through words and movements that maintain contact

**1/14 10:30 a.m.** After individual work time: Kay **asks** the class to clean up their tables and come to the carpet for Author's Chair to read their original creative writing to each other. Kay **helps** them clean. At the same time she **watches** children move to the carpet. **Observing** each child Kay **says**, "I like the way Misty is ready. I like the way Kevin is ready." She **calls each child's name** as they settle into the group until each child's name has been called. The children sit on a special carpet and Kay **sits** in a chair. She **is visible** to all children.

Category: actions that maintain flow of class and individual recognition

**1/15 9:00 a.m.** Individual work time: After the children moved to tables, Kay spent about five minutes **rotating to each table** where she quickly **checked** on each individual's work. She **moved** by a child, leaned closer to him, and in a **very soft voice asked** a question. When the child answered, **she put her hand on that child's shoulder**. She **moved** to the computer with one child to **publish** his story. They **seated** themselves side-by-side at the computer. The child opened his notebook and briefly told Kay about his story. Kay **asked** what was the title of the story then typed it on a title page. She **asked** the student, "Is this the way you want your title page?" The book conversation continued with Kay **asking questions and seeking the child's opinion**. Kay points to words on the computer screen, **leans closer** to the child, and **makes direct eye contact** with him.

Category: movements, voice and touch that recognize and affirm children

**1/20 1:45 p.m.** Group time: Kay **sits** in a chair with children on the carpet. Kay **involves** children in **planning** their next activity. Braden stood, walked to the door, then turned around and looked toward Kay. She **smiled and waved** to him. Braden left the room for special reading class and seemed to need Kay's reassurance signaled through her **facial and hand gestures**.

**1/22 2:10 p.m.** Individual Work Time: Kay **smiled, nodded her head, and made direct eye contact** with students. She **leaned forward** to talk with one child to answer questions. She **squatted low** to be at child's eye level when she responded. She **winks** at individual children when she **answers questions**.

Category: movements and gestures than maintain flow

**1/24 2:10 p.m.** Individual Work Time: Several children lined up beside Kay to ask her questions. She **asked** them to sit down and said, "If you need help, raise your hand (she **demonstrated**) and I will come to you. That is less confusing." Kay **moves closer** to Kristen to **assess her reading**. Gage goes to Kay to ask a question. Kay **holds up one finger** to Gage while continuing to follow Kristen's reading. Gage returned to his table and raised his hand. When Kristen was finished reading, Kay **went** to Gage's table to help him. Jessica was fidgeting and squirming. Kay **patted her on the back**. She continued to be restless. Kay **touched her shoulder** but she continued to squirm. Kay **called her name**. When Jessica looked at her, Kay **made a circling motion with her finger** pointed toward the floor indicating for Jessica to sit down and she did.

Category: movements and gestures for positive guidance

Codes from categories: M=movement, A=activity, G=gesture, EC=eye contact, Q=asks question, AQ=answers question, T=touches, CL=gets at child's level, V=verbalizes not a question, O=observes. Codes can be used to classify additional text in the process of doing multiple readings.

**FIGURE 6.5** *Continued*

## Theme Analysis

After categorization and coding are complete, the researcher can analyze for what predominant themes or major concepts are reflected in the categories and codes. Themes can be viewed as clusters of similar categories and codes that cluster together based on a common element. Themes represent the main idea in the cluster. Categories and codes are consolidated to become themes. Types of themes include main or primary themes that predominate in the data, secondary themes that may be subsets of the primary themes, unexpected themes that contradict what was expected, and missing or absent themes that one would expect to find but are not in the data. Missing themes can be just as powerful by their absence as primary themes. In presenting the themes found in a study it is important to present them with support from several viewpoints or data points to illustrate main themes. Theme analysis continues until you reach **saturation,** that is the point at which no new themes are emerging. When no new information or evidence comes from multiple readings of text for themes, then the researcher has reached saturation and makes a decision to stop searching for additional themes.

During theme analysis it is important to be open and recognize any evidence that contradicts or does not support a theme. A diligent researcher does not ignore contradictory evidence but attempts to understand it, explain it, or recognize it in presenting findings.

As an example of how to do theme analysis, van Manen (1990) defines theme phenomenologically (from a lived experience perspective) as the structure of an experience or the sense we make of an experience. In this approach, the researcher is reading not so much to identify words or phrases but to identify them in terms of the day-to-day experiences of classroom life. A theme analysis is an attempt to grasp the essential nature of something. "Theme is the means to get at the notion. Theme gives shape to the shapeless" (p. 88). In qualitative research there are many types of theme analysis available to researchers. For example van Manen (1990) describes three approaches to theme analysis commonly used in teacher research: holistic, selective highlighting, and detailed line-by-line (pp. 92–93). The three approaches are listed in descending order of the amount of information in the text that is coded. A holistic approach involves analyzing the complete text for overall meaning. A researcher would read the entire text and ascribe a basic or holistic meaning to it. A selective highlighting approach would highlight any phrases that stand out to the researcher as being relevant to the study. A researcher would read and highlight words, phrases, or whole sentences that reflect key concepts in what is being studied. A line-by-line approach involves carefully reading each sentence for relevant meaning then coding each one. A selective highlighting approach is often preferred in teacher research because it provides an opportunity for identifying all the major themes in the data that a holistic approach might miss, and it seems to make sense to focus on the key concepts and not on each sentence as in the line-by-line approach.

**REFLECTIONS**

In the previous example of a teacher research study on what it means for a teacher to be physically present to young children, the researcher focused on the highlighted phrases, categories of the phrases, and codes for the categories to generate some themes from the text. What may be a primary theme/s? secondary theme/s? unexpected theme/s? missing theme/s? Compare your ideas to the identified themes listed below and remember that you may identify themes different from the themes identified by other researchers. Each person may see something different in the data. That is why it helps to collaborate with others when possible.

Primary theme: to be physically present to young children means to be bodily active (movements, verbal expressions, gestures, and touches)

Secondary theme: body actions set and maintain the flow of classroom life

Unexpected theme: body actions are used for positive guidance

Missing theme: where is the teacher's physical energy level evident in the data?

**Explorations**

For additional practice of theme analysis, see Appendix C Teacher Interview Transcript of the teacher observed in the preceding example. Do multiple readings of the interview text, do selective highlighting of phrases of significance, create categories and codes from the highlighted phrases, and identify primary, secondary, unexpected, and missing themes emerging from the text.

## Document Analysis

Typical documents sometimes referred to as archived artifacts (Hendricks, 2009) that may be used as data sources in teacher research include curriculum guides and handbooks, textbooks, published mandated learning outcomes, attendance and other school records, lesson plans, report cards, portfolios, minutes of meetings, reports, and sets of email messages. Documents may be analyzed both qualitatively and quantitatively depending on the question asked. For example, if a teacher is studying attendance records and wants to compare the records of one class with another, he may chose to do a quantitative analysis using frequency counts. Or he may do a qualitative analysis of a child's work produced the day after being absent to determine the effects of being absent on performance. Qualitative analysis of documents is often done using a theme analysis and analyzing for emerging themes in the document. For example the NAEYC Position Statement on Developmentally Appropriate Practice (2009) can be analyzed for themes that define what is meant by developmentally appropriate.

Another type of qualitative analysis of documents is **content analysis** similar to theme analysis. Content analysis is used to show what is in the document being analyzed (Lankshear and Knobel, 2004). Content analysis tends to focus on the message in the document, the author/s of the document, and the intended audience. For example one could analyze their state mandated curriculum or learner outcomes recorded in public, accessible documents for the content related to how learning is defined, assessed, and determined in order to do research that compares the teacher researcher's practices to the state mandates. One may find that learning is written about primarily as performance on tests. Other typical documents in teacher research are curriculum guides that can be analyzed for the type of content that is emphasized and the concepts of primary focus. Teacher researchers can compare student work to the concepts to be covered in the curriculum guide.

## Analysis of Child Artifacts

Child artifacts can be anything that a child produces as part of the educational program such as drawings, artwork, written work, journal entries, constructed projects, block constructions, performances, etc. Chapter Five provides several examples of child artifacts that can be qualitatively analyzed. For example, a second grade teacher researcher analyzed her students' invented games for state mandated learner outcomes. Another example shows three drawings done by Ben in August, October, and February. Ben's drawings can be compared for evidence of emergent writing. Ben's February drawing shows an incorporation of alphabet letters not evident in the earlier drawings. In the previous example in this chapter on the Underground Railroad study, the second grade teacher researcher analyzed children's drawings and journal entries for evidence of learning. The following artifact is a journal entry written by a boy from the perspective of a slave escaping to freedom.

The teacher's analysis of the child's learning focused on his knowledge of the role of the Underground Railroad. The teacher wrote:

> His journal entry illustrated his understanding of the role of the Underground Railroad. His reference to the house he stayed in at one point in the journey demonstrated his understanding of safe houses and their role in aiding escaping slaves. He incorporated knowledge of the journey of escape being over a long period of time and attempted to illustrate this in his writing. When he wrote, "We all don't like walking. We will hurry so we can be free." this indicated that he had conceptual knowledge of the hardships slaves endured along the Underground Railroad. He exceeded goals for the project when he incorporated knowledge of states and countries (Georgia, Tennessee, and Ohio; Canada) along his journey.

The teacher researcher noticed that children were incorporating mapping skills into their study of the Underground Railroad so she integrated mapping into the project. She asked children to make a map to correspond with part of their written journey. The teacher analyzed one child's map for learning (see Figure 6.7). The teacher wrote:

> When I looked at Caleb's map, I concluded that he had much factual knowledge about the Underground Railroad. He incorporated important elements

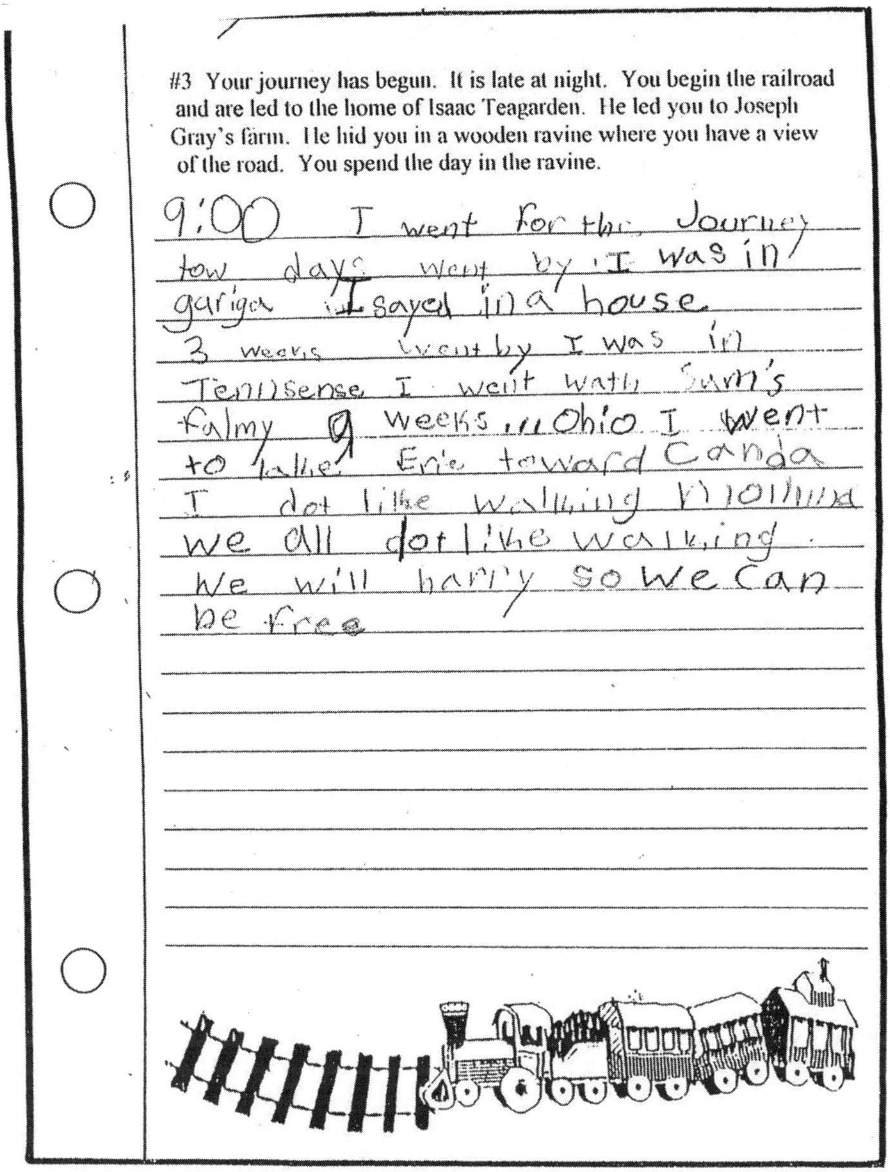

#3 Your journey has begun. It is late at night. You begin the railroad and are led to the home of Isaac Teagarden. He led you to Joseph Gray's farm. He hid you in a wooden ravine where you have a view of the road. You spend the day in the ravine.

9:00 I went for the Journey tow days went by I was in gariga I sayed in a house. 3 weeks went by I was in Tennsense I went with Sam's falmy 9 weeks in Ohio I went to lake Erie toward Canda I dot like walking niothind we all dot like walking. We will harry so we can be free

**FIGURE 6.6 Underground Railroad Journal Entry**

Source: Courtesy of Kristi Dickey

such as the big house, slave's cabin, safe houses, woods, river, North Star, boat and slave hunters. Finally his path lead him into Canada. The stars at the top of his map indicate that his travels occurred at night. He understands the significance of the Big Dipper in leading slaves to freedom as he included this feature in his night sky. When I questioned Caleb about his map, it was evident to me that he had an understanding of the role the Underground Railroad played in aiding the escape of slaves, the main goal of this project. His excitement in telling me about his map indicated his level of engagement. "Look! There's a slave catcher right here so I had to change my route!" This method of analysis gave me specific information about Caleb's thinking.

**FIGURE 6.7  Underground Railroad Map**

Source: Courtesy of Kristi Dickey

## Interpreting and Reconceptualizing Data

Interpretation of the data can occur during data analysis and following data analysis. The purpose of data interpretation is to clarify what the findings or results of the study mean. The researcher may call upon professional literature on the topic under study to help make sense of the findings. For example, the researcher may decide that the findings support what other researchers have found or that findings contradict what is in the professional literature. The researcher may also interpret the findings from a specific theoretical framework that can be used to make sense of the findings. For example, if the researcher finds that boys and girls show differences in their approaches to problem solving, the researcher may draw upon feminist theory as a lens through which to interpret these differences.

In interpreting findings it is important for researchers to reflect on their own beliefs and preconceptions of what is being studied and even write these ideas in their teacher journal for later reference. What some refer to as researcher biases, others consider the importance of researcher stance declaring one's position and beliefs about the topic of study. In qualitative research, it is assumed that the researcher has ideas about the topic of study because the researcher has chosen to study the topic. It is important to declare those ideas up front and to be open to alternative perspectives during the study. The teacher researcher needs to consider how his/her role as teacher might influence the interpretation of the data. The social context of the study including the classroom, school, and community need to be considered in interpreting findings. In interpreting what the study means a researcher can ask: "What is important in the data? Why is it important? What can be learned from it? So what?" (Gay et al., 2009, p. 456) The "So what?" question asks the researcher to stretch in terms of thinking about the findings and their significance or importance. The researcher may answer that based on the findings, changes will be made in the program that will improve teaching and learning. That would be an answer to the "So what?" question.

It is also important in interpreting findings to return to the original research questions being asked and relate each finding to the questions in such a way to show to what extent the original questions have been answered, whether additional study is necessary, and what new questions arise that need attention. In this way the study may be reconceptualized or reconsidered from a new perspective.

## Ongoing Data Analysis

**Ongoing data analysis** (Phillips and Carr, 2010), interim data analysis (Hendricks, 2009), and constant comparative analysis (Mertler, 2009) refer to analyzing data as it is collected and comparing data across data sources. There are several reasons to do ongoing data analysis including obtaining information early on whether the data sources are giving you the information you need to answer the research questions so that you can change data sources if they are not working. It allows you to compare data across data sources for similarities and differences in emerging themes. It gives you a sense of accomplishment without having to wait until the end of data collection to find out answers to your research questions.

During ongoing data analysis it is helpful to make written summaries or **memos** about what you are seeing in the data and about questions that arise when analyzing data. This process of memoing or having an ongoing dialogue about the data helps the researcher to explore thoughts about the data including possible explanations (Creswell, 2008). Writing memos and including memos in the margins of text that is being analyzed help the researcher to think through what the data mean and if they are helping shed light on the research questions. Memoing can be a sort of brainstorming the researcher needs to do to construct meaning and position it within a theoretical framework. It is recommended that teacher researchers engage in ongoing data analysis in order to sustain their interest in the research and to sustain the study through the analysis and interpretation stage of the research.

## Mixed Methods Data Analysis

Research studies that collect both quantitative and qualitative data in a single study are called **mixed methods** studies (Creswell, 2008). While the history of teacher research shows it to be predominately qualitative in nature, it is not uncommon for teacher research questions to require the collection of quantitative data and employ mixed methods for data collection and analysis. In the example in this chapter on the study of what children learn from a project on the Underground Railroad, a qualitative analysis of the teacher researcher's observation field notes and child artifacts was presented. The teacher researcher may help to answer the question, "What will children learn about the role of the Underground Railroad in the escape of slaves?" through an assignment in which the children are asked to answer a series of questions about the role of the Underground Railroad with quantifiable answers. Scores can be given based on learning reflected in children's answers as assessed by the teacher. The teacher would then have both qualitative and quantitative evidence of children's learning. One advantage to a mixed methods approach is the fuller and more balanced picture it gives of the data.

Quantitative data could also be gathered in the teacher research study on what it means for a teacher to be physically present to young children. The teacher researcher could use frequency counts of the number of times the teacher makes direct eye contact, moves her body, gestures, touches, and uses verbalizations to maintain communication and classroom flow. The observational data provide the researcher with the qualities involved in being physically present while the frequency counts of the teacher's movements quantify how often and to what extent a teacher engages in the movements. The purpose of the research and the questions asked may lend themselves to a mixed methods analysis that requires both quantitative and qualitative analysis.

## Establishing Rigor and Trustworthiness

The rigor of research refers to its level of quality. It is important for teacher researchers to demonstrate quality of research through accuracy and credibility of the study in order for others to have confidence in the results. In quantitative experimental design, research credibility is established primarily through demonstrating **internal and external validity and reliability** of the study. Internal validity means the study is accurate and the measures used in the study actually measure what they are intended to measure. To show internal validity, the researcher should control as many of the variables involved in the study as possible to demonstrate the cause–effect relationship of the independent variable to the dependent variable (Lankshear & Knobel, 2004). Control of variables gives explanatory power to the researcher to be able to adequately and thoroughly explain results. Also, sampling methods, including random assignment to groups, can be used to increase the likelihood of representative groups and thus validity. External validity refers to the extent to which results can be generalized to a larger population. External validity can also be created through random assignment to groups making sure that participants are representative of the population to whom results will be generalized. Reliability means there is consistency in the data and results across time and repeated measures. Validity and reliability of a study can be demonstrated through existing statistical tests and formulas such as correlational tests like the Kuder-Richardson split half test or formulas for correlating interrater reliability among two or more observers. Other tests of consistency in measures used include the Spearman-Brown formula and the coefficient alpha test (Creswell, 2008).

The quality of qualitative research is determined primarily by its usefulness to others. While qualitative studies are not designed to be generalizable to populations, results can transfer to similar contexts. For example, teachers reading teacher research studies may find relevance and meaning in results and may apply those to their own similar contexts. In qualitative research, rigor is also established by demonstrating **trustworthiness** of the study (Lincoln & Guba, 1985). Trustworthiness refers to the extent to which the study is truthful and accurate. Lincoln and Guba (1985) identified aspects of trustworthiness including **credibility, dependability, transferability,** and **confirmability.**

- **Credibility** refers to how believable the study is and to the demonstration of authenticity in data and methods.
- **Dependability** refers to the adequacy of research procedures, thoroughness in data collection, analysis and interpretation that are clearly articulated for others to understand and agree to the trustworthiness of what was done.
- **Transferability** refers to the extent the results of the study are applicable to other situations. Qualitative research is not generalizable to other contexts in the way that quantitative experimental research may be generalizable. But if described in enough detail, results may fit or transfer to other situations. The determination of whether the results are transferable is made by others who read the report of the study and decide for themselves that the results may fit their situations.
- **Confirmability** refers to sufficient documentation and description of data to assure others that the study results can be confirmed by the evidence presented.

Additional ways to establish trustworthiness include prolonged engagement, member checks, audit trails, participant debriefing, and triangulation of the data (Stringer, 2008). **Prolonged engagement** means that the researcher engages in data collection for an appropriate length of time to gather enough data to inform the research. For example, observing once in a classroom is usually not sufficient to gather enough data to demonstrate results. **Member checks** refer to providing participants in the study opportunities to review data and reports to ensure the information represents those who have participated in the study. Member checking is frequently done when participants have been interviewed. The researcher makes a transcript of the interview that is given to the participant to check for accuracy of information. Some teacher researchers view their research participants as co-researchers involved in all processes of the study. **Audit trail** means that the researcher maintains organized records of all data collected and all data analysis procedures. In addition the researcher makes available other documents such as field notes, journals, and artifacts so that others may review these items and procedures to determine if results are accurate based on the data collected. **Participant debriefing** occurs when the researcher tells participants about various aspects of the study and gives them an opportunity to clarify or interpret events. For example, in the teacher research study on interest children express in their free choice journal writing, the teacher researcher may share a list of all interests he has identified in children's writing and ask the children if the list truly represents what they like to write about. Teacher researchers may also do a type of debriefing in which they share with participating parents what they are seeing in their research results. A similar process is **peer debriefing** in which the researcher shares aspects of the study with a critical friend or peer who may help to clarify aspects of the study.

**Triangulation** is borrowed from the nautical procedure of establishing a location by using two known points to locate a third point. In teacher research it refers to the process of including in the study multiple data sources for cross validation. Three or more data sources are used so that data analysis occurs across all data sources. The researcher attempts to cross validate findings from one data source to others so that different data sources confirm results and thus add rigor to the study. The researcher looks for patterns from one data source in all other data sources. Triangulation enhances the accuracy of the study and is used to corroborate findings across data sources.

## Explorations

Do multiple readings of the text describing a first grade classroom in Appendix A. How might this ethnographic description be used as data in a teacher research study? Then think of an appropriate way to analyze this ethnographic description. Then apply your approach to analyze this description.

### Exploration of Resources

The following is a list of resources for computer software programs and websites for data analysis. Explore at least one resource and share what you learned with others.

*Programs for categorizing data*
Ethnograph http://www.qualisresearch.com/
Hypersearch http://www.researchware.com
MAXqda http://www.maxqda.com
NUD*IST and NVivo http://www.qsrinternational.com/products_nvivo.aspx
WinMAX http://www.agry.purdue.edu/max/

*Programs for qualitative analysis:*
AnSbWR http://www.cdc.gov/hiv/software/answr.htm
ATLAS.ti http://www.atlasti.com
EZ-Text http://www.cdc.gov/hiv/software/ez-text.htm
Qualrus http://www.ideaworks.com/qualrus/index.html
XSight http://www.qsrinternational.com

*Programs for statistical analysis:*
Microsoft Excel http://www.internet4classrooms.com/excel_functions.htm
SPSS http://www.spss.com
StatCrunch www.statcrunch.com
SYSTAT http://www.systat.com

*Guidelines for data analysis:*
Madision School District Classroom Action Research Site: http://www.madison.k12.wi.us/sod/car/caranalyzingdata.html

## References

Altrichter, H., Feldman, A., Posch, P., & Somekh, B. (2008). *Teachers investigate their work.* New York: Routledge.

Creswell, J. W. (2008). *Educational research planning, conducting, and evaluating quantitative and qualitative research* (3rd edition). Columbus, OH: Pearson Merrill Prentice Hall.

Fromberg, D. P. (2002). *Play and meaning in early childhood education.* Boston: Allyn & Bacon.

Frost, J. L., Wortham, S. C., & Reifel, S. (2008). *Play and child development* (3rd edition). Columbus, OH: Pearson Merrill Prentice Hall.

Gay, L. R., Mills, G. E., & Airasian, P. (2009). *Educational research competencies for analysis and applications.* Columbus, OH: Merrill Pearson.

Hendricks, C. (2009). *Improving schools through action research*. Columbus, OH: Pearson.

Kirk, R. E. (1995). *Experimental design: Procedures for the behavioral sciences* (3rd edition). Pacific Grove, CA: Brooks Cole.

Krathwohl, D. R. (1998). *Methods of educational and social science research* (2nd edition). Long Grove, IL: Waveland Press.

Lankshear, C., & Knobel, M. (2004). *A handbook for teacher research*. New York: Open University Press.

Lincoln, Y. S., & Guba, E. G. (1985). *Naturalistic inquiry*. Newbury Park, CA: Sage.

Mertler, C. A. (2009). *Action research: Teachers as researchers in the classroom* (2nd edition). Los Angeles, CA: Sage.

NAEYC Position Statement on Developmentally Appropriate Practice. (2009). Retrieved June 2, 2010 from http://www.naeyc.org/positionstatements/dap.

Parten, M. B. (1932). Social participation among pres-school children. *Journal of Abnormal and Social Psychology, 27*, 243–269.

Phillips, D. K., & Carr, K. (2010). *Becoming a teacher through action research* (2nd edition). New York: Routledge.

Shea, M., Murray, R., & Harlin, R. (2005). *Drowning in data? How to collect, organize, and document student performance*. Portsmouth, NH: Heinemann.

Stringer, E. (2008). *Action research in education* (2nd edition). Columbus, OH: Pearson, Merrill Prentice Hall.

van Manen, M. (1990). *Researching lived experience*. New York: The State University Press.

# seven
# Who Might Be Interested?

*I have thought of 3 ways to do teacher research: **informal**—I notice things and try to learn from them; **formal**—systematic attempt to keep records, collect data, reflect on data looking for patterns, do comparisons of data, and use results to change how I teach; and **more formal**—I think in advance to a larger audience such as teachers in general with whom I would share results in written form.*

Andrea Rains, Teacher Researcher

The focus of this chapter is on how to share research findings. Examples will be given for presenting results in informal and formal ways including sharing with colleagues, presenting at professional meetings, posting results on websites, blogs, and chat rooms, and writing results for publication in professional magazines, journals, and other documents. This chapter also provides information on existing teacher researcher collaborative groups and on forming collaborative groups.

## Prelude to Sharing Results

Upon completion of a study, the teacher researcher reflects on the results and findings of the study and what they mean in terms of making changes in the program and in teaching for improved learning. The most exciting part of a teacher research study is the application of findings to making improvements in teaching and learning. Once the data collection and analysis are complete and the findings have been obtained, it is important to ask:

- Now what?
- What do my findings tell me that I can use to make changes?
- Did I ask the right questions or do my results indicate I need to rethink my research questions and begin a new study?
- Did I involve the appropriate participants or should I have involved others?
- How can I best use results to improve my teaching and student learning?
- What are the most significant things I have learned from doing teacher research?
- Who might be interested in my results? Who might benefit from what I have learned?

Answers to these questions will provide guidance to the teacher researcher in showing necessary next steps or what some call taking "action" (action research) based on results. Action research, similar to teacher research, involves action that can be taken following results of a research study in the application of results to a situation in order to improve it. Action research may also refer to action that is taken during the course of a study in which a teacher studies the effectiveness of the action or intervention she wants to research. Some action research refers to the political actions that teacher researchers engage in when they advocate for policy changes based on their research results.

The teacher researcher may decide that results of the study can be applied to teaching in significant ways and that others may also benefit from knowing about the results of the study. This chapter explores ways to share results with those who might benefit from research results and provides reasons for the importance of sharing results. Early childhood teachers may be reluctant to share results of their teacher research studies for several reasons including thoughts that the results may not be important enough to share, a lack of confidence, or a feeling that colleagues may not be receptive. Overcoming this reluctance and realizing that others may be truly interested in your study and may actually benefit from what you have learned will help you find ways to share results. If you hide your results from others, then only you will benefit from all the hard work you have done. When results are shared, others benefit as well.

Teacher research findings can be shared in many ways including informal and formal sharing such as conversations and meeting reports, in presentations at the local, state, and national levels, on the Internet at teacher researcher websites, and in written formats such as reports, narratives, and journal publications. Results can be shared in more than one format. It is not uncommon for a teacher researcher to share results with colleagues, then at a conference presentation, and finally as a manuscript submission for publication. As you will see in the examples that follow, there are many ways to share results with a variety of audiences.

---

## REFLECTIONS

Reflect on a time you completed a project that was important to you and that represented your best work. With whom did you share your work? Why was it important to you to share your work with someone?

---

## Purpose for Sharing Results

Think of a time that a friend of yours accomplished something that you were interested in doing yourself. You may have asked your friend for all the details in how she did what she did so that you could do it too. Perhaps your friend took a yoga class, began to practice yoga, and improved her fitness, energy level, and overall attitude with results noticeable to you. Your friend might not have thought you were interested in what she had done or perhaps she didn't want to boast about improvements to her health and therefore didn't talk much with you about what she had done even though you could have benefited from the information. It's useful to think about the results of your teacher research study in a similar way. While you may not want to impose your results on others, there are probably teachers who would want to know how you did what you did so that they might try it too. There are many reasons for sharing results with others.

## Communication

Sharing results is a form of communication that keeps all participants in the research and those who might be affected by the results informed about what you have done and what it might mean for them. If you have kept written records of your study as a form of documenting what you have done, the next step is to share that with those who have a stake (**stakeholders**) in the study. These stakeholders may be other teachers, parents, or community members who may be affected by your results or who may be participants who are curious about your findings. In doing teacher research, it is important and also ethical to keep all parties informed. In addition to informing participants, think to a larger audience who may benefit from hearing about your study. For example, if your study was focused on the role of choice in first graders' learning, other first grade teachers may find what you have done to be not only interesting but also something they might use in their own programs. Consider a local as well as a broader audience for your research.

## Finding a Voice

When you share teacher research results with others, you find your voice not only in your own program but also in the profession at large. When you are the teacher who is the one who has done the study and know the most about it, you are more likely to speak with a strong voice of confidence in providing to others research based evidence to support the educational program. Teachers are increasingly expected to support their practices with research-based evidence. Results from teacher research studies provide the evidence you can use to explain to others the importance of what you do and thus strengthen your professional voice.

## Professional Development

Not only do others benefit from hearing about your study, but they can also provide meaningful questions and feedback that help teacher researchers grow in professional knowledge. When results are shared, others ask questions that lead to reflection and insights for teacher researchers that can be used to improve their educational programs. Feedback from others helps teacher researchers better understand what they have done and what needs to be done next in future studies. Such exchanges result in professional growth.

## Contribution to the Field

If you complete your teacher research study to the point of getting results, it is important to put your results out there for others to benefit from what you have done, even though you may think your results are not that important. Some consider this an ethical, professional responsibility of the teacher researcher. Participating in a teacher research group or teacher learning community is a great way to share results and benefit from the research of others. Such groups, especially within a school context, can be quite contagious in involving teachers to collaborate in doing teacher research for the benefit of children in the school. Research on teacher research communities shows they greatly benefit the educational program of the schools where teachers do teacher research (Myers & Rust, 2003; Hendricks, 2009).

You may want to view sharing results on a continuum from starting small then branching out to a larger audience. For example, you may share your results first in conversations with colleagues, then present results at a workshop or conference, then make a written report to your administrator, principal or director, and finally submit a manuscript of your research for publication in a teacher magazine, website, or professional journal. Reaching a larger audience makes an even more significant contribution to the field.

## Audience for Your Research

It is important to consider your audience when sharing teacher research results. Thinking about the audience will help the teacher researcher to determine how results will be shared, informally or formally, and which aspects of the results will be of most interest to a particular audience. For example, colleagues may be most interested in how your results may apply to them and their own teaching, and less interested in the details of data collection and analysis. In conference presentations, you may not know your audience and decide to present a brief summary of all aspects of your study followed by a question and answer session in which the audience may ask for more details. A journal audience may require a report of as many details about your study as possible in case someone reading your report has a desire to replicate what you have done in their own situation. Typical audiences for sharing results include the following.

### Other Teachers

Think about which early childhood teachers in your school or program might want to hear about your study. You might share results over lunch or at a break or at a school faculty meeting. There may be teachers at other levels, such as elementary teachers, who may also benefit from what you have done. When news of your study goes through the grapevine, you may get requests to share results with other teachers you might not have expected would be interested. For example, news of one teacher's study got around to others including a book editor, a friend of another teacher, who then asked the teacher to write a chapter summarizing her study for an upcoming book on early childhood mathematics. The teacher's initial sharing of results and subsequent book chapter brought her study to a much wider audience than she had expected.

### Administrators

Your principal, program director or supervisor is an important audience for your work because they are in positions of facilitating staff meetings and conducting professional development opportunities for others including putting your study on the agenda. They also have access to other audiences at the local and district levels giving a wider coverage of your study. In their positions, they need to know what teachers are doing and to be informed of teachers' professional development activities. Sharing results with administrators helps them get to know your interests and program at a deeper level than sporadic visits to your classroom. When they know about your efforts, they have a better idea of how to support your work.

## Parents

Sharing results with parents of children who have participated in your study is an important way to communicate with them as well as get their feedback on what you have done. Interested parents will want to hear about how results from your study will benefit their children and improve the educational program. Other parents of children in the school may also want to know about your study, particularly if their children will have you as their teacher in the future.

## Community

People in the community such as school board or advisory board members may be interested in your study. You can share results at community gatherings or in written reports distributed locally. Many communities have foundations that grant funds to teachers for various projects including teacher research projects. If you have shown that you conduct teacher research, they may be more likely to fund your next study.

## State/National/International

Many teacher researchers want to reach a broader audience beyond the local level. Blogs, websites, Facebook, and other internet resources serve as forms of digital communications and networks that can be used for sharing results to extensive audiences. Professional publications such as teacher magazines and journals will get results to an even broader audience including teachers in other countries.

## Informal Sharing

There are many ways teacher research results can be shared informally, from conversations with others who are interested in the study such as teacher colleagues, to sharing results at faculty meetings or other teacher meetings such as school district curriculum committee or grade level meetings. Teacher researchers can present their studies at parent-teacher meetings such as back-to-school events or curriculum nights when families visit the school to find out more about the educational program. Teacher researchers informally share results by making class displays of results of the study including displays of children's work, drawings, photos, or other representations of the data accompanied by brief descriptions of what the artifacts/data mean. Such displays may be in the form of class posters, murals, table displays, or media displays.

Documentation panels can be used to display results including the progress of the study from beginning to end. **Documentation panels** are displays of children's learning that use graphic representation as well as written narrative to tell the story of what children have learned from the activities they have participated in. Documentation panels are often used in a (Reggio Emilia approach, Gandini, Etheredge, & Hill, 2008) project approach to teaching in order to communicate the richness and extent of children's creativity and learning. For example, in a teacher research study of young children's ideas about shadows, kindergarten children's project work with shadows could be displayed in a documentation panel, to include children's initial questions about shadows, captioned photographs of children experimenting with making shadows using an overhead projector and sheet for projecting shadows, children's captioned drawings of shadows, and the teacher's written commentary about the project.

Teacher researchers can informally share their studies in letters and newsletters that go home to parents or are posted on the classroom website to give parents information about classroom activities and events. Upon the conclusion of a study, a teacher researcher may wish to schedule an appointment with her principal, director, or other administrator in order to share with them verbally the results of the study, what the study has meant to the teacher researcher, and to discuss ideas for next steps to take in applying results to the program. Administrators may encourage teacher researchers to present their results in a formal atmosphere such as at a professional conference and may even provide monetary support for conference travel or suggest funding possibilities.

## Formal Sharing

Formal sharing is usually done by preparing a more structured presentation or manuscript that is then shared in a formal setting such as at a conference or in a professional publication. There is usually a format to follow for formal presentations that is given in the call for presentation proposals from professional associations conducting conferences and workshops. Formal sharing may be done in a newsletter, conference presentation, or journal article.

## Newsletters

Many state early childhood associations publish newsletters of events including informational articles and are always looking for submissions. Most newsletters are not peer reviewed and have only an editor who approves content. Consider submitting a summary of your study to a newsletter. Write the summary as if you are telling a friend about your study, use first person, and write in a conversational tone including only the details you think readers would want to know about. For example, I shared a teacher research study I did involving my students over a semester in a state newsletter. My newsletter article (see Appendix D The Wonder of Learning) described how I assigned students to visit the Reggio Emilia exhibit, The Wonder of Learning: The Hundred Languages of Children, that was touring our state. In the article I described what I asked my students to do, what they learned about children's constructed knowledge from the assignment, and what I learned about my teaching.

## Conference Presentations

Professional conferences at the local, state and national levels provide opportunities for sharing results with other interested educators and a wider audience than just teachers in one school. Most conferences call for program presentation proposals that are reviewed and accepted as part of the conference program. Writing a conference proposal is a good first attempt to organize and summarize your teacher research study. A logical sequence is for teacher researchers to present their work first at a conference and then as a manuscript submitted for publication. Doing a presentation first may give you some feedback from conference participants about things that are of interest to them in your research or questions they have that may further stimulate your thinking about the study. The presentation experience may then help you improve your written report of the study that would also possibly enhance your chances of getting it published. A format is usually given by the conference for writing a conference proposal which typically includes a brief summary including objectives of the presentation, who might be interested in the content, how participants will be involved in the presentation, media equipment needed to do the presentation, and length of presentation. For example, the following conference proposal was submitted by a group of teacher researchers who had collaborated on a study of mapping with children.

## CONFERENCE PROPOSAL NARRATIVE

**TITLE:** Project Work on Mapping with Teachers and Children

**INTENDED AUDIENCE:** This session is aimed at early childhood/elementary teachers

**OBJECTIVES:**

- To display results (text and photos) of teacher research on mapping with children (4 to 11 years) using the Project Approach to curriculum (Katz & Chard, 1989)
- To show that the Project Approach to curriculum can be used effectively with all age groups from early childhood through elementary
- To show the developmental progression in understanding mapping as a set of concepts
- To provide implications for teaching from project inquiry
- To support a constructivist view of curriculum through project work.

**CONTENT:** Seven early childhood teachers studied project work on mapping inquiring into the meaning of mapping, following maps, creating maps, and generating research questions on mapping to study in their own classrooms (7 total) with children aged 4 to 11 years. Then the teachers did research on mapping in their own classrooms and schools over an eight week period.

Modes of inquiry included questioning, discussing, problem solving, analyzing, reflecting, and interpreting all done within the context of Project Work. A project is an in-depth study of a topic to deepen understanding of the topic (Katz and Chard, 1989). Teachers began the project with a brainstorm session on what it means to map. Teachers discussed mapping experiences and identified key concepts of mapping, such as sign/symbol representation, location, vertical/horizontal space, and perspective/viewpoint. Project work included interpreting, following, and creating maps. Teachers formulated questions for inquiry including:

What do children think a map is?

In what ways do children map space?

How can a teacher promote mapping through various types of play?

How will children map their class garden?

What maps do families use and how can we help parents to become involved in mapping with young children?

How do children's maps at different ages/stages vary in how they look and how does this reflect changes in their thinking?

How do children make use of or construct maps during a mapping project and what are the roles that girls choose within the group?

What literature will enhance children's desire to engage in mapping activities?

Children involved in the project work ranged in age from 4 to 11 years. Teachers engaged their own students in questioning, researching, interpreting, and creating maps. They gathered artifacts of children's writing, drawing, discussions, and map creations that they shared with each other. They analyzed the developmental aspects of mapping.

**RESULTS AND CONCLUSIONS:** Data were analyzed for understanding of mapping. Evidence of increased understanding came from increased complexity in discussing and writing about mapping and in self-reported increased ease at map interpretation. Evidence supported that both teachers and children deepened their understanding of what it means to map. Analysis of teachers' ideas about mapping indicated greater understanding as a result of collaborative participation in mapping activities and engagement of children in mapping and analysis of children's work. Analysis of children's artifacts supported the developmental aspects of children's understanding of mapping (Sobel, 1998). It can be concluded that teachers who participate in project work will use project work in their own teaching with young children because they have personally experienced project work as meaningful learning.

**EDUCATIONAL IMPORTANCE OF THE STUDY:** Mapping and map interpretation are long standing curriculum objectives that pose difficulties for teachers and children. Mapmaking can be a valuable tool in elementary schools (Sobel, 1998). However, teachers who have difficulty understanding mapping concepts will not be in the best position to teach those concepts. Project work can be a meaningful way for teachers to reconstruct their knowledge of topics such as mapping. Collaborative project work provides a non-threatening context in which teachers can deepen their understanding of a topic through questioning, personal research, and exposure to the thinking of peers. This deeper understanding translates into rethinking their work with children and refocusing on understanding children's understanding of curriculum. Results from this study support a constructivist approach to teaching at all levels (Fosnot, 1996).

**References**

Fosnot, C. (Ed.) (1996). *Constructivism: Theory, perspectives, and practice.* New York: Teachers College Press.

Katz, L. G. & Chard, S. C. (1989). *Engaging children's minds: The project approach.* Norwood, NJ: Ablex.

Sobel, D. (1998). *Mapmaking with children.* Portsmouth, NH: Heinemann.

**TECHNIQUES FOR PRESENTATION:** Results of the inquiry will be represented on a free-standing poster in text and photos depicting mapping activities and child artifacts. One teacher/presenter will do a 10 minute presentation on the topic of a constructivist view of curriculum through project inquiry. The presenter will use the poster to exemplify the relevance of a constructivist approach to curriculum with all age groups. Participants will be engaged in a question and answer session in which they will have an opportunity to share their mapping experiences. The presentation will be one hour in length to fit the length of the conference poster presentation session.

## Writing for Publication

Teacher researchers may want to submit their research for publication. Since publication is a public sharing of the work, it is important to maintain confidentiality including protection of identities and to obtain written releases from parents and from those whose work you intend to share in the publication. Many possibilities exist for sharing written results including electronic and paper submissions to listservs, blogs, websites, newsletters, magazines, journals, and books. The publication gold standard of quality in the field of education is publication in a **peer-reviewed journal**. A peer-reviewed journal is a journal that has a blind review process in which submitted manuscripts are sent to a few reviewers in the field. The author and reviewers remain anonymous to each other.

But some teacher researchers may prefer to get their results to an audience as quickly as possible and may not want to take the time and effort to prepare a full-blown manuscript for publication. Results can usually be shared more quickly by posting to an electronic system such as to a listserv, blog, or Facebook page. The advantage to electronic postings is the speed of sharing results with a potentially wide audience. Most paper publications such as magazines and journals go to a set of subscribers or members of associations who get the publication as a subscription or member benefit. Magazine and journal audiences may or may not be as large as electronic social networks. However, magazines and journals usually have a more rigorous review process to ensure quality of the publication to readers who can assume that the study has met certain professional standards for conducting research. Publishing in professional journals is considered a professional contribution to the knowledge base in the field.

Publishing your teacher research results in a professional journal is a good way to reach a wider audience beyond your local setting. While writing a manuscript for publication takes time and effort, it represents a contribution to the field that will benefit others who might have only known about your study from reading about it. The following information will help you explore ways to write up your results and get your teacher research manuscript published.

## Professional Journals

There are hundreds of professional journals in the field of education. There are journals sponsored by professional associations, universities and publishing houses. There are journals published in a paper format, others that are totally online, and still others that are both paper and online. Each journal has a special mission that targets a specific audience. Many professional journals publish teacher research studies along with other types of manuscripts such as those that focus on practical applications, theoretical and conceptual pieces, program evaluations, and reader opinion pieces. There are some professional journals that are teacher research journals and publish only teacher research studies. In order to determine the most appropriate place to send your manuscript, you will need to explore journal possibilities by reading some of them. Select journals that you think might be good possibilities for your work and then explore each one to ascertain the journal's targeted audience, mission, upcoming themes, and author guidelines. Then review a few issues of the journal to get a feel for the types of content and format of published articles in each one.

### Examples of professional journals in the field of education

*Educational Leadership*
*Phi Delta Kappan*
*The Journal of Curriculum and Teaching Dialogue*
*The Journal of Supervision and Curriculum Development*
*The American Educational Research Journal*
*Educational Researcher*
*Teachers and Teaching*
*Teaching Children Mathematics*
*The Reading Teacher*

### Examples of early childhood education professional journals

*Young Children*
*Childhood Education*
*Early Childhood Journal*
*Dimensions of Early Childhood*

### Examples of early childhood education research journals

*Early Childhood Research Quarterly*
*Research in Childhood Education*

### Examples of teacher research journals

*Collaborative Action Research Network* (http://research.edu.uea.ac.uk/links/care/
    collaborativeactionresearchnetworkuk)
*Educational Action Research* (http://www.tandf.co.uk/journals/titles/09650792.asp)

*Networks: An Online Journal for Teacher Research* (http://journals.library.wisc.edu/
   index.php/networks)
Early Childhood Education Teacher Research Online Journal:
*Voices of Practitioners* (http://www.naeyc.org/publications/vop)

Professional journals usually include announcements of upcoming theme issues and
guidelines for authors to use to write and submit manuscripts to the journal. Author
guidelines are usually included in each issue of a journal or on the journal website. For
example, author guidelines for the NAEYC journal, *Voices of Practitioners* can be found
at http://www.naeyc.org/publications/vop/about/manuscript. Before submitting your
manuscript, make sure that it conforms to the format described in the author guidelines.
The following example is the set of author guidelines for submitting to the *Networks
Online Journal for Teacher Research*, retrieved from http://journals.library.wisc.edu/
index.php/networks/about/submissions

## Author Guidelines

We plan to have four sections of the journal. When submitting a contribution,
please indicate the section for which your submission is intended.

- full-length articles (normally 2,000–3,500 words). These will typically report a
  completed investigation or offer a critical review of a number of investigations
  that share a common theme or topic.
- shorter articles and notes (about 300–750 words). These might describe work in
  progress, raise issues arising from such work, or discuss general issues related to
  methodologies, ethics, collaboration, etc.
- book reviews (about 750–1,000 words). These will typically provide a sense of
  the main arguments and presentation style of the author. In addition, reviews
  will take the perspective of a critical friend in terms of the author's assumptions,
  arguments and evidence, drawing, where possible, on other work on the same
  topic or issue.
- resources for teacher-research. These notices will keep teacher-researchers
  informed of upcoming events, opportunities, and resources.

### Submission Preparation Checklist

As part of the submission process, authors are required to check off their submission's compliance with all of the following items, and submissions may be returned
to authors that do not adhere to these guidelines.

1. The submission has not been previously published, nor is it before another journal
   for consideration (or an explanation has been provided in Comments to the
   Editor).
2. The submission file is in Microsoft Word, RTF, or WordPerfect document file
   format.
3. All URL addresses in the text (e.g., http://pkp.sfu.ca) are activated and ready to
   click.

4. The text is single-spaced; uses a 12-point font; employs italics, rather than under-lining (except with URL addresses); and all illustrations, figures, and tables are placed within the text at the appropriate points, rather than at the end.
5. The text adheres to the stylistic and bibliographic requirements outlined in the Author Guidelines, which is found in About the Journal.
6. The text, if submitted to a peer-reviewed section (e.g., Articles), has had the authors' names removed. If an author is cited, "Author" and year are used in the bibliography and footnotes, instead of author's name, paper title, etc. The author's name has also been removed from the document's Properties, which in Microsoft Word is found in the File menu.

Many professional journals in the field of education require that manuscripts follow the format of the most recent edition of the *Publication Manual of the American Psychological Association* commonly called the APA Guidelines. This manual is currently in its sixth edition (2009). The manual covers all aspects of writing for publication from the mechanics of style to crediting sources to creating a references list. It also includes the ethics of writing and publishing including citations and authorship.

## Manuscript Structure

A typical manuscript structure for a teacher research journal submission now follows.

### *Cover letter*

Author guidelines usually indicate how manuscripts are to be submitted. Email submissions are becoming more common, but some journals may want submissions through regular mail. Regardless, a cover letter to the journal editor should be included that tells the title of the manuscript that is being submitted and a statement that the manuscript has not been submitted to any other journal. Ethically manuscripts can be submitted to only one journal at a time. This process prevents a situation in which two journals might publish the same article. That would be a waste of journal space and resources and considered unprofessional. The following cover letter is brief but gives the pertinent information.

9-21-2012 (Date of Submission)

Dear (Name of Journal Editor):

The manuscript entitled "Young Children's Computation Strategies" is being submitted for review for the Voices of Practitioners Journal. The manuscript summarizes a teacher research study I conducted. I think it is a good fit for the mission and audience of the journal. This manuscript has not been submitted elsewhere.

Sincerely,

(Name of Author)

## Title page

This page includes the title of the manuscript and author information. The title of the manuscript should clearly indicate what the study is about so that readers searching for specific topics will find it easily. If the study is about the computation strategies that children use, then this information should be in the title. The author/s' name/s, professional affiliation, and contact information including an email address would also be included on the cover page. No author information should appear in the manuscript itself so that reviewers will not know the identity of the author/s and can review without bias. Similarly, the author is not given the identities of the reviewers. The process of concealing identities is called **blind peer review**. It is a much more rigorous review than one in which the reviewer may be swayed by the identity or location of the author. An example of a title page follows.

(Running Head) Young Children's Computation Strategies

(Title of Manuscript) Young Children's Computation Strategies

(Author Information)  Dr. Kathryn Castle
Oklahoma State University
245 Willard Hall
Stillwater, OK 74078
405 744-7125
kathryn.castle@okstate.edu

## Abstract

The abstract is a brief summary (about 200 words) of the teacher research study including research questions and findings. The following is an example of an abstract.

**Abstract**

This teacher research study focused on identifying the computation strategies used to solve arithmetic problems by 21 students in a first grade classroom. The teacher researcher analyzed computation strategies in children's math journals, project work, and group discussions. Findings indicate the most frequent computation strategy used by children was *adding on* even when the problem was one of subtraction. Recommendations call for teacher recognition of the role of addition in all types of computation, not just in addition problems. Teachers need to be aware of how children approach computation and encourage their use of a variety of computation strategies.

## Body of the manuscript

The body of a manuscript includes an introduction, a literature review, a methodology section, a findings or results section, a discussion of results section, a conclusion, references, and possibly appendices.

## Introduction

The introduction tells the reader what the study is about and why it is important to the teacher researcher as well as to other educators. The introduction often gives an explanation of how the teacher researcher came to do the study, the issues involved that lead to the study, and ways in which the study is connected to professional literature on the topic of the study. The introduction may include a problem statement about difficulties experienced by the teacher that may get resolved or better understood through the research. A statement of purpose may also be in the introduction such as "The purpose of this teacher research study is to identify various computation strategies children use in problem solving."

The introduction describes the context of the study including the location of the study such as in a kindergarten classroom. It lists the research question/s. For example, there may be a main question followed by a few subquestions that help answer the main question. Each subquestion has a more specific focus than the main, umbrella question, and all subquestions taken together will give a comprehensive coverage of the main question.

## Literature review

The literature review includes a summary of professional literature relevant to the topic of the study. The researcher uses a summary of the literature to build a case for why the research study is needed, such as gaps in the literature that the study might fill, in order to build upon what is already known about the topic from previous research.

## Methodology

The methodology section of the manuscript describes which methods were used to collect and analyze data, and is usually composed of several subsections such as setting, participants, data sources, data collection procedures, and data analysis. Details about the classroom context including organization and set up help the reader better understand the location of the study. It is also important to include information about child participants such as ages and other demographic information that conceals child identities but communicates characteristics of the children involved in the study as well as characteristics about all participants. Details of data collection and analysis should be specific enough that readers would be able to reproduce the study in their own settings.

## Findings

The findings or results of the study are described in terms of what the teacher researcher learned from doing the study. Examples of results taken from the data are necessary to document and validate findings. For example, if an interview were used to collect data, then some representative samples of participant comments would help confirm the findings. A description of how the teacher researcher established credibility of the study is also included. See Chapter 6 on how to establish credibility.

## Discussion

This section is focused on what the findings mean to the teacher researcher, their significance for what comes next, and how they might be connected to professional literature and/or other studies. Implications are drawn for teaching and for additional research that might build on the study including other research questions that arose during the research.

## Conclusions

The Conclusions section provides a summary of the study and includes implications for teaching and future research. Recommendations based on research findings are given.

## References

A list of references for all citations in the manuscript is given usually using the APA guidelines for format such as an alphabetical listing by authors' last names.

## Appendices

Items that are relevant to the study but may be too lengthy to include in the body of the manuscript can be included in an appendix or appendices following the References section of the manuscript. Typical items to include in an appendix might be a copy of the survey, questionnaire, or interview questions used to collect data. Appendices may be used when the information is very detailed and may distract or burden the reader if included in the body of the manuscript. In the case of a manuscript having only one appendix, it would be labeled Appendix. When two or more appendices are used, each is labeled with an alphabet letter in the order it is mentioned in the manuscript, such as Appendix A, Appendix B, etc. (APA, 2009).

## Manuscript Review Process

The journal editor will log in the manuscript upon submission and send it to two or three reviewers who are knowledgeable of the topic and who have agreed to review the manuscript. It may take as long as three to six months before authors are notified of the outcome of the review process. It is typical for the blind review process to involve three reviewers who evaluate the manuscript and complete an evaluation form that is sent to the journal editor who makes a final decision. A typical evaluation form might include criteria scored along a Likert scale, as in Table 7.1.

It is typical for the final decision from each reviewer to reflect one of the following categories:

Accept as written; no revisions required

Accept with minor revisions

Accept with major revisions

Rewrite and resubmit

Reject manuscript for one of the following reasons: it doesn't fit the mission/audience of the journal; it lacks clear conceptualization and/or methodology; writing skills are lacking; other reasons_____

Reviewer Comments to Editor (confidential)

Reviewer Comments to Author: may include ideas for revision of manuscript.

### Outcome of review

The editor will send a letter to the author indicating the outcome and any revisions needed as well as comments from reviewers that guide the author in making revisions. A revisions deadline is given for receiving revisions from the author. Once revisions are submitted, there may be an additional review and an additional request for revisions. Once the revised manuscript is accepted for publication, the author will have one final opportunity to make minor corrections to the page proofs in the final stage prior to publication.

Most professional journals accept only the best manuscripts and publish only about 20% of submitted manuscripts. Therefore, rejection of submitted manuscripts is the rule more than the exception. It is very common to have a manuscript rejected on the first submission. Rejection is just a part of the publication journey and should not be taken personally. When a manuscript is rejected, it is best to focus on the reasons. If it was rejected because it was not a good fit with the journal and journal audience, then research other journals for those that would be a good fit and submit it to a different journal. Take a look at the reviewer and editor comments to the author and use those constructive comments to improve the manuscript before submitting to another journal. If no guidance is provided in the rejection letter, then having a critical friend read and critique the manuscript might help to improve it before submitting to a different journal. A **critical friend** is a professional person or colleague you trust will give you honest and constructive feedback you can use to make your work better (Costa & Kallick, 1993). Members of teacher research collaborative groups (discussed in detail below) serve as critical friends to each other. For example, the National School Reform Faculty website provides a forum for a critical friends approach to collaborative work and describes the functioning of critical friends groups (http://www.nsrfharmony.org).

## Writing Tips

- Keep a Teacher Researcher Journal
- Establish a schedule and routine for writing
- Aim the writing for an intended audience or journal
- Write narratives in first person
- Narrative writing should be clear and well organized using simple language
- Draft and redraft
- Engage a critical friend and proof-reader
- Join a Teacher Research Collaborative Group.

Writing can and should become part of a teacher's daily/weekly routine. Write often both at regularly scheduled times and on the fly as events occur. As an early childhood teacher, I kept index cards and sticky notes on me at all times for taking short hand notes when something of significance occurred. A simple note to yourself followed up by a regularly scheduled time to "flesh out" the notes goes a long way in helping draft your written account of events. Your teacher research journal can be the repository where you record field notes as well as manuscript drafts. Some teacher researchers schedule an early morning, quiet time for writing, even as little as 15 minutes, to reflect and write before the day begins. Spreading the writing out over a period of time not only prevents it from becoming a chore but also allows reflection time in between that can help in the organization and clarity of the written work.

Find out something about the journal audience and write with them in mind. Put yourself in the role of the reader and include all the details that you would want to know if you were reading the manuscript or wanting to reproduce the study. If the audience is teachers, then think of what in your research would be important to them that they would want to know about. An outline will facilitate the writing of a first draft. Remember that first draft work, or the "sloppy copy" as one teacher put it, is meant to just get it down on paper. Once it's down, revisions are in order. Anne Lamott (1994) describes the first draft as the down draft in which the emphasis is just on getting it down on paper. She says the second draft is the up draft when you fix it up and make it better. If you strive for a perfect manuscript, then you may never get to the point of submitting it for publication. But when you have a clearly organized and conceptualized draft, it is time to enlist a critical friend's suggestions for improvement. Their constructive review and comments will only help the work and help you to make it better. If you are not a member of a teacher research collaborative group, then consider joining or starting one in your area. Such groups meet regularly to ponder and help each other's work whether preparing for National Board Certification or for manuscript submission. The following section describes what such groups do.

## Teacher Research Collaborative Groups

Teacher research collaborative groups can take the form of:

- Teacher Writing Groups such as the National Writing Project (NWP) and the Teacher Inquiry Communities of the NWP
- Professional Learning Communities
- National Board for Professional Teaching Standards Groups
- Teacher Research Groups.

Teachers feel more supported when they have a collaborative group of other teachers with whom to share the planning, implementation, results, surprises, joys, and difficulties of doing teacher research. Teacher learning communities that have come together to discuss various aspects of teaching may quite naturally evolve into a teacher researcher group. Teachers are more likely to do teacher research when participating in a teacher research group. Teachers can join local, state, national, and even international teacher research groups, although participation in a local group is more immediate and satisfying when group members can get together on a regular basis. As one second grade teacher commented, "I see myself taking full advantage of the resources around me. There is evidence of internal and external collaboration with colleagues. I seek out colleagues who stretch me as an educator." Teachers sharing insights and projects can help each other in conceptualizing their teacher research studies, making sense of results, and communicating results to others.

Teacher research communities and inquiry groups support the work of individuals and teacher groups and provide the type of collaboration that supports teachers' work as well as communicates this work to members of the group as well as to a broader audience beyond the group (Lieberman & Miller, 2008; Mohr, Rogers, Sanford, Nocerino, Maclean, & Clawson, 2004; and Myers & Rust, 2003). Participation in or formation of a teacher research collaborative group provides a support network of like-minded teacher researchers with a common mission to facilitate each other's work. A form of collaborative group is Teacher Professional Learning Communities (DuFour & Eaker, 1998) that can provide the type of collaboration that teachers need in order to do their own teacher research studies. For example, Eleanor Duckworth's (1997) book, *Teacher to Teacher*, summarizes the work of a teacher group she formed that worked meeting regularly for a year in an effort to become better teachers. Each teacher-authored chapter in the book summarizes what teachers learned from participating in the group that they applied to their own teaching situations.

Guidelines for forming a teacher research group can be found at the George Mason University Teacher Research website: Teacher Research, George Mason University, http://www.gse.gmu.edu/research/tr/. Guidelines include having a group leader who is experienced in doing teacher research and can facilitate functioning of the group including scheduling the time and location of group meetings, sending meeting reminders, setting meeting agendas, providing guidance during group meetings, and facilitating publication of group findings. They recommend a group size of three or more teacher researchers. They suggest trying to get funding for teachers to meet during the school day, or after school with dinner out. They cite organizations that support and fund teacher research such as Met Life Fellows, the Carnegie Foundation for the Advancement of Teaching, the Reading Teachers Network, and the National Education Association (NEA) Foundation for the Improvement of Education.

Annie Ortiz, a fifth grade teacher, teacher researcher, and Director of the National Writing Project Teacher Inquiry Communities, organized a teacher research collaborative group composed of teachers representing each grade level in her elementary school (K-5th grade). The teachers worked together for a year on a project focused on boys' literacy. Their interest in such a project came from many conversations about why boys did not write as much as girls and seemed to lack interest in literacy activities. The teachers were concerned that boys were not as engaged in literacy activities, such as writing, as girls were. Annie led the group in a teacher research study on how to promote boys' literacy. She wrote a grant to an educational foundation to purchase several books on boys' literacy for each teacher in the study. The grant was funded and the research began with meetings to discuss the professional readings the teachers were doing. For a year they met monthly and communicated through a listserv where they discussed their data and findings. Results from their research described the teaching strategies and school activities that increased boys' interest in reading and writing across all grade levels. They learned more than just how to promote boys' literacy. They also learned how to work collaboratively in doing teacher research that benefited each teacher, the boys in their school, and even the community. They presented their results locally and nationally and are currently writing a manuscript for publication in a professional journal.

One of the most well-known teacher collaborative groups is the Teacher Inquiry Communities (TIC) of the National Writing Project. This group has an active website and listserv for teachers to share their projects. Teachers and TIC group members have participated in the National Writing Project at the local, state, or national levels. Many states have active Writing Projects that offer summer workshops for teachers. Teachers who complete the workshop can then serve as consultants to other teachers interested in the work of the Writing Project and can participate in sharing their teacher research studies with local, state, and national Teacher Inquiry Communities.

The American Educational Research Association (AERA) offers several special interest groups (SIGs) on teacher research including the Teacher as Researcher SIG, the Action Research SIG, and two early childhood SIGs, Early Education and Child Development and Critical Perspectives on Early Childhood Education. The SIGs have listservs and newsletters for sharing information and research results plus annual meetings at the AERA conference.

In addition, there are increasing numbers of website groups that support and mentor teacher researchers including:

> Action Research for sharing teacher research studies, http://actionresearch.altec.org/
>
> Fairfax County Virginia Public Schools for online teacher research support, http://www.fcps.edu/plt/tresearch.htm#
>
> The United Kingdom National Teacher Research Panel, http://www.standards.dfes.gov.uk/ntrp/?version=1
>
> The United Kingdom Teacher Research.net for support and mentoring, http://www.teacherresearch.net/index.htm
>
> University of New Hampshire at Manchester for information about the annual teacher as researcher conference, http://www.unhm.unh.edu/community/teachers-as-researchers-conference/index.php

Some school systems such as Fairfax, Virginia and Madison, Wisconsin support and facilitate teacher research groups as part of their commitment to teacher professional development. Teacher inquiry has become an important tool for educational systems in promoting teacher professional development and thus reforming schooling (Helterbran & Fennimore, 2004). For example, a teacher research group supported by a Florida federally funded regional educational laboratory (SERVE) and university teacher educators created a collaborative model in the form of a "Teachers as Researchers Academy" in which teachers were selected to participate. Teachers conducted teacher research studies that led to improved student performance (Bingham, Parker, Finney, Riley, & Rakes, 2006). One teacher commented,

> I discovered in the process of doing my TR that my ideas and thoughts have merit. Why rely on someone else labeled the 'experts' to tell me what is going on in my own classroom? I know my students, and I know my school climate and situations. Who better to make observations and decisions about my

situation? My opinions and conclusions are applicable and do have professional merit.

(Bingham et al., p. 688)

## Explorations

Go to a teacher research website such as *Networks Online Journal for Teacher Research*, retrieved from http://journals.library.wisc.edu/index.php/networks/about/submissions. Review some of the teacher research articles posted there. Then find the guidelines to authors for submitting teacher research articles. How do these guidelines compare to the ones on the NAEYC website for the teacher research journal, *Voices of Practitioners*?

### Websites of Teacher Research Groups

Berkeley Teacher Research Group: http://csmp.ucop.edu/programs/view/73775/meeting-at-berkeley-teacher-research-group

LSJTRG Literacy for Social Justice Teacher Research Group, St. Louis, Missouri: http://www.umsl.edu/~/sjtrg/

NWP: Teacher Inquiry Communities Network: national network that links sites interested in developing leadership and resources for teacher inquiry and in sharing information and disseminating practices with other sites (Western Massachusetts Writing Project; South Carolina WP; Tennessee WP): http://www.nwporg/cs/public/print/programs/tic

University of California, Davis, School of Education, CRESS Center Teacher Research Group (classroom teachers): http://education.ucdavis.edu/cress-teacher-research

### Teacher Research Online Journals and Networks

AR Expeditions: Action Research Journal: http://arexpeditions.montana.edu/index

Collaborative Action Research Network, CARN international network for promoting collaborative action research:

http://www.did.stu.mmu.ac.uk/carnnew/

http://research.edu.uea.ac.uk/links/care/

Educational Action Research: http://www.tandf.co.uk/journals/titles/09650792.asp

National School Reform Faculty: http://www.nsrfharmony.org

Teacher Research, George Mason University: http://www.gse.gmu.edu/research/tr/

**Additional Resources**

Allen, D., & Blythe, T. (2004). *The Facilitator's book of questions: Tools for looking together at student and teacher work*. New York: Teachers College Press.

Chandler, K., & the Mapleton Teacher-Research Group. (1999). *Spelling inquiry: How one elementary school caught the mnemonic plague*. York, ME: Stenhouse.

Chiseri-Strater, E., & Sunstein, B. S. (2006). *What works? A practical guide for teacher research*. Portsmouth, NH: Heinemann.

Falk, B., & Blumenrich, M. (2005). *The power of questions: A guide to teacher and student research*. Portsmouth, NH: Heinemann.

Fishman, S. M., & McCarthy, L. (2000). *Unplayed tapes: A personal history of collaborative teacher research*. New York: Teachers College Press.

Mohr, M., Rogers, C., Sanford, B., Nocerino, M. A., MacLean, M. S., & Clawson, S. (2004). *Teacher research for better schools*. New York: Teachers College Press.

## TEACHER RESEARCHER NOTEBOOK ENTRY #7

Select an upcoming professional conference that you would like to attend and the requirements for submitting a conference presentation proposal. Using the ideas from this chapter and the proposal guidelines, prepare a proposal for a teacher research conference presentation that you could submit to this conference.

# References

American Psychological Association. (2010). *Publication manual of the American Psychological Association* (6th edition). Washington, DC: American Psychological Association.

Bingham, S. S., Parker, S., Finney, P., Riley, J., & Rakes, J. (May, 2006). The Teachers as researchers academy: Building community, expertise, and a knowledge base for teaching. *Phi Delta Kappan*, 681–688.

Castle, K. (Spring, 2009). The wonder of learning: The hundred Languages of children. *Early Childhood Association of Oklahoma News*, 12–14. Oklahoma City, OK.

Costa, A., & Kallick, B. (1993). Through the lens of a critical friend. *Educational Leadership*, 51(2), 49–51.

Duckworth, E. (1997). *Teacher to teacher*. New York: Teachers College Press.

DuFour, R., & Eaker, R. (1998). *Professional learning communities at work: Best practices for enhancing student achievement*. Alexandria, VA: Association for Supervision and Curriculum Development.

Fosnot, C. (Ed.). (1996). *Constructivism: Theory, perspectives, and practice*. New York: Teachers College Press.

Gandini, L., Etheredge, S., & Hill, L. (Eds.) (2008). *Insights and inspirations from Reggio Emilia: Stories of teachers and children from North America*. Worcester, MA: Davis Publications.

Helterbran, V. R., & Fennimore, B. S. (2004). Collaborative early childhood professional development: Building from a base of teacher investigation. *Early Childhood Education Journal*, 31(4), 267–271.

Hendricks, C. (2009). *Improving schools through action research*. Columbus, OH: Pearson.

Katz, L. G., & Chard, S. C. (1989). *Engaging children's minds: The project approach.* Norwood, NJ: Ablex.

Lamott, A. (1994). *Bird by bird: Some instructions on writing and life.* New York: Anchor Books & Doubleday.

Lieberman, A., & Miller, L. (Eds.) (2008). *Teachers in professional communities: Improving teaching and learning.* New York: Teachers College Press.

Mohr, M. M., Rogers, C., Sanford, B., Nocerino, M., MacLean, M. S., & Clawson, S. (2004). *Working together: A guide for teacher researchers.* New York: Teachers College Press.

Myers, E., & Rust, F. (2003). *Taking action with teacher research.* Portsmouth, NH: Heinemann.

Sobel, D. (1998). *Mapmaking with children.* Portsmouth, NH: Heinemann.

# eight
# What Comes After Research is Completed?

It is here that "rubber meets the road", where people take specific actions to modify teaching practices, develop new classroom procedures, or engage in new learning processes.

Ernie Stringer (2008, p. 147)

This chapter presents information on using teacher research results to take action, make changes, and make improvements in teaching and children's learning. The chapter addresses action plans and advocacy efforts at the individual, program, and community levels. It also shows how to use results to decide what to research next and thus begin a new teacher research cycle. This chapter presents the role of protocols in facilitating the beginning and end of teacher research studies and describes several protocols and their use. The book ends with examples of how teaching has been transformed through teacher research.

It takes much courage and hard work to bring a teacher research study to completion. But merely finishing a study is not enough. To stop after reflecting on results or even with a written report would be to stop too soon and shortchange all the work you have done. It is important to ask at the conclusion of a teacher research study: Now what? What comes next? How can this study benefit my students, my professional development, and the educational community at large? What needs to be done to apply this study in ways that will make a difference? Is there something about this study that will lead into a new teacher research study? Who would care and how can I involve them in next steps? This chapter will help you to know how to begin to answer some of these questions and to recognize the power that teacher research can have in transforming teaching and learning.

## Using Results

Completing a teacher research study can be tiring but also exhilarating once you realize what can be gained from results. There is a temptation to stop with results because so much time has been spent on the study and because results are now in hand. But it is important to consider the various ways to use results to make a difference in your teaching and a contribution to others who may also benefit from knowing your results.

It is important to take some time to consider what to do with the results you have worked hard to get.

Making some type of written report will help you to think about your results and possible implications for you, your program, and for others. Chapter Seven gives many suggestions for written reports, presentations, and journal manuscripts. When you write up your results, then you can share them with a larger audience beyond yourself and even beyond your program. In addition to written reports summarizing results, you can also create an action plan. An **action plan** provides an itinerary about how to apply results to solve a problem, develop an appropriate intervention based on results, implement program-wide changes, and/or engage in advocacy efforts. For example, based on their teacher research results, a small group of teacher researchers who studied their teaching methods for teaching mathematics, advocated at their district level for changes in the adopted mathematics curriculum. Through knowledge gained from their research, they were able to convince others and took a leadership role in the adoption of a new math curriculum for the district. The following section describes action plans and how to create them based on research results.

---

**REFLECTIONS**

Reflect on your own courage to take action and the characteristics you possess that enabled you to take a stand. Recall any experiences you have had in taking a stand on certain causes or educational issues. What action/s did you take? What were the effects of your actions? What would you do differently today compared to your initial actions?

---

## Taking Action

It takes courage and teacher autonomy to put research results into action (Castle and Ethridge, 2003). A type of research similar to teacher research called Action Research (Castle, 2006) puts the focus on the action that follows teacher research. Sometimes that action is in the form of an intervention that a teacher then plans another research study around in order to determine the effectiveness of the intervention. The type of action described in this chapter focuses on action after the fact of doing teacher research in the application of research results to addressing some problem or situation.

The terms teacher research and action research are sometimes used interchangeably to mean the same type of research and sometimes to make a distinction in which action research refers to political activity teachers do based on research results. An action plan in this chapter refers to what teacher researchers plan to do or actions they plan to take with the results of their study, either in making improvements in their individual classrooms, engaging in advocating for political change, or other activities based on results. Taking action may be done by an individual teacher whose results show a need to make changes in his program or by a group of teachers whose research results indicate some needed changes in the entire program or school or even beyond to the district or community level as in the preceding example of changes to the math curriculum adoption. Regardless of whether it is at an individual teacher level or with a larger group, it is important to consider how and when to go about the application of results through creating an action plan. What follows are some suggestions and examples of how to create an action plan.

## Individual Action Plan

Common steps in formulating any action plan include the following:

Reflection on results and what they mean for teaching and learning

Decisions about necessary changes/interventions based on results

A timeline for changes indicating:

- What changes will be made
- Who is involved in making changes
- How changes will be made
- When changes will be made
- Where (location) changes will be made, and
- Assessment of action plan.

You may have noticed that the "why" is missing from what, who, how, when, and where. The "why" consists of the results of the study that has already been done. The "why" or rationale for each step of the action plan is because results call for a change—this is the nature of the teacher research. The last step in the process is to assess the action plan. It is important for the assessment step to lead back to the initial research question. It is important to ask whether the original problem has now been solved or the original situation necessitating the research has been improved. If the answer is "no", then further steps may be necessary to do additional research or to revise the action plan. In this way, teacher research comes full circle back to the need for the research in the first place. If the problem no longer exists, or if the situation has been improved through the action steps, then teacher knowledge has grown beyond the original research problem and plans for new teacher research and development can be generated. The process then is not so much circular as it is an upward spiral of teacher development (as noted in Chapter One).

What follows is an example of an individual action plan of a teacher of 4 year olds based on the preceding steps.

## 8 Week Action Plan for 4 Year Old Classroom

### Reflection on Results and What They Mean for Teaching and Learning

My initial problem was what I perceived as too much disruptive behavior in my classroom of twenty 4 year olds. I have been a teacher for three years but had never had such a disruptive group. My teacher research question focused on when and where in my classroom were the most disruptive behaviors occurring. Data collection involved frequency counts of disruptive behavior, keeping a teacher journal about my perceptions of disruptive behavior, and interviews with the other 4 year old teacher and two kindergarten teachers about disruptive behavior in their class rooms.

My results showed that the greatest frequency of disruptive behaviors (62% of all disruptions) occurred in the area housing the blocks followed by the dramatic play area (31%). In addition, two boys and one girl accounted for 87% of all disruptions.

To apply what I learned from my results, I decided that changes needed to be made in the arrangement of the blocks and dramatic play areas; the number of children allowed in each area at any one time; the composition of individual children playing together in these areas; whole class efforts to build community and friendship bonds; and individual interventions for the three children with the greatest frequency of disruptive behaviors.

The teachers I interviewed gave me new insights on making these changes plus encouragement that changes could be made. In addition, they shared what they did when encountering disruptions that might be helpful to me in making changes such as remaining calm and using logical consequences. I created an action plan to implement needed changes.

**Decisions About Necessary Changes/Interventions Based on Results**

I decided to try some changes in a systematic way and then to assess the outcomes. I decided to relocate the blocks away from the dramatic play area; to restrict play in both areas to not more than three children at any one time in the block area and not more than four in the dramatic play area; to assign the three children with the most frequent disruptive behaviors to play with other children and not with each other except for brief intervals; to hold individual conferences with each of the three children about changes to their behavior including keeping a daily log to send home to their parents complete with what logical consequences I was using with their children; to conduct weekly whole group community building discussions on the importance of peaceful behavior and what it means to be a friend in the classroom; to focus more on recognizing appropriate behaviors and responding to those; and to focus on my own reactions and my teaching behavior and the effect I am having on children's behavior. I will keep a teacher journal for recording my thoughts on what I am doing and my reactions to what is happening.

**A Timeline for Changes**

I will implement the action plan for a period of 8 weeks and then assess how it is working.

**What, When, Where and How Changes Will Be Made**

*Weekend Afternoon Before Week 1*

Relocate blocks and dramatic play areas giving more space between and in each area.

*Week 1*

Post population cards in areas and show and tell class that only three can be in blocks and only four in dramatic play at a time; follow up with reminders and redirection of children to other areas.

*Week 2*

Conference with three children about restricting their play with each other allowing them to play together only during outside time and assigning each a buddy, another child to befriend and play with, to help them establish themselves in new small play groups; begin whole group discussions on appropriate behavior and building friendship relationships.

*Week 3*

Conference individually with three children about behaviors to substitute for their disruptive behaviors; logical consequences to disruptive behaviors; keeping a daily behavior log that goes home to parents; and what it means to be a friend and a contributor to classroom community. Explain plan to parents of three children. Continue to conduct whole group discussions on appropriate behaviors and friendship relationships. Begin keeping behavior logs.

*Weeks 4–8*

Continue to conduct whole group discussions on appropriate behaviors and friendship relationships plus add how to be a contributing member of our classroom community; continue to have individual conferences with the three children by helping them develop appropriate relationships with all children in our program; continue to send home their daily behavior logs and conference with their parents about their behaviors at home; monitor for disruptive behavior and implement new logical consequences; and monitor my own responses to disruptive behavior by writing in my teacher journal.

*Week 8*

I will assess the success of the action plan by comparing frequency of disruptive behaviors prior to implementing the action plan to frequency at the end of the 8 week period.

### Who is Involved in Making Changes

I plan to implement changes to my own classroom and teaching. I will need the help of all children in my program, especially the three children who are the most disruptive and whose behaviors will hopefully change with the interventions. I will also need the help and cooperation of the three children's parents and the support of my administrator. I will continue to rely on the support and encouragement of my teacher colleagues.

### Assessment of Action Plan

During **Week 8** I will assess the implementation of my action plan. I will tabulate frequency counts of disruptive behavior I have made during the previous weeks. I will review my teacher journal for signs of success including changes I have made in my teaching and in my attitude. If the disruptive behaviors have significantly been reduced, then I will decide what further implementation will be necessary, if any. If there has been no change in the level of disruptive behavior, then I will need to rethink a new plan, possibly involving others more knowledgeable about the problem of disruptive behavior. I will also delve more deeply into the professional literature on disruptive behavior and how to manage classrooms.

**REFLECTIONS**

Reflect on the preceding example and think about what you might have done differently in this situation. Then discuss this example with another early childhood teacher and compare your reactions plus any other changes you might make in this teacher's action plan.

## Program Level Action Plan

Teachers who work together in doing a teacher research study can proceed through the same steps as in the example of the individual teacher. They may reflect on their results and decide that program level changes are necessary. In order to apply results, the entire program or parts of the program must be involved in order for improvements to be made. The teachers who have done the research together may decide to meet on a weekly basis to create an action plan for the program. In order for the action plan to be successful, there must be buy-in among all teachers involved in the program. This may be more feasible if all teachers in the program have also participated in the teacher research study. If some teachers did not participate but may stand to benefit from applying results, then the teacher researchers may want to try to elicit the participation of the other teachers. However, it is not uncommon for some teachers not involved in the research to resist any changes coming from results of the study. In this case the best outcome may be to obtain agreement of the other teachers that they will not stand in the way of changes in the program.

But if resistance is too great, then the best outcome may be to get the resisting teachers' agreement that while they're welcome to opt out, other teachers will be making changes and no one should be getting in the way of anyone else's decision. This may be the best compromise that can be reached in situations in which teachers resist changes. Program level action plans contain all the elements of individual teacher action plans plus the element of negotiated changes. Teachers who have served a leadership role in the research or administrators supportive of teacher research may serve as facilitators of these negotiations. It is always a good idea to involve administrators and keep them informed of what is happening with the research and the application of results. The main focus should always be on improving teaching and learning for all children in the program.

## Advocacy and Community Level Action

There are times when teacher research results have implications for action beyond the teachers involved in the research, and even beyond the local or district levels. Teacher research results can be used for advocacy efforts in which teachers advocate for changing certain situations based on research results. Advocacy efforts involve speaking out in favor of making changes and bringing certain issues, such as equity issues, to an awareness level so that those in decision making positions can make changes in policy or laws to address these issues.

Occasionally an issue will activate teachers to take a stand and advocate for what is in the best interests of children. If you are familiar with the history of the Developmentally Appropriate Practices movement in the 1980s, then you may be aware of teachers' advocacy efforts to change developmentally inappropriate practices such as the highly didactic teaching practice of focusing only on children's rote memorization of content that could be regurgitated on tests. Teachers used the child development and learning research literature to advocate for change. Advocacy efforts took place at the local, state, and national levels. Because of its size and advocacy history, the National Association for the Education of Young Children (NAEYC) formed a task group that worked for five years on the issue. One result of this work that has made a major impact on education in this country was the NAEYC Position Statement on Developmentally Appropriate Practice (1986) and the subsequent publication in its third edition of *Developmentally Appropriate Practice in Early Childhood Programs Serving Children from Birth through Age 8* (Copple and Bredekamp, 2009). This book has become a highly significant resource in early childhood practice and has resulted in beneficial changes for educating children. All of this started with teachers who were concerned about the negative effects of some teaching practices and who worked to make changes.

Another example of such an action plan involved several elementary teachers advocating for increased resources, including additional teachers qualified to teach children who were English language learners (ELL). These teachers advocated for change at the state level, based on results from their teacher research study that clearly showed ELL children in their program were not getting appropriate education and subsequently had very low performance in all areas including end of instruction tests. Based on their research results, teachers concluded that more efforts were needed to get ELL teachers into classrooms and to equip existing teachers with the knowledge and skills needed to address the learning needs of ELL children.

The group of teacher researchers formulated an action plan that involved sharing their research results with other educators at the local and state levels and sending a written report of their research results and advocated changes to their school district and to their state department of education. A few of the teachers were able to attend legislative hearings about the issue of the need for more ELL teachers, and one of the teachers was appointed to a state task force created to address the problem and make recommendations for change.

Turning teacher research results into action plans can take many forms at the individual, group, program, local, and state levels. Action plans enable the results of teacher research to have a greater impact on a wider audience than just the individual teacher. Teacher research action plans have been shown to reform education from the inside out (Altrichter, Feldman, Posch, and Somekh, 1993/2008; Cochran-Smith & Lytle, 2009; Pine, 2009).

## Explorations

Explore the websites of early childhood professional associations such as the NAEYC website, www.naeyc.org, for advocacy efforts of these associations and their results. Look for evidence of position papers on various topics plus reports of advocacy groups, committees, and task forces. Then interview an experienced early childhood teacher about her experiences doing advocacy work. Find out what issues are most important to her that she would like to see changed at higher levels, such as in her state or at the national level. Identify one early childhood advocacy group and review their work looking for action plans and implementation of those plans.

## A Classroom Culture of Inquiry

Teachers who have conducted teacher research and recognize the benefits to be gained can become leaders among other teachers in helping to create a classroom culture of inquiry by modeling what this means for other teachers and children in their classrooms. One entry point for other teachers to become teacher researchers is the case in which teachers engage children in doing their own research or inquiry that results in children's meaningful learning of content as well as research skills and strengths. Teachers who have witnessed children's enthusiasm and energy in doing their own inquiries may become interested in their own teacher research inquiries and may even engage children in inquiry as they do teacher research on children, as pointed out by Mardell, LeeKeenan, Given, Robinson, Merino, and Liu-Constant (2009, p. 13), "As we promote the culture of inquiry, we learn about teaching young children; and as we learn about supporting children's capabilities, we strengthen our adult culture of inquiry."

Involving children in research is not a new approach to teaching and can be seen in the history of education dating back to project work during the progressive education movement (Foster and Headley, 1936). One example of today's approach to project work involving children's inquiry comes from the influence of the Reggio Emilia approach (Katz and Chard, 2000) in which children's interests determine the direction that inquiry will take. Typically in using the project approach, teachers encourage children to generate questions they want to get answered about a topic. Teachers then provide appropriate resources for children's inquiry including materials, books, computer programs, field trips, speakers, and activities. Children do project activities and represent their learning in many ways in their constructions, writings, drawings, dramatic play, and other activities. Teachers also encourage children to share their learning with other children and adults. Teachers create documentation panels that display children's learning through work samples, photographs, and captions describing the work. A culminating project of the inquiry may require children to share their work and what they learned about their questions with another class or with their parents during a special events night. Kindergarten teacher, Isauro Michael Escamilla (2004), engaged his children in a project on shadows and writes, "As I record and document the children's drawings, conversations, and ideas, I then engage in my own research process of understanding the power of the children's learning and of my teaching". (p. 4)

Teacher research done in a collaborative fashion by groups of teachers fosters a culture of inquiry within the local context of their environments. Teachers researching together tend to get the interest and attention of other teachers within their location who then join the group and establish a culture of inquiry. As Stringer (2008) states, "As a 'culture of inquiry', action research therefore becomes an integral part of the teaching/learning, curriculum, assessment, and planning processes of classroom and school" (p. 148). There are various ways that such a culture can become established and thrive.

Teacher research groups can work in many ways to create such a culture or what Cochran-Smith and Lytle (2009) call an "inquiry stance." Teachers who perceive a problem to study can become leaders of teacher research groups encouraging other teachers and serving as role models for creating such a culture.

Those teachers who collaborate in teacher research projects focused on studying the same or similar research questions across classrooms—such as how best to teach mathematics—need to decide together how to apply results. There are many ways to make these decisions and many group formats that can help with these decisions such as participation in self-studies, lesson studies, critical friends groups, or protocol groups. Regardless of the format, deciding how to apply results is usually done by meeting with those teachers who have been involved in the study to discuss next steps. Such group decision-making sessions can be open-ended discussions or can involve a more structured format such as using protocols to have structured conversations. Either established or emerging teacher leaders can take an active part in facilitating these group sessions. If higher education faculty have also been involved with the research, they may be called upon to facilitate group discussions. Or the group may also decide that leadership in the discussions will rotate. Either way, it is important to have someone or a few people to initiate getting the group together, schedule meetings, find appropriate meeting locations, and attend to the convenience and comforts of group members such as procuring refreshments, meals, comfortable surroundings, and appropriate technical equipment.

## Collaborative Group Approaches

### Japanese Lesson Study Group

Japanese lesson study was brought to the United States and became a model for studying teaching in the 1990s (Stigler & Hiebert, 1999). It is a format that can be used by teacher researcher groups to address how best to make changes based on research results. It is a collaborative approach among teachers who know each other and feel comfortable working together to critique and give feedback to each other through observing each other teach, analyzing teaching episodes or lessons, and then meeting with the presenting teacher to ask questions and give feedback (Watanabe, 2002).

A type of Japanese lesson study focuses on a research lesson in which the presenting teacher presents research on certain approaches to teaching. The research lesson study can be used in collaborative teacher research groups considering certain teaching interventions as either part of the research to be implemented or as an implication for the application of the intervention based on teacher research results. Japanese lesson study can be a format to help teacher researchers analyze and learn to apply certain teaching approaches that seem called for based on the results of the teacher research study.

### Critical Friends Group

A critical friends group is a group of teachers who come together to support each other and give each other critical and constructive feedback within an atmosphere of care, trust, and encouragement (Bambino, 2002; McDonald, Mohr, Dichter, & McDonald, 2007). Critical friends groups form for many reasons including to promote teacher professional development, to facilitate teachers' writing, to study student work, and to do teacher research. Time is spent in the group initially building trust and making connections. Activities in critical friends groups center on community building, reflection, and sharing perspectives on teaching. Being open to others' perspectives is important and can be very insightful into one's own teaching. Critical friends groups meet regularly and may use protocols for some group meetings to have a more structured format for presenting student work or other teaching issues and getting feedback from group members. Critical friends groups where teachers get together with trusted colleagues can provide a meaningful format for discussing applications of teacher research results.

## Protocol Groups

Protocol groups can function at the end of a study in order to determine where to go next, or at the beginning of a study to help formulate and refine research questions. Protocols can be used by teacher researchers to raise research questions or issues, to plan research studies, and to consider the meaning of student work. Such group meetings focus on the meaning of the research. While problem solving may occur through protocol group discussions, it is a by-product, and not the main purpose of using protocols that is to deepen understanding.

## The Role of Protocols in Teacher Research

**Protocols** are conducted in groups such as when teachers meet to discuss mutual concerns, issues, innovations, students, and ideas for teacher research. Protocols are structured group discussions and conversations on topics relevant to the group participating in the discussion. There are many different kinds of protocols to fit a great variety of topics and objectives. For example, there are protocols to discuss student work, approaches to teaching certain content such as mathematics, teacher need for clarification of issues, and generation of mutual teacher research topics and questions.

Protocols are conducted by a group, such as a group of teachers, for the purpose of increasing understanding and enlightenment of the object or topic being discussed (McDonald et al., 2007). For example, the Descriptive Review of the Child protocol (Himley and Carini, 2000) is used by groups of teachers to come to a deeper understanding of the growth and development of individual children for whom teachers are responsible. This particular protocol is very appropriate for early childhood teachers who want to better understand children and their role in teaching them. The benefit of teachers using protocols in a collaborative way is that multiple perspectives shared in the group can enhance everyone's thinking in ways that individual reflection cannot. Many heads are better than one in discussing problems and dealing with issues.

The format of doing a protocol is very structured. Protocols have phases or steps that are worked through within a time schedule (Allen and Blythe, 2004). Each phase of a protocol is timed. Protocol discussions adhere to the time limits for each phase in order to accomplish the purpose of each protocol. Most protocol discussions can be completed in about 45 to 60 minutes, with some shorter than others. An appropriate group size for a protocol discussion is about 8 to 10 individuals. When more than 10 need to be involved, then a smaller inner circle of 8 to 10 conduct the protocol while the rest form an outer circle of observers who at some point may have input into the discussion.

Larger groups are more difficult to facilitate so it is best to keep the group small, especially at the beginning when learning to use protocols for the first time. It is also important for the participants to know each other, to trust each other, and to feel comfortable discussing issues with each other. There are some protocols that help with getting acquainted and establishing community within the group.

A facilitator of the protocol is designated to guide the discussion. The facilitator makes sure that the time schedule is followed by reminding participants when it is time to move on from one phase to another. The facilitator also guides the group in keeping to the format for each phase of a protocol discussion such as when a phase calls for a round of one question per participant. The facilitator makes sure the structure is followed and the discussion does not become just a gab session (Allen and Blythe, 2004).

Protocol discussions begin with a teacher who presents a piece of student work, a question, or an issue for the group to consider. Then depending on the protocol in use, participants have a chance to ask clarifying questions and/or give feedback to the presenting teacher to consider. The presenting teacher then has a chance to reflect on the ideas presented by the participants and to respond to them. Group members can rotate the roles of being the facilitator and presenting teacher on a voluntary basis. Protocol group discussions may occur on an "as needed" basis or on a regular meeting schedule such as every other week.

## Using Protocols During Teacher Research

In collaborative teacher research studies such as when a group of teachers within a school is working together doing the research, protocol discussions can be a useful tool in facilitating the research. Teachers may agree to meet every two weeks, for example, to consider issues emerging from the research or to discuss pieces of data in order to understand what the data are telling them about the study. It is recommended to begin with a protocol or two that will help teachers become better acquainted and gel as a community working together within a safe environment. One such protocol is the Postcard protocol (McDonald et al., 2007) in which the facilitator asks participants to select a black and white postcard and consider in what ways the picture on the postcard represents their views of themselves as learners or as teachers. Each participant then takes a turn showing their selected postcard and describing how it fits them as a learner or teacher.

The facilitator may begin with a round focused on how the postcard represents the participants as learners and then do another round on how the postcard or a different selected postcard represents them as teachers. To initiate the protocol, the facilitator may pass a deck of postcards face down around the group and ask each participant to select a postcard sight unseen or display the postcards face up on a table and ask participants to select one after viewing the whole set. Through sharing their ideas, participants come to know each other better as teachers and learners and come to a deeper understanding of their various perspectives on teaching and learning. Black and white postcards are used to better facilitate interpretations of the postcards, although color postcards may be used as well.

Once there is a commitment of participants to work together doing teacher research and once a sense of community in the group has been established, other protocols may be used periodically during the teacher research phase to discuss research issues, clarify the meaning of data, or to find ways to move beyond obstacles to the research.

An appropriate protocol for studying student work or analyzing a piece of data is the Tuning protocol (McDonald et al., 2007). In the Tuning protocol, the presenting teacher may present a data piece, such as an example of a child's work, and some questions she has about it. Participants then give feedback about their reactions to the teacher's questions and to the data piece in terms of what it might mean, and how it might be relevant to the research. Participants may give feedback or ask questions of the presenting teacher who listens carefully but does not speak until a later round after she has a chance to reflect and then give her reactions to what has been said by participants. The idea is not to challenge the teacher or to put her on the spot, but rather to offer ideas or questions that she may not have previously considered.

This step is then followed by an open discussion about the data piece and any insights coming from the rounds. For example, the presenting teacher may show a data piece that is a child's journal writing replete with the child's invented spelling of words the teacher thinks the child should be able to spell conventionally. Participants may ask the presenting teacher why she thinks the words should be spelled correctly, what this work might mean about the child's ability to do narrative writing, and what it tells the presenting teacher about her research question on determining the stages of individual children's writing development. The teacher's thinking may then be expanded based on feedback received from the group. She may develop insights about the data and what it is telling her that she may not have previously considered.

Peeling the Onion is a protocol that might be used to help teachers decide on what types of data to collect to answer their research questions (McDonald et al., 2007). This protocol helps teachers peel away various parts of a problem until getting to a more basic understanding of the various aspects of the problem in order to address it in meaningful ways. For example, a presenting teacher may want to initially study why certain children in her program exclude other children with special needs. She gives the example of two children in her program who are diagnosed as autistic and are excluded from certain play groups. Through exploring this issue with her group and peeling the layers, she gets to a point where she realizes the question she really wants to study is how to create an inclusive classroom community that involves all children in the program. Through better clarification of her research focus, she can begin to identity more appropriate data sources to help answer her research question.

There are many appropriate Protocols available for use. The book, *The Power of Protocols* by McDonald, Mohr, Dichter, and McDonald (2007) is a great resource for many protocols helpful to teacher researchers. Another good resource, especially for protocol facilitators, is *The Facilitator's Book of Questions* by Allen and Blythe (2004). These two resources may benefit newly formed collaborative research groups wanting to begin using protocols. Many of the existing protocols have been developed by individuals and groups in the National Writing Project for teacher collaboration in general and for teacher research collaboration as well. An additional protocol resource is the National School Reform Faculty (NSRF) website, www.nsrfharminy.org.

## Using Protocols Following Teacher Research

At the conclusion of a teacher research study, it is important for the collaborating teachers to consider implications of the study for their own teaching, for the entire program in general, and possibly for the broader community. Teachers come together to discuss what went well, what didn't go so well, and how best to apply results to their individual situations.

Two Protocols, among others, can be used to deliberate a teacher research follow-up. The Constructivist Learning Groups Protocol takes advantage of everyone's thinking about the implications of the research. This protocol helps participants analyze what the research means and how best to use results to improve the program. Participants work in small groups and the facilitator gives the groups specific questions to discuss and propose workable answers such as how best to use research results. Several rounds of questions and answers are conducted. Following the rounds, participants are asked to reflect and respond to what they have learned in the process. The end result is a workable plan for the application of the research results to improving the program for children and teachers. For example, in a teacher research study of various teaching approaches to mathematics, teachers may participate in this protocol and conclude that one approach involving engaging children in thinking through their own problem solving strategies is a worthwhile approach that participants agree to implement in their teaching and then revisit at a later date.

A second protocol for following up a teacher research study is The Success Analysis Protocol in which participants discuss and analyze the successes of the teacher research study and even those things that were major challenges. This is also a protocol that can be used for exploring what works best in teaching and for sharing various success techniques with group members.

## Using Protocols to Determine Future Teacher Research Studies

A protocol, Inquiry Circles (Bisplinghoff, www.nsrfharmony.org) or a modified version of it can be used at the beginning of a study to determine appropriate research questions to study and can also be used when a study has been completed to determine next steps and a future teacher research study to conduct next. This protocol values the role of narrative in constructing meaning about one's professional work.

At the beginning of the protocol in the first phase, the facilitator asks each participant to write a teacher research question to be the focus of each participant's teacher research and to share that question with the group. Then the facilitator asks participants to think of a time when they felt successful in their professional work or felt that they made a difference. Each participant writes a narrative about this successful professional experience and then tells her story to a partner who listens carefully and takes notes. The partner then tells her story as they take turns sharing narratives. Each partner then shares her partner's story with the whole group. Participants then do a round of asking clarifying questions of the author of the story who responds. Other rounds involve giving warm and cool feedback about the story and its meaning to the author.    Each partner completes a storytelling sheet on which they are asked to list the top ideas or themes found in the story plus other aspects of the story that stand out to them. These storytelling sheets are given to the partner/author of the story. The author reflects on what their partner has written. The facilitator then asks participants to return to their original research question written at the beginning of the protocol and re-write their question in light of what they have learned from participation in the protocol.

The rewrite is usually a changed and more refined version of the original question that has also become more personalized for the author. The rewrite is usually a clearer and more relevant version of the research question. In addition, having an opportunity to reflect on one's professional success tends to rejuvenate teachers with new energy and enthusiasm for doing the research.

Using protocols at the beginning and throughout the teacher research study will aid in the collaboration of the work. Participation in protocol groups helps in teacher professional development and results in providing a supportive network for those who participate.

## Transforming Teaching Through Teacher Research

Teachers who do teacher research are transformed by it (Castle, 2006; Cochran-Smith & Lytle, 2009; Helterbran and Fennimore, 2004). They do not go back to the status quo but continue to change and grow in their knowledge of their teaching and how to improve it as stated by Jeffrey Wood (2005):

> I can no longer teach without using teacher research, whether it is a formal study … or the daily analysis of my classroom practices. Teacher research gives me the attitude of a learner and helps me see how to shape my classroom practice to better guide my students and support their learning. Through collecting and analyzing daily events I have a heightened sense of what is happening in the classroom, freeing me up to better listen to and respond to the needs of my students, allowing me to learn from them.
>
> (p. 10)

Teacher research can be transformative in the sense that once you do it, you are changed as a teacher and will look at teaching and learning differently. There is often a desire to share one's research experience with others and to encourage other teachers on the benefits of doing teacher research. You are no longer just a teacher, but a teacher who is capable of generating important research questions and seeking answers to those questions for the improvement of teaching and learning.

Cochran-Smith and Lytle (2009) write about teacher research, or what they prefer to call practitioner research, as a way to take an Inquiry Stance in education. They describe practitioner research as being transformative for teachers. "We regard 'inquiry as stance' as a grounded theory of action that positions the role of practitioners and practitioner knowledge as central to the goal of transforming teaching, learning, leading, and schooling." (p. 119) Teachers who take an inquiry stance continuously question not only their teaching but the entire educational enterprise in terms of social justice and equity. Inquiry as stance focuses on the knowledge generated by teacher inquiry and inquiry communities and the perspectives taken in the inquiry including the positions taken by teachers applying the generated knowledge to their practice. According to Cochran-Smith and Lytle, inquiry as stance can transform education leading to a more just and democratic society through inquiry, critical reflection, and action. They say,

> In educational settings where teachers, students, and other stakeholders are engaged in inquiry and mutual deliberations, common assumptions about the roles and outcomes of teaching, learning, and schooling are debated and transformed. So too are ideas about teachers as leaders.
>
> (p. 148)

Cochran-Smith and Lytle view teacher research as a social movement transforming the landscape of education. They call for teacher researchers in the US to connect and collaborate with others around the world to work for educational change focused on social justice and to move away from the idea of the transmission of knowledge approach to teaching. Their book, *Inquiry as Stance*, gives numerous examples of teacher researchers who have been transformed and whose work has transformed others resulting in significant educational change. After concluding a project on social justice in a primary classroom, teacher researcher Elizabeth Goss (2009) concluded:

> The project reinforced my belief that classroom community can be built around sharing, discussing, and working to resolve social justice issues. It showed what democracy in action looks like in my classroom. It reinforced my belief in using education to transform our ways of thinking and our ways of living in this complicated world.
>
> (p. 14)

## Conclusion

Teaching experience alone will not necessarily result in better teaching. But teacher research will almost certainly result in better teaching because it involves a thinking teacher looking for answers and motivated to make changes. A teacher researcher is seeking the answer to the general question, How can I do things better? This inquiry will take a teacher through a lifetime career of professional development and lead to a wisdom about teaching that can't be gained in any other way. What is unique about early childhood teacher research is the continuing focus on making things better for children. According to Stribling and Kraus (2007):

> Teacher researchers are reflective practitioners who don't just teach the children a certain way because "that's the way it has always been done." They examine how the children are learning and try to figure out a better way to teach the concepts so the children can grow into productive thinkers and learners.
>
> (p. 16)

### From the Field

Annie Ortiz, a National Board Certified teacher and teacher leader in her state and in the National Writing Project's Teacher Inquiry Communities, perceived a problem among her male elementary students who were not as engaged in writing and literacy as the girls. She found a similar concern among fellow teachers who were also concerned about their male students' lack of interest in reading and writing. Annie decided to do a teacher research study on boys' literacy. She asked a teacher from each grade level in her elementary school to participate. She wrote a grant to get funding to give each teacher a small stipend for participation as well as to purchase some books giving the most recent research findings on boys' literacy. The main research questions focused on why boys are less engaged in literacy and how to get boys more engaged in literacy activities.

During a school year, the teachers read the professional literature and met regularly to discuss data collection and analysis. Their study yielded results that helped the teachers make changes in the entire program at their school, pre-K through fifth grade. This example of a collaborative teacher research study is evidence that teacher research can be used to change school climate and improve education for children and teachers. What follows are some reflections that Annie made at the conclusion of the study:

### Boys' Literacy Study: Implications and Action Plan

*Annie Ortiz*

My study involved facilitating a group of teachers in researching their own teaching practices focused on boys' literacy choices. The teachers involved with me in the study changed their teaching, interactions, and responses to boys' literacy choices. Their knowledge of teaching and teacher research shifted throughout the year the study was done and continues to change.

I became interested in boys' literacy after reading a book called *Misreading Masculinity* by Newkirk (2002). This book suggested since most elementary teachers are white females, they might not read what boys like to read. At the same time, school board members questioned why Black and Hispanic boys were scoring lower in literacy. I applied and received a $5,000 grant from the National Foundation for the Improvement of Education (NFIE) to conduct a study of boys' literacy and provide some books and a small stipend to teacher participants in the study. Eight teachers (all female) participated, one from each grade level and the art teacher and library media specialist. Our research question focused on the ways in which we support boys' literacy specifically in reading, visual literacy, and writing. Data sources included teachers' field notes, child surveys, and child artifacts such as their writings and drawings. Findings indicated similar themes in what boys read, write, and draw. The themes in their literacy activities were nonfiction and real things, monsters and superheroes, action, and humor, especially gross humor.

There are two major implications coming from our study of boys' literacy. One has to do with what I learned as the facilitator of the study. I realized how much impact teacher research could have to change the professional atmosphere of a school. Conversations in the hallway were about things teachers had tried, noticed or wondered about instead of gossip. I realized how inclusive instead of exclusive this process could be. Other teachers asked us about what we were finding out, shared articles they found, or suggested books boys might like to read. Now I'm wondering based on this study about facilitating this group of teachers further, such as with developing a professional publication reporting our results. I would like to help them lead their own grade levels through a teacher research project. Or I might even possibly facilitate another group of teachers in a school-wide project.

I noticed that my questioning skills developed through this process. I learned that I need to have more types of ways to find a research question to study.

I know it takes time to find a question but maybe if I had more ways to keep identifying a question the group might have come to our research question sooner. I have since identified some techniques that might be possible to use in a different circumstance.

The second major implication focuses on the group and how the results have impacted group members. For example, the kindergarten and first grade teachers have begun to collaborate with the librarian about how to check out books for younger children. Books are selected by both the teacher and the librarian and set out for children to choose from. Teachers and children selected more nonfiction books than they had before because our results showed boys like to read nonfiction more than fiction. The importance of searching for books has lead to more time in the library spent on book selection.

The fourth and fifth grade teachers facilitating book clubs are now for the first time adding nonfiction books into their clubs. Because of the grant funding, each teacher researcher in the group had $300 to spend in their classrooms. Most of them bought graphic novels (popular among boys) or added to their nonfiction collections. Because of her participation in the study and her budget, the library media specialist added many more graphic novels and nonfiction books to the library based on what we learned about boys' book preferences.

Results from our research have also impacted communications with parents. For example, one member of our teacher research group overheard a parent tell his son he could buy two "real" books, but not comic books at our annual school-wide book fair. The teacher researcher, based on learning about how much boys like comic books and read them, shared this information with the parent who then let his child select both a real book and a comic book.

The afterschool reading tutor, a member of our teacher research group, and who had only boys in her program, based her reading selections on our results and began to incorporate more graphic novels, nonfiction books, and drawing activities as strategies to get boys more interested in reading. Similarly, our library media specialist in our summer program consisting mostly of boys, taught the boys how to make book bags and how to check out books of interest. She also selected sets of nonfiction and graphic novels for the reading teachers to use.

The second and fifth grade teachers in our group had their classes become reading and writing buddies. The fifth graders became scribes of the second graders and they wrote stories together. Drawing before writing became another strategy teachers used to encourage writing.

The art teacher used the results about boys' interests in superheroes to bring in a cartoonist to teach all fourth grade students how to draw and design superheroes. Based on the finding that boys rely on visual information, teacher research members identified state learner outcomes for visual literacy to incorporate in each grade level. Since the fifth grade curriculum and assessment focuses on learning about explorers, the teachers along with the library media specialist developed a plan for students to design explorer trading cards.

Based on the finding of the writing survey and quick writes we used that showed topics boys like to write about, the fourth grade teachers implemented girl or boy only writing groups. Cartooning became a series of writing lessons for third and fourth graders. The fourth graders turned biographies into comic books and third graders did book reviews as comics. Whereas it hadn't been accepted in the upper grades, drawing as a way into writing became accepted in each grade level. Drawing also became a tool for revision.

The realization that boys will draw and write about violence helped teachers in this group change how they responded to boys. One teacher who had sent a boy to the office for violence in his writing before the study took place, learned to react differently to boys' writing.

The effects of the implications of our research study impacted not only the teachers who collaborated in the study but also involved other classrooms in the school as well. The teachers who participated shared with their grade levels. Collaboration between the art teacher and the library media specialist impacted all students in the school. Responses to what boys would read, write, or draw would now be very different for the teachers involved in the study. The implications from the study will be far reaching and long lasting.

## Explorations

Explore various protocols and find one for studying children's work. Share what you have learned about doing this protocol with a friend. Put yourself in the role of the presenting teacher and identify an example of a child's piece of work or artifact you might present to a protocol group to gain a deeper understanding of the child's work and its meaning for the child's learning. If possible, engage with a group in the protocol you have chosen.

## TEACHER RESEARCHER NOTEBOOK ENTRY #8

Review your previous journal entries and reflect on what you have learned from reading this book. Record in your journal any new questions you have about early childhood teacher research based on what you have learned to this point. You may have learned that teacher research often begins with a question, then comes a journey to find results and wisdom, and finally some new questions emerge. We continue to develop as professionals through teacher research in our mission to make things better for children.

### Additional Resources

Looking at Student Work Collaborative (LASW) www.lasw.org

National School Reform Faculty (NSRF) www.nsrfharmony.org

National School Reform Faculty New York Center www.nsrfnewyork.org

# References

Allen, D., & Blythe, T. (2004). *The facilitator's book of questions.* New York: Teachers College Press and Oxford, OH: National Staff Development Council.

Altrichter, H., Feldman, A., Posch, P., & Somekh, B. (1993/2008). *Teachers investigate their work.* New York: Routledge, Taylor & Francis.

Bambino, D. (2002). Critical friends. *Educational Leadership, 59*(6), 25–27.

Bisplinghoff, B. Inquiry Circles Protocol. Retrieved January 22, 2011, from www.nsrfharmony.org

Castle, K. (2006). Autonomy through pedagogical research. *Teaching and Teacher Education, 22,* 1094–1103.

Castle, K., & Ethridge, E. A. (2003). Urgently needed: Autonomous early childhood teacher educators. *Journal of Early Childhood Teacher Education, 24,* 111–118.

Cochran-Smith, M., & Lytle, S. L. (2009). *Inquiry as stance: Practitioner research for the next generation.* New York: Teachers College Press.

Copple, C., & Bredekamp, S. (Eds.) (2009). *Developmentally appropriate practice in early childhood programs serving children from birth through age 8* (3rd edition). Washington, DC: National Association for the Education of Young Children.

Escamilla, I. M. (2004). A dialogue with the shadows. *Voices of Practitioners,* 1–5. Retrieved January 22, 2011, from www.naeyc.org/publications/vop/articles

Foster, J. C., & Headley, N. E. (1936). *Education in the kindergarten.* New York: American Book Company.

Goss, E. (2009). If I were president: Teaching social justice in the primary classroom. *Voices of Practitioners, 10,* 1–4. Retrieved January 22, 2011, from www.naeyc.org/publications/vop/articles

Helterbran, V. R., & Fennimore, B. S. (2004). Collaborative early childhood professional development: Building from a base of teacher investigation. *Early Childhood Education Journal, 31*(4), 267–271.

Himley, M., & Carini, P. F. (2000). *From another angle.* New York: Teachers College Press.

Katz, L. G., & Chard, S. C. (2000). *Engaging children's minds: The project approach* (2nd edition). Norwood, NJ: Ablex.

Mardell, B., LeeKeenan, D., Given, H., Robinson, D., Merino, B., & Liu-Constant, Y. (2009). Zooms: Promoting schoolwide inquiry and improving practice. *Voices of Practitioners, 11,* 1–15. Retrieved January 22, 2011, from www.naeyc.org/publications/vop/articles

McDonald, J. P., Mohr, N., Dichter, A., & McDonald, E. C. (2007). *The power of protocols* (2nd edition). New York: Teachers College Press.

NAEYC. (1986; 1996). Developmentally appropriate practice in early childhood programs serving children from birth through age 8. A position statement of the National Association for the Education of Young Children. Washington, DC: NAEYC.

Newkirk, T. (2002). *Misreading masculinity: Boys, literacy and popular culture.* Portsmouth, NH: Heinemann.

Pine, G. J. (2009). *Teacher action research: Building knowledge democracies.* Los Angeles: Sage.

Stigler, J. W., & Hiebert, J. (1999). *The teaching gap: Best ideas from the world's teachers for improving education in the classroom.* New York: Simon & Schuster.

Stribling, S. M., & Kraus, S. M. (2007). Content and mechanics: Understanding first grade writers. *Voices of Practitioners.* Retrieved Januaary 22, 2011, from www.naeyc.org/publications/vop/articles

Stringer, E. (2008). *Action research in education* (2nd edition). Columbus, OH: Pearson, Merrill, Prentice Hall.

Watanabe, T. (2002). Learning from Japanese lesson study. *Educational Leadership, 59*(6), 36–39.

Wood, J. W. (2005). Moses's story: Critical literacy and social justice in an urban kindergarten. *Voices of Practitioners,* 1–12. Retrieved January 22. 2011, from www.naeyc.org/publications/vop/articles

# appendix A
# Ethnographic Description of a First Grade Classroom

## *Peggy Lisenbee*

**Date:** 2-12-2008
**Time:** 1:20 p.m.
**Temperature:** 75 degrees inside (it was too cold to go outside so they had inside recess at lunch today)
**Setting: Physical Elements of the Classroom:**

The room is quiet. There are no children here right now, but there is a low humming sound emitted from the fan for the white board projector. The blinds are closed on the two middle windows of the six windows on the far wall of the rectangular shaped classroom. The side walls of the classroom are not parallel to each other but instead are angled towards the back wall making the room bigger at the back wall and smaller by the doorway (the entire school building is round in its shape).

The floor is covered with blue indoor/outdoor carpet except for a four foot square area by the doorway with white rubber tiles speckled with gray and black dots and lines. The room is lit by florescent lighting with three additional lamps located throughout the room—one on the back shelf, one on the table by the computers by the doorway and one by the teacher's desk. Only the back half of the florescent lights are on at this time so that the white board projects the images more vividly.

The walls around the classroom display 18 Lifeskills, 8 Multiple Intelligences, and 71 Learning Community Guidelines that the school district promotes being taught to students as well as student work, inspirational posters, phonics skill posters and calendar/school informational items. There are stuffed animals, books, baskets of glue/scissors/pencils, beach balls, animal figurines, markers, crayons, erasers, and photographs located throughout the room. The classroom didn't have a smell possibly because I am stopped up with sinus issues, but since there aren't any children in the room, I would hope that there wouldn't be any smells lingering in the classroom.

Upon entering the classroom through double wooden doors in the middle of the wall, there is a table to the left of the doorway draped with some blue/green material that has two computers on it. Next to the computer table, there is a three foot by three foot by three foot horizontal storage cabinet angled in the corner of the room with student mailboxes sitting on top of it. The side wall to the left of the doorway has blue felt covering a three foot tall bulletin board that starts about two feet off the floor and runs the entire length of the wall with green corrugated wavy borders surrounding the blue felt of the bulletin board.

The rest of the wall is composed of concrete blocks painted a whitish/blue color. A white board is attached to the bulletin board on the other side of the angled storage cabinet. On the other side of the white board, there is another small computer table located beneath the bulletin board with a computer monitor, hard-drive, and printer. Above the computer table, the bulletin board is filled with birthday posters, a large tooth to list "lost teeth," and a student of the month poster. Continuing on down the left side wall on the bulletin board are helper lists, calendar/school information, an agenda, a season poster, and a mini-word wall. A wooden chair is angled between the wall and a horseshoe table that is angled in the back corner of the room. Behind the horseshoe table are shelves and two storage cabinets for storing teacher materials and a large word wall—an alphabetical listing of words—is directly behind the horseshoe table on the last space left on the bulletin board.

On the back wall from left to right is one five foot tall by six feet wide bookshelf, a small mobile white board, a listening center with a tape player and two headphones, a five foot tall by two foot wide bookshelf, and another bookshelf that is four feet tall by three feet wide. All the bookshelves are covered by a blue sheet. The side wall to the right of the doorway has a three foot tall white board on it, the kind that uses dry erase markers, running the length of the wall beginning about two feet off the floor with an additional one foot tall bulletin board above the white board covered in the blue felt/green border combination described for the bulletin board on the opposite wall. Underneath the white board are two bookshelves that are two feet tall and three feet long each. They too are covered with a blue sheet.

To the immediate right of the doorway on the wall is a double light switch and thermostat knob plus the side of an eight foot tall wooden storage cabinet that has many boxes sitting on top of it and extra paper towel rolls. On the side of the wooden cabinet are emergency procedure instructions, lunch duties, fire drill evacuation signs/information and a four foot tall rectangular trash can. The wooden cabinet has two doors on it that open from floor to ceiling facing the back wall of the room and it is approximately two feet wide and has a two foot depth.

In the corner of the room, are twenty desks with blue molded plastic chairs for the students to sit in at their desks. Each desk has a standard imitation wood-grain top with a 6 inch rectangular opening by the student's tummy to store books, journals, workbooks and pencil boxes inside their desks. The desktops have a large puzzle piece laminated with their name written in black sharpie on it taped to the right hand upper corner of the desktop while taped to the left hand upper corner of the desktop is a handwriting list of numbers and alphabet letters. In between these two items on the desktop is a molded yellow plastic square clock made to be interactive with a moveable red hour hand and a moveable blue minute hand. The desks are situated facing the whiteboard with about two feet between each desk and in four parallel rows of five desks in each row.

# appendix B
# Reflection on National Board Video of Class Discussion

## Second Grade Teacher: Kristi Dickey

## What is the Event Shown on the Videotape?

The event shown on the videotape took place on Friday, January 22, at 11:10 a.m. It occurred in our classroom in our group time area. It involved 18 of 19 members of our class (one person was out of the room for a special class).

The discussion took place to determine if our current schedule of reading activities was still meeting children's individual needs. Our class schedule had previously allowed a 45 minute time block for self-selected reading (15–20 minutes of *silent reading*, then 15–25 minutes of *partner reading*). A kitchen timer's bell would identify the transition from the former activity to the latter. Following these activities was whole group reading instruction. However, I assessed that my children needed to have more time during the day to choose from a variety of other kinds of self-selected activities (listening centers, science observations, math games, puzzles, etc.). I asked my class to come up with a list of activities that would be appropriate for a *choice time* that could take place during the time slot that partner reading had once occupied. Partner reading became one of the several choices on the list for appropriate activities during choice time. Our schedule became *silent reading*, then *choice time* for which partner reading was one choice. During choice time, most children were choosing not to partner read, but to participate in all the other activities on the list.

After this change, I noticed that many children were not reading silently during silent reading time. They began to cluster up and quietly talk about books that they were reading. Although this was certainly an acceptable learning experience, it did not fit the guidelines we had established for silent reading. Once other children noticed that some were not reading silently, they were confused. I began hearing the question, "Is it still silent reading time?" even though the kitchen timer was obviously still ticking to indicate that silent reading time was still in progress. Other comments were, "If they are reading together it must be choice time. Can I start choice time now?" Understanding the reason for the confusion of the children, I began to reflect on the decision to do away with the special time slot that had previously been devoted to partner reading. I was seeing children who obviously still cared very much about reading with partners and still needed that experience. Changing partner reading to an option only during choice time had created a situation where children were choosing other activities, thus not spending enough time reading books with others. I began to wonder if I should put a time slot back into the schedule devoted only to partner reading. If I did, there would not be enough time for choice time, which the children obviously enjoyed and needed. I reflected on silent reading time. Maybe silent reading was not meeting everyone's needs. Confused and frustrated myself about the lack of time in the day to do everything I wanted to do for the children, I decided to ask them about the situation and let them express their opinions about which activities we should include in our mornings. I wanted my class to have input regarding our schedule so that together we could come up with a plan that would better meet everyone's needs. The activity on the videotape features the whole group discussion regarding this schedule change.

## How Does the Interaction on the Videotape Reflect Ways You Strive to Meet a Portion of One of Your Goals?

My overall objective in involving my students in decision-making processes is to contribute to our atmosphere of mutual respect (DeVries & Zan, 1994). Any time there is a sharing of opinions and ideas, children learn to respect and tolerate each other's differences. By giving students the opportunity to participate in the dilemma with our schedule, I was striving to create ownership of the routines. From experience I know that children are more committed to following rules and routines when they feel ownership. I felt the opportunity to give input regarding our schedule change would give my students this ownership of our routines; therefore they would feel more compelled to follow and not vary from them.

I first wanted students to recognize that there was a problem during silent reading time. One of the first interactions on the videotape is when I ask my class if they noticed something about silent reading that day. Three children gave responses that demonstrated to me that they were aware of the problems. "We were louder than usual." "People were reading with others." "We were talking." Their willingness to share enlightened me that they were taking responsibility for their actions, and were not afraid of any kind of punitive action on my part. These students did not feel that they were in "trouble," but recognized their actions resulted in a problematic situation. By owning the problem, children would be more willing to take part in the solution decided upon.

My first step in guiding children to solving the problem was to ask them if silent reading time was important to them. I then gave them the opportunity to share opinions. I asked for help to change our current schedule to include the things that were the most important to them. I also made it clear to them that I didn't feel it would be fair for me to make this decision on my own. I wanted children to feel that it was okay to express that our current routine was not meeting their needs. I also wanted children to feel that their opinion was needed and valued. I did this in the video by responding in such a way that they knew I heard them and was genuinely interested in what they had to say. I often paraphrased answers and encouraged children to respond to others by saying, "What does anybody else think about that?" This kept the children from responding just to me; rather they shared opinions and responded to each other. This allowed me to be a facilitator in the discussion without exercising any unnecessary authority (DeVries & Zan, 1994). By telling students that I needed their help in changing our schedule, I was letting them know that I respect their opinions.

The responses of the children show a great deal about the community in our classroom. Some children are more comfortable raising hands during discussions, while other children express opinions as they come up. I have encouraged my class throughout the year to have discussions *without* hand raising. I feel that this is more natural and allows children to respond to others more spontaneously. Of course it can also create the problem of too many children talking at once. This happened in the video. I brought them back together as a group by saying, "Did you hear Mei's idea?" and "I'm having trouble hearing Chris." Discussions without hand raising can also mean that quiet, undemanding children can get overlooked (DeVries & Zan, 1994). I try to keep this from happening by calling on children who have hands in the air, although I noticed in the video that Pat raised his hand, waited patiently, then finally put it down before being called on.

From the video, I observed that my class is comfortable sharing ideas and listening to each other. I became more aware that children were able to disagree in an agreeable way. When one person suggested that we change writer's workshop from its own separate time to be included as a choice along with silent reading and partner reading, Sabrina stated, "I think that would be too much at once. Some people might want to do all three and just not have time."

Time and time again the conversation among the children returned to this solution: Silent reading and partner reading would take place during the same block of time, with choice of which one to do. I saw evidence of children respecting others when a few children made the comment that it would be important to partner read with soft voices to respect those people who were choosing to read silently. I asked the children if this was the solution that they would like to try. Henry felt comfortable sharing his concern that he was afraid we weren't going to have choice time. Once I assured him that having silent reading and partner reading in the same time block would allow time in our schedule for choice time, he enthusiastically agreed to the solution. We ended the discussion with the decision to try this solution the next day, then to get back together to discuss its success. I addressed the goal of mutual respect by providing the opportunity for ideas and opinions about our schedule change.

## How Successful Were Your Efforts to Meet Your Goals?

If I did this activity again, the first thing I would do is seat the children in a circle. In order for more faces to be seen on the video, I seated some in chairs and some on the floor (which is natural for some settings). Normally in situations regarding classroom decision-making, I ask children to sit in chairs in a circle for class meeting. This arrangement allows us to see and respond to each other. Although I do feel that our videotaped discussion allowed for sharing of opinions and ideas, there were still six children in my class that gave no input in the discussion. I feel that more people might have shared ideas if our seating arrangement had been different. In retrospect, another approach would have been to pass around the beanbag that we have used in class meetings. Students respond to each person's idea as in other discussions, but this way each person finds him or herself with the beanbag in hand with the opportunity to speak. This approach might have encouraged more participation from some of the quieter students.

Another thing I would have done differently would have been to write down the ideas and opinions that children had as they came up. Summarizing children's ideas was difficult without a visual to refer to. Writing down ideas would have also assured that children were accurately represented. In the middle of our discussion, our fourth grade buddy class arrived a few minutes early for a scheduled reading time. My distractibility with this unexpected issue during videotaping caused me to inaccurately represent Jay's idea. Writing down his idea as he stated it would have given me a visual to refer to when summarizing ideas.

The idea of having silent reading and partner reading in the same block was definitely the idea that came up most often with the children. However, there were other children that had completely different ideas. Although all the children agreed with the prospect of trying out this solution the next school day and getting back together to discuss the issue, I could have asked the children if they wanted to vote on each idea. Again, if ideas had been written down, then I could have given the children the opportunity to ask for a vote, then those with different ideas might have felt more represented.

Overall, I feel that the videotape discussion was a success. Children were able to give their input and see that it was used to come up with a solution to a problem in our classroom. After trying the solution, I asked the children if it was working for them and they all agreed that it was. The solution agreed upon is still working in our classroom.

## Reference

DeVries, R., & Zan, B. (1994). *Moral classrooms, moral children.* New York: Teachers College Press.

# appendix C
# Teacher Interview Transcript

**Teacher:** Kay
**Interviewer:** Kathryn Castle
**Interview Focus:** Kay's relationships with adults.
**Interview Setting:** In Kay's classroom after school. We sat across from each other at a table in child-sized chairs. Kay seemed relaxed and happy to meet with me.

## Interview

**Kathryn: What is your family background?**
**Kay:** In curriculum meetings I tell parents about my family background. I come from a very loving family. I am the youngest of 7 children. When I was born, my oldest brother was 18 and my youngest sister was 8. I was a little child in a house of grown-ups. I always felt I was living under an umbrella of love all the time. That contributes to who I am. I had lots of young nieces and nephews that I would dress up and we would do plays.

**Kathryn: Who have been your significant mentors?**
**Kay:** First, my "saintly" sister teaches kindergarten. She has mentored me in life, not so much in teaching. She has great love for the children she teaches. We communicate often.

Second, my major mentor is Liz a kindergarten teacher at my school. When I was an undergraduate student, I went into many classrooms to observe. I remember the first day I went to Liz's room. She was in her closet and she came out with a huge smile on her face. She was so nice to me. I could tell I was going to love being in her room.

The next year I requested to do my student teaching with her. She was an excellent role model. She modeled all the things I had read about as appropriate practices. The way she talked to children and handled their behavior were what I considered examples of good teaching.

We hit it off from the beginning. She would tell me I was good with children. We had many discussions about developmentally appropriate practice. I would return to her room often to discuss things with her.

Liz gave me suggestions, guided me, supported me, put out her things to let me use—I would use her things and add to them. She stressed that things I prepared for children should look professional—this was important. She is a real perfectionist. Her closet has so much stuff organized in little boxes—it's amazing. She knows where everything is. She is the ultimate professional. She never says anything she would regret. She is always prepared. I go to her first when I need to make an important decision.

After student teaching, I subbed in her class and in Naomi Sander's classroom. Liz was instrumental in my getting the job here. She took my evaluation to the principal and told her I was getting ready to take another job. So the principal at that time, Kit, hired me.

**Kathryn: What was your first year of teaching like?**

**Kay:** I was in a portable building my first year in first grade. Liz was the one I went to for advice. The other first grade teachers weren't thrilled that I was going to Liz for help. At that time, teachers above kindergarten were not doing developmentally appropriate practice or fun things or noisy activities.

There were five new teachers, one in each grade, all coming from different philosophies. It was wild. One of them made chicken soup with rice with her class and got in trouble. I was told that the other first grade teachers were going to wean me away from kindergarten and that I shouldn't be going to a kindergarten teacher for help. They were threatened by kindergarten parents who were wanting developmentally appropriate first grade. Some parents wanted their kids in my class because it was so different. They stayed with me and were happy.

During that time, the principal was pressuring me to be like the other first grade teachers. Liz would come up to my room late at night and work with me. She said, "You have to do what you have to do to get by the first year." I would be in my room late at night getting my materials ready for the next day. I was told to use work sheets and I tried to figure out what the children might learn from them. I was forced to do reading groups.

Liz's advice took the pressure off me because people expected me to fight for the kids, but I started doing what the other teachers told me to do. The teacher assigned to serve as the Mentor teacher on my Entry Year Committee, told me my centers were wrong and that I needed to rotate children through the centers in a prescribed way. I don't think she had wanted to be assigned as a mentor teacher. And she thought I wanted and needed her guidance. She came into my room and made nametags and made a rotation system for my centers.

Kit, the principal, was coming into my room everyday to tell me I was wrong. Soon they began to leave me alone. Gradually I started changing things one at a time. Liz told me to roll with it and that I could gradually put myself back into it.

That year, I had a dialogue journal with the kids who could read. One parent told me that she was so glad that her gifted daughter was with me and that we were doing the journal together.

The teachers and principal made me spend one half day in my assigned mentor's classroom. Now that teacher has changed a lot. She changed slowly after moving next door to my room. She became very interested in what my kids were doing: center time and the book bags that went home. She did help me with art and we shared center activities and math games. Now she is very dear to me.

**Kathryn: How would you describe your relationship with your first principal?**

**Kay:** She was busy responding to parent confusion about what they wanted for their children. Once she saw that parents wanted what I was doing, she left me alone.

I cried everyday my first year. I was up until 2 a.m. every night. But I had support from Liz, Gwen and the group of new teachers I started with. Liz spent hours listening to me and validating what I was doing. She gave me so much time and made me feel like a good teacher. She would listen, agree with me, and cry with me. She stood up for me a few times. She told Kit, "You never gave her the opportunity to figure things out for herself. You never told her how you were evaluating her."

**Kathryn: Please tell me about your relationship with Liz during the time the two of you were working on National Board certification?**
Kay: I've always held Liz here (arm above her head). She does everything perfectly. She fights every battle to extremes. She never quits. She is very tenacious and will fight with the legislature if she needs to.

We all felt confident in the National Board process, but your weaknesses do hit you in the face. Through this process, I am beginning to see myself on an equal level with Liz. For example, I helped her plan units. We discussed units in terms of the national standards. I gave her my materials. We did more planning together than we have ever done. We read each other's writing and gave each other input. I saw that she needed my help as much as she helped me. I would tell her what was good in her writing.

The process just beats you down. You have to see it through someone else's eyes. I put her labels on her evidence the night we taped our boxes up. Her sister-in-law died in Tennessee and she was gone for three days. She was gone the week she was supposed to collect artifacts. One day I typed up artifacts for her. I had already figured out how to do it. I told her. "If you're not mailing your box, I'm not mailing mine." I knew she would do it. She stayed up all night writing interpretive summaries. Her husband helped her. She is a perfectionist—it had to be the way she wanted it.

**Kathryn: Please tell me about your relationship with Gwen during the National Board process.**
Kay: We started teaching the same year and have always been friends. This last year we have become closer. We bonded when we went through the ropes course together. Gwen had my guideline. She was my partner and your partner talks you through everything. That really bonded us.

For awhile, Gwen was frustrated with education and with low pay. She was considering getting another degree in something. She decided to do the National Board certification instead. We read each other's work even though I was doing early childhood and she was doing middle childhood. We bared our souls on paper.

We would send notes to each other back and forth during the day with candies attached. If I was having a bad day, she would pick me up with chocolate chip cookies. We have confided in each other on issues about our principal.

**Kathryn: What was your relationship with your second principal, Wendy?**
Kay: Wendy projects two different sides of her personality. She can fool you by being nice and then not so nice. She can say one thing one minute and then the opposite the next minute. She constantly feeds us inconsistencies. We don't have many faculty meetings. She meets with grade levels and gets "input". She is very contradictory. She says we have shared governance but we don't. She has committees on paper, but they don't meet.

It always has to be her agenda. She doesn't want us to have information. She can be vindictive. For example, the counselor who was her follower crossed her and Wendy stopped speaking to her. She would purposely not tell her things and leave her out in the cold. When one of our fifth graders died, Wendy didn't bother to tell our counselor that she had called in counselors from other schools.

I had an incident with Wendy on the looping I wanted to do by following my first grade class into second grade. Wendy had encouraged looping. All year we told parents that we were going to loop. Then Wendy moved a teacher to a grade level that would not make looping possible. When I questioned her, she said she couldn't tell me whether we would loop and to trust her. Parents were calling me wanting to know if we were going to loop. I told them I didn't have an answer.

I went to Liz who suggested I follow procedures and write a formal letter to Wendy. I wrote the letter and explained that parents were wanting to know. When I went to see her, she put her hands on her hips and said, "Kay, you're asking and me granting it are two different things." I didn't hear from her for several days. She had been holding a position for one of her pets. I told her I had thought she was more committed to looping than that.

Wendy has pets. Once she hired someone without an interview. She just announced that the person was hired. She acquired a following among the weak teachers, but it has dwindled lately.

**Kathryn: In your writing, you mention asking Wendy to be a guest reader in her class. Why did you do that?**
**Kay:** I had invited our superintendant to be a guest reader in my room and I felt I had to ask Wendy too.

**Kathryn: What is your relationship with the superintendant?**
**Kay:** I have been a United Way volunteer on the United Way Team and we met there. I was amazed that he knew who I was: he knew my name, grade, and school. Every time I saw him he would say hi. I related this at the Board meeting when his contract was in question and they were considering letting him go. He has been to my classroom several times and he wrote me a congratulatory letter for National Board selection. My own principal, Wendy, never did that.

When he had back surgery, I went to see him. He favors shared governance. He is a teacher and child advocate. That threatens the principals. He listens to what teachers want. He says we all have to own the process before it can be fixed.

He hired a wonderful curriculum director who works very hard. She also listens to teachers and is insightful. She knows more about me as a teacher than my principal does. She has encouraged us to document concerns we have. I have a notebook of examples of what our principal has done. For example, during opening in front of the whole school, she berated the child care kids for not respecting things. She also singled out one child as her favorite because the child has "wild and woolly" hair. One day she called out the August birthdays and said, "You all are really young or really old for your group."

I have avoided Wendy this year, but my evaluation was good. She didn't volunteer to help us one bit with National Board certification. We had to ask her for a mandatory letter of support. Another teacher in another district is getting released time and other support from her principal. We are getting nothing. I shared my Board notebook with her. When she didn't return it, I had to ask for it. I don't think she even read it. But our curriculum director sent me a nice note and a keychain.

Wendy doesn't give compliments. It's depressing working with her. Morale is low. But because we have each other, we made it through the process. We say we will outlast her, but we get weary at the end of each year.

# appendix D
# The Wonder of Learning Newsletter Article

## The Wonder of Learning
### The Hundred Languages of Children

by Kathryn Castle
Oklahoma State University

It isn't too late to visit the Wonder of Learning: The Hundred Languages of Children exhibit that documents the Italian Reggio Emilia approach. It will be with us until the end of June and is located on two floors of Building A on the NSU Broken Arrow campus, 3100 E. New Orleans St.

It is free and open to the public during the week or by appointment on the weekends. You can also call Riverfield Country Day School to schedule a tour (918 446-3553).

We owe thanks for this wonderful exhibit to the people of Reggio, the teachers of Riverfield, the people at NSU Broken Arrow, and the Kaiser family for their contributions to bring the exhibit to the Tulsa area.

Every teacher, parent, and administrator should visit this exhibit because it brings the ideas of the Reggio schools to life in the displays of children's artifacts, Reggio books, video clips, interactive areas, and documentation panels. The great respect and love for the Reggio children are obvious in the exhibit.

Encourage all those you know who try to eliminate play in schools to visit the exhibit to see for themselves the value that play has in children's lives.

The exhibit includes a variety of displays and projects including children's dialogue with the environment; children's representations of their knowledge through running, drawing, painting, constructing, and using computers; explorations of sound, black and white, wire, and light; children's literacy and metaphors; color and natural objects; and children with special rights (special needs).

Although you could breeze through the exhibit, to get the most from the experience requires several hours. It is best to schedule several visits if possible to take it all in. It is comfortably spread out on the first and second floors of Building A in a very lovely facility with plenty of comfortable chairs for relaxing and visiting with friends about what you are seeing. Vendors and vending machines are available and local restaurants are not far.

## References & Resources

Children, art, artists: Catalogue of the exhibition "The Expressive Languages of Children, the Artistic Language of Alberto Burri". (2004). Reggio Emilia- Italy: Reggio Children.

Dialogues with places. (2008). Reggio Emilia-Italy: Reggio Children. Edwards, Carolyn, Gandini, Lella, & Forman, George. (1998). The hundred languages of children, 2nd edition. Greenwich, CT: Ablex/JAI Press.

Forman, George. (1996). A child constructs an understanding of a water wheel in five media. Childhood Education, 72(5), 269-273.

Gandini, Lella, Etheredge, Susan, & Hill, Lynn. (2008). Insights and inspirations from Reggio Emilia. Worcester, MA: Davis.

Gandini, Lella & Edwards, Carolyn Pope. (Eds.). (2001). Bambini, The Italian approach to infant/toddler care. New York: Teachers College Press.

Lewin-Benham, A. (2005). Possible schools: The Reggio approach to urban education. New York: Teachers College Press.

Murray, Mary & Valentine-Anand, Lesley. (December, 2008). Dinosaur extinction, early childhood style. Science and Children, 36-39.

Topal, Cathy Weisman & Gandini, Lella. (1999). Beautiful stuff. Worcester, MA: Davis.

Wien, Carol Anne. (2008). Emergent curriculum in the primary grades, NY: Teachers College Press and Washington, D. C.: NAEYC

# Teaching with the Exhibit by Kathryn Castle

Some of us in higher education are taking/sending our students to experience the exhibit. There are even some universities giving course credit for the experience. I decided to feature the exhibit in my graduate curriculum class at OSU Tulsa.

I chose a Reggio inspired required text for the class, Emergent Curriculum in the Primary Grades by Carol Anne Wien (2008). Each chapter of this text is written by a different early childhood teacher who describes using a Reggio approach to do projects with children. The Reggio books I purchased at the January conference served as great resources to my class.

I also used George Forman's Reggio inspired research in his article on how a child constructs an understanding of a water wheel in five media. Forman's research shows that the medium a child uses (drawing, constructing, using clay, etc.) influences, changes, and deepens the child's thinking on the topic and affects the child's representation of the thinking. There are numerous examples of this in the exhibit such as project work on representing sound in various ways.

I asked my students to visit the exhibit on their own and for multiple times if possible. I also asked them to attend the OU Seed Sower's speakers on the Reggio approach. Jennifer Armstrong from Canada and Louise Cadwell from St. Louis were featured speakers and advocates for the Reggio approach.

I held one class at the exhibit. Dr. **Kay Grant,** Dean of NSU's College of Education, provided a nice classroom next to the exhibit

where we met to discuss students' reactions to the exhibit. We were joined by a Riverfield teacher, **Kirsten Redmond,** who talked with my class about the exhibit, her experiences at the Reggio schools in Italy, and her classroom at Riverfield. She was very patient in answering questions and showing us around the exhibit. She also invited us to visit her school.

I directed my students to start at the beginning of the exhibit because it provides historical information about the Reggio schools and the ideals of Loris Malaguzzi, founder of the approach. Since the exhibit is not ordered in a linear fashion, the beginning of the exhibit is not readily obvious. But for those new to the Reggio approach, I think it is appropriate to start there to provide a rich context for the rest of the exhibit. At the beginning of the exhibit, found on the first floor on the east side of the exhibit, there is a sign-in book, Reggio books, a documentation panel, a video of Loris Malaguzzi talking about his ideas, and a video of children.

Next I took my students to the second floor to the light display that has documentation panels, boxes of objects, an overhead projector, and two light tables. As a provocation (Reggio term to refer to something that encourages interest), I asked my students if they would try to explain how the images cast on the wall got from the overhead projector to the wall. I asked this question because it was a similar question asked by the Reggio children who explored light and colored objects. The documentation panel in the display shows how the children explored this question with objects and the overhead projector.

My students pondered the question for a while and then offered a few explanations. Along with their explanations were comments about how they should know the answer but couldn't give a scientific explanation. They wondered what they would do if a child asked them for a "scientific" explanation.

I think they were somewhat uncomfortable in thinking that their explanations weren't scientific enough. I tried to assure them by telling them I didn't know the scientific explanation either, but it might be fun to explore the materials and the overhead projector to learn more. In doing so, they offered a few explanations about the change in color, the relationship of the lens to the light sources, and the mirror reversal of the projected images from the real objects.

After several minutes of exploration and explanation, I encouraged them to read the documentation panel. They were pleasantly surprised that their adult explanations had much in common with the explanations of the Reggio children documented in the panel. They also concluded that these very young children were very smart! They were impressed at the creativity, thinking and problem solving demonstrated by the Reggio children. I think this is a common conclusion that people viewing the exhibit for the first time come to, that the Reggio children are very creative and smart.

*continued next page*

# Exhibit *continued*

What we discussed later in class was the important role of the teacher and the environment as the third teacher in Reggio schools. We also discussed the importance of children having time to work on their questions and projects.

Project work may take place over just a few weeks to a year and even two years as one project that was documented did. Children's work is collaborative including guidance from an atelierista and the teacher. It is sometimes difficult to see in the exhibit the amount of time and effort that has been given to the project activities. To include all of it would probably make the exhibit too large and unwieldy.

Students explored the exhibit on their own using a handout I prepared. The handout asked them to notice the different types of projects, how they are documented, what children learn from them, and what stands out to them about the entire exhibit. They were also asked to:

Select one example of project work and observe and take notes on:

(a) Children's purpose, inquiry questions, reasons for the project work including any hypotheses children posed.

(b) Ways in which the work was documented so that you could understand what was done.

(c) What the child/children learned; the knowledge they constructed from the project work.

(d) Identification of an Oklahoma PASS objective that might have been achieved in the project work.

(e) Your own ideas about the project and how it might be implemented, possibly in your own classroom.

We met after their exploration of the exhibit to discuss their reactions and findings. Students had no trouble identifying children's purposes and learning.

Their favorite areas of the exhibit seemed to be the column project in which children explored the numerous large white columns in the Malaguzzi Center and then represented their knowledge and connections to the columns in various ways including using aesthetic coverings to "dress" the columns; the black and white project; the sound project showing how children drew and represented various sounds and rhythms that they had made on a stairway; and the light display including children's constructions of the light catching machines.

Since our class meeting at the exhibit, we continue to discuss it including how some of the ideas could be implemented in public school classrooms.

My students are concerned that public schools might not be condu

cive to Reggio activities because of the accountability concerns related to curriculum mandates. When they asked me if I knew of public schools in Oklahoma moving toward a Reggio approach, I couldn't give them many examples- just a few isolated teachers here and there.

I did learn from the Riverfield teachers and the Seed Sower speakers that some public schools in St. Louis, Utah, Chicago, Portland and California are using the Reggio approach. And the Riverfield teachers have welcomed us to visit their school where the Reggio approach is alive and well!

Still, my students are reluctant to accept that this approach can be done with older children in public elementary schools. They cited many cultural differences between the Reggio schools and American schools in terms of American expectations for orderly and quiet classrooms where children work on PASS objectives and teacher directed lessons.

They feel American children may lack the self-regulation and interest shown by the Reggio children. They also bemoan the lack of American parent involvement compared to the Reggio schools.

I think some of their concerns are warranted, but I continue to encourage them to find ways to try projects in their own programs.

One option they can choose for an assignment in my class is to write a paper about the exhibit and what they have learned about a Reggio approach to curriculum.

## Share Your Exhibit Experiences!

As a university professor, I appreciate access to the exhibit and think it has benefited my students and deepened their understanding of curriculum and teaching. I also think the exhibit has opened up possibilities for my students to ponder in rethinking their programs. The exhibit provides a multitude of ideas to try with children. I hope all educators will take advantage of this opportunity. For those of you incorporating class assignments around the exhibit, I would love to hear about your experiences. Please email me at **kathryn.castle@okstate.edu.**

# Glossary

**action plan** A plan to apply results from a teacher research or action research study to solve a problem, develop an appropriate intervention based on results, implement program-wide changes, and/or engage in advocacy efforts to make social changes.

**action research** A type of research similar to teacher research or practitioner research focused on taking action based on results. Taking action may mean action for social changes.

**alpha level** A percentage used (typically .05 in educational experimental research) to indicate significance level (confidence level) of results. A p (probability) value at an alpha level of .05 or less indicates the difference would be due to chance in about 5% of the cases. If the p-value is greater than 0.05 then the difference would not be considered statistically significant.

**analysis** Refers to data analysis and means breaking data down into its parts, organizing the parts into relevant categories, and then interpreting or making sense of the parts, the categories, and the relationships among them to reach a deeper understanding of the problem under study.

**analysis of variance (ANOVA)** A test from inferential statistics used to show significant differences among three or more groups.

**anecdotal notes** Teacher recordings or notes of children's behaviors and classroom events.

**anonymity** Concealment of identity of research participants.

**artifact** An object, typically a sample of a child's work such as a drawing, that represents what a child has done or learned that can be analyzed.

**audit trail** A researcher's organized records of all data collected and all data analysis procedures maintained for possible review to verify research procedures.

**bar graphs** A type of graphic representation of data recorded in a graph.

**Behaviorism** A worldview that holds that truth exists "out there" in the world to be discovered through experimental research and that all behavior is caused or controlled by certain variables that can be predicted and determined by highly controlled experimental studies.

**Belmont Report** A report created in 1979 by the National Commission for the Protection of Human Subjects of Biomedical and Behavioral Research under the direction of the Department of Health and Human Services that gives three ethical principles for human subjects research: "respect for persons, beneficence, and justice" (Nolen & Putten, 2007, p. 401).

**blind peer review** *See* **peer-reviewed journal**

**categorizing data** Assignment of conceptual labels or categories to data. A form of textual analysis.

**chi-square test** A statistical test of significant differences used with frequency data.

**codes of ethics of professional associations** Codes or positions taken on ethical conduct adopted by professional groups.

**coding** Assignment of codes or labels for analysis of data either determined prior to or following data collection.

**coding systems** Conceptual systems using categories or codes to assign labels or codes to data.

**confidentiality** Assurance that data will be kept private and confidential.

**confirmability** Refers to sufficient documentation and description of data to assure others that the study results can be confirmed by the evidence presented.

**Constructivism** A theory that knowledge is actively constructed rather than passively received.

**content analysis** Analysis used to show what is in (ideas, concepts, information, etc.) a document being used as data in research.

**control group** In experimental design the group that does not get the treatment or intervention in order to make comparisons between two or more groups to ascertain the effectiveness of the treatment.

**correlational studies** Designed to show the degree to which a relationship exists between two attributes.

**credibility** Degree of believability or authenticity of a research study.

**critical friends group** A group of teachers who meet to support each other and give each other critical and constructive feedback within a collaborative and safe environment to promote teacher professional development, facilitate teachers' writing, study student work, or do teacher research.

**data** Bits of information collected and analyzed to help answer research questions.

**data analysis** Scrutiny of data for what it means.

**data collection** Systematic gathering of data to help answer research questions.

**dependability** Adequacy of research procedures, thoroughness in data collection, analysis and interpretation that are clearly articulated for others to understand and agree to the trustworthiness of what was done.

**dependent variable** The variable under study, such as performance level, that may be affected by the independent variable controlled by the researcher, such as teaching approach.

**descriptive statistics and measures of central tendency and dispersion** A type of data analysis used to describe characteristics of the data in a numerical fashion that shows general tendencies or trends in the data such as the **mean, mode, median, range,** and **standard deviation.**

**document analysis** Scrutiny of documents used as data in research.

**documentation panel** Displays of children's learning that use graphic representation as well as written narrative to tell the story of what children have learned from the activities they have participated in.

**documents** Papers, policy manuals, reports, curriculum guides, etc. used as data in research.

**ethics** The study of what is considered good or right.

**ethnography** A type of research design common in the social sciences including anthropology and sociology that involves the study of certain groups or cultures (such as schools and classrooms) to ascertain how the group functions, the language and rituals typical of the group, and all the written and unwritten rules and codes for social behavior that exist and regulate the group.

**evidence based teaching** Teaching focused on documenting that learning has occurred with evidence of that learning, such as assessments of child performance and achievement.

**experimental design** A research approach to determine cause and effect relationships among independent and dependent variables

**factor analysis** Used in inferential statistics to determine which factors or which independent variables affect the dependent variable under study both separately and in combination.

**field notes** Recorded notes that describe what a teacher sees children doing in an activity that is the focus of research.

**formative assessment** Evaluation that shows progress or development of what is being assessed.

**frequency counts** A research procedure in which events such as interactions are tallied or counted.

**hypotheses** Predictions of results in experimental research.

**independent-measures *t* test** A test for statistically significant differences in the means of measures when comparing a treatment or intervention group with a control group.

**independent variable** Condition or variable manipulated by the researcher to ascertain effects on the dependent variable.

**inferential statistics** A type of experimental design data analysis to show causal relationships between and among variables to allow researchers to draw generalizations from a representative sample of students to a larger population of students.

**informed consent** Permission or consent to participate in a research study given after all pertinent information about the research has been disclosed and is understood.

**internal and external validity and reliability** Demonstration that the research study is accurate and the measures used in the study actually measure what they are intended to measure and with consistency across time and measures.

**interpretist paradigm** Worldview that holds that truth does not exist externally to be discovered, but rather is internally constructed by each individual. All understanding and truth are interpreted.

**interview** A set of questions used to get information from research participants.

**IRB** Institutional review board that reviews human subjects research for approval.

**Japanese Lesson Study Group** A model for studying teaching that can be used by teacher researcher groups to address how best to make changes based on research results.

**Likert scale** A scale used for surveys which is in the form of a continuum, where survey choices range from strongly agree to strongly disagree. A numeric value is usually associated with each response choice where 1=strongly disagree, 2=disagree, 3=no opinion, 4=agree, and 5=strongly agree.

**mean** The numeric average of a set of scores.

**measures of dispersion—the range and the standard deviation** of a set of scores Descriptive statistics that tell how much spread or diversity exists in a set of scores.

**median** The score that splits the data set in half. It is the middle score of all the scores around where 50% of the scores fall above the median and 50% of the scores fall below it.

**member checks** Opportunities provided to participants in a study to review data and reports to ensure the information represents those who have participated in the study.

**memos** Writing in the margins of text that is being analyzed to help the researcher to think through what the data mean and if they are helping shed light on the research questions.

**mixed methods** Research design using quantitative and qualitative data more likely to give rich results than one type of data alone.

**mode** The score in the data set that occurs most frequently and indicates the most common score in the set of scores. The mode tells what score is most represented in the group.

**multiple regression analysis** Inferential statistics approach used to find the combined relationship of multiple independent variables on a single dependent variable.

**NAEYC** National Association for the Education of Young Children.

**narrative inquiry** A form of research sometimes used in teacher research in the study of the lives of students and teachers as perceived by the teacher researcher as stories told by the lived experiences of those studied.

**NBPTS** National Board of Professional Teaching Standards.

**NCATE** National Council for the Accreditation of Teacher Education.

**observations** A type of data collected by observing children and activities.

**ongoing data analysis** Also called interim data analysis or constant comparative analysis that refers to analyzing data as it is collected and comparing data across data sources.

**outliers** Scores at the extremes of the data set.

**paradigm** A worldview with a loose set of assumptions about the goals of education, how learning occurs, what teaching is most likely to lead to student learning, and what methods are most useful for studying educational problems.

**participant debriefing** Occurs when the researcher tells participants about various aspects of the study and gives them an opportunity to clarify or interpret events.

**participant observer** A form of qualitative researcher stance in which the researcher is both a participant and an observer within the research setting being studied.

**peer debriefing** Communication in which the researcher shares aspects of the study with a critical friend or peer who may help to clarify aspects of the study.

**peer-reviewed journal** A journal that has a blind review process in which submitted manuscripts are sent to reviewers in the field who remain anonymous to the author and the author anonymous to the reviewers.

**pie chart** A type of graphic representation of data charted in "pie" slices or categories.

**portfolio and portfolio assessment** Collection and evaluation of work such as writing samples that represents a long- term record of progress reflecting a teacher's evaluation of the materials as well as the possible self-evaluations that children do when asked to compare an item they produced at the beginning of the year to one at a later point in time and when asked to select and give reasons for their best work. Often shared with parents to show child's progress.

**prolonged engagement** Involvement in data collection for an appropriate length of time to gather enough data to inform the research.

**protocols** Structures for having group discussions and conversations on topics relevant to the group participating in the discussion and that contain phases and instructions for each phase, such as the Inquiry Circles protocol.

**p-value** A numerical probability value or statistic of the difference between groups occurring by chance.

**qualitative data** Data that is interpreted for meaning or for its qualities.

**quantitative data** Numerical data that can be counted or measured.

**randomization** Random (by chance) and representative assignment of subjects to research conditions or groups and the use of randomized trials in experimental studies. A standard used for judging the quality of experimental research.

**range** The spread of scores obtained by subtracting the lowest score in the data set from the highest score.

**reflection** Thinking deeply about a topic and its meaning.

**repeated-measures *t* test** Test used in inferential statistics to test for significant differences among the same individuals due to the intervention.

**rubric** A chart or matrix that describes a set of criteria for various levels of performance on an assignment or learning outcome from low to medium to high levels.

**saturation** The point in qualitative data analysis in which additional/new data will not provide any new themes beyond those that have already emerged from analyzed data.

**scientific method** A systematic approach to research in order to show significance of results.

**stakeholders** Those who may be affected by research results or who may be participants who are curious about findings because they have a stake in the study.

**standard deviation** The average distance of scores away from the mean.

**statistically significant difference** From inferential statistics in which the effect studied (dependent variable) is not likely due to chance.

**summative assessment** A final evaluation.

**teacher (pedagogical) autonomy** The ability to make professional judgments and actions based on the right thing to do, taking into consideration all relevant perspectives, and in spite of the reward system in place (Castle, 2006; Kamii, 1985).

**teacher research plan** A systematic plan for conducting a teacher research study including a timeline.

**theme** A term used in qualitative analysis to refer to a major idea or unit of meaning or the essence of what is being analyzed or interpreted.

**theme analysis** Qualitative analysis for what predominant themes or major concepts are reflected in the data.

**time sampling approach** A type of data collection method in which events are coded according to a time interval such as every 60 seconds.

**transcript** A written narrative of data taken from field notes, observations, or interviews.

**transferability** Refers to the extent the results of a qualitative study are applicable to other situations. The determination of whether the results are transferable is made by others who read the report of the study and decide for themselves that the results may fit their situations

**treatment group** In experimental research it is the group that is given the treatment, intervention, instructional approach, or program whose effectiveness is being studied and can be compared to the control group.

**triangulation** Refers to the process of including in the study multiple (at least three) data sources for analysis and cross validation. Triangulation enhances the accuracy of the study and is used to corroborate findings across data sources.

**trustworthiness** The extent to which a qualitative study is truthful and accurate. Lincoln and Guba (1985) identified aspects of trustworthiness including **credibility, dependability, transferability,** and **confirmability.**

**unitizing the data** Examining the parts of data and making holistic sense of the parts. This process involves breaking down the data from the text into smaller pieces such as words, phrases, sentences, or units of meaning.

## References

Castle, K. (2006). Autonomy through pedagogical research. *Teaching and Teacher Education, 22,* 1094–1103.

Kamii, C. (1985/2000). *Young children reinvent arithmetic.* New York: Teachers College Press.

Lincoln, Y. S., & Guba, E. G. (1985). *Naturalistic inquiry.* Newbury Park, CA: Sage.

Nolen, A. L., & Putten, J. V. (2007). Action research in education: Addressing gaps in ethical principles. *Educational Researcher, 36*(7), 401–407.

# index